MARY IN EARLY CHRISTIAN FAITH AND DEVOTION

MARY

IN EARLY CHRISTIAN
FAITH AND DEVOTION

STEPHEN J. SHOEMAKER

YALE UNIVERSITY PRESS
NEW HAVEN AND LONDON

For information about this and other Yale University Press publications please contact:
U.S. Office: sales.press@yale.edu   yalebooks.com
Europe Office: sales@yaleup.co.uk   yalebooks.co.uk

Typeset in Adobe Caslon Regular by IDSUK (DataConnection) Ltd
Printed in Great Britain by TJ International Ltd, Padstow, Cornwall

Library of Congress Cataloging-in-Publication Data

Names: Shoemaker, Stephen J., 1968– author.
Title: Mary in early Christian faith and devotion / Stephen J. Shoemaker.
Description: New Haven : Yale University Press, 2016.
LCCN 2016004005 | ISBN 9780300217216 (c1 : alk. paper)
LCSH: Mary, Blessed Virgin, Saint—Devotion to—History. | Church history—
    Primitive and early church, ca. 30–600.
Classification: LCC BT645 .S53 2016 | DDC 232.9109—dc23
LC record available at http://lccn.loc.gov/2016004005

A catalogue record for this book is available from the British Library.

10 9 8 7 6 5 4 3 2 1

For my goddaughter and niece Grace Ann Shoemaker

Χαῖρε, κεχαριτωμένη

CONTENTS

Preface and Acknowledgments   *ix*

INTRODUCTION
Mapping a New Approach to Early Marian Piety   1

CHAPTER ONE
A Virgin Unspotted: Devotion to Mary in the First
Two Centuries   30

CHAPTER TWO
Mother of God and Mother of Mysteries:
The Third Century   64

CHAPTER THREE
Mother of the Great Cherub of Light: The *Book of
Mary's Repose*   100

CHAPTER FOUR
A Cult Following: The *Six Books Dormition Apocryphon*   130

CHAPTER FIVE
The Memory of Mary: The Fourth and Early
Fifth Centuries   166

CHAPTER SIX
The Scepter of Orthodoxy: The Cult of the Virgin and
the Council of Ephesus   205

CONCLUSIONS   229

Notes   *241*
Bibliography   *266*
Index   *284*

PREFACE AND ACKNOWLEDGMENTS

THIS BOOK HAS BEEN in the works for a long time, sitting on the back burner while I completed other projects. It is in many ways the logical successor to my first book, *The Ancient Traditions of the Virgin Mary's Dormition and Assumption*, and it was conceived not long after that volume appeared. I owe Sarah Jane Boss a large debt of gratitude for inadvertently inspiring this project. Over ten years ago Sarah approached me about contributing an article on Marian liturgies in Early Christianity to a Marian resource book that she was editing. On receiving the initial invitation, I recall thinking, oddly enough, that I don't really know much about that. This recognition, however, also brought awareness that the topic had not really been covered very well in a systematic way by previous scholarship, and I thought, if I didn't tackle this, who would? While writing the article, which would eventually be published as "Marian Liturgies and Devotion in Early Christianity" in *Mary: The Complete Resource*, I came to realize that the early Christian apocrypha were a largely untapped resource that had much to add to this topic even though they had been largely overlooked to this point. I decided to write a book on early Christian devotion to Mary before the explosion of

Marian piety that ensued after the Council of Ephesus. For the past decade I have worked steadily on this topic, and this book draws on a number of previously published articles, all of which have been indicated in the notes. It does not simply reproduce these articles, however, but instead provides a fresh and more accessible synthesis of these studies, along with significant new material regarding early Christian devotion to Mary.

I would especially like to thank the Institute for Advanced Study and the National Humanities Center for a membership in the School of Historical Studies and a Rockefeller Foundation fellowship respectively during the academic year 2013–14. Support from both of these institutions was invaluable for the timely completion of this project. Not only did their financial generosity make it possible for me to write this book, but both centers provided extraordinary intellectual communities. Conversations with the members and fellows contributed significantly to this project, and these exchanges sowed the seeds for many new ideas that I am certain will open up new directions for my research in the near future. I also wish to thank the superb staff at these institutions: their extraordinary assistance greatly assisted in the completion of this project. In particular, I would especially thank Karen Carroll of the National Humanities Center for her copyediting while I was a fellow there. I would additionally thank all those who offered comments and suggestions in response to presentations of various parts of this book at the meetings of the North American Patristics Society; the Society of Biblical Literature; the American Academy of Religion; the International Conference on Patristic Studies, Oxford; the Byzantine Studies Conference; l'Association pour l'étude de la littérature apocryphe chrétienne; the Mariological Society of America; the Conference on the Origins of the Cult of the Virgin at York St. John University (7/06); the Conference on Christian Apocryphal Texts for the New Millennium: Achievements, Prospects, and Challenges at the University of Ottawa (10/06); the Fifth International Symposium of the International Centre for Christian Studies at the Orthodox Church of Georgia (05/14); and at the University of Tübingen; Duke University; the University of North Carolina at Chapel Hill; and Virginia Commonwealth University.

Given the long gestation of this project, it is impossible to remember all of the individuals who have contributed their thoughts and comments along the way, and I fear that I will inevitably forget to mention some. Nevertheless, I especially wish to thank for so many helpful exchanges related to the topics in this book: Pauline Allen, Rina Avner, Jane Baun, David Brakke, Jorunn Jacobson Buckley, Averil Cameron, Elizabeth Clark, Kate Cooper, Mary Cunningham, Theodore de Bruyn, Alain Desreumaux, Jan Willem Drijvers, Bart Ehrman, Deirdre Good, Susan Ashbrook Harvey, Scott Johnson, Jean-Daniel Kaestli, Ally Kateusz, Derek Krueger, Julie Kelto Lillis, Vasiliki Limberis, AnneMarie Luijendijk, Chris Maunder, Enrico Norelli, Bernard Outtier, Leena Mari Peltomaa, Michael Peppard, Pierluigi Piovanelli, Richard Price, Walter Ray, Brian Reynolds, Miri Rubin, Timothy Sailors, Philip Sellew, Alexander Toepel, and Lily Vuong. I also thank the two anonymous reviewers for the press for their helpful comments. Finally, I am most grateful to Malcolm Gerratt at Yale University Press for his strong interest in this project and for his help and advice in seeing it through to publication.

Mapping a New Approach to Early Marian Piety

IT IS RATHER REMARKABLE, I think, that even at this late date there is still no satisfactory study of the development of Marian piety in ancient Christianity. In view of the considerable importance that devotion to the Virgin Mary has had over the course of Christian history, one might expect that by now there would be any number of historical studies on this topic. But as others have noted before me, such a comprehensive study remains lacking.[1] This absence became quite clear to me some twenty years ago as I began research for my first book on the ancient traditions of Mary's Dormition and Assumption. In setting out I simply assumed that the origins of Marian piety would already be well mapped onto the history of early Christianity. And I still recall my astonishment when a specialist on early Byzantine piety suggested that I might find in the early Dormition and Assumption traditions the origins of Marian intercession: surely such a matter had long been settled, I (naively) thought. Yet, despite the existence of a number of fine articles and even several monographs on specific aspects of devotion to Mary in late antiquity, there was then—and is now—still no adequate treatment of Marian piety's emergence within the history of early

Christianity. It is almost as if, as Peter Brown once wrote of the early cult of the saints, Marian veneration, "as it emerged in late antiquity, became part and parcel of the succeeding millennium of Christian history to such an extent that we tend to take its elaboration for granted."[2]

Of course, there has been much previous investigation of Marian doctrine during the early Christian period, but such studies generally pay scant attention to the emergence of Marian devotion and cult, preferring instead to focus on Mary's position in the development of early Christian dogma. And, likewise, there has been a significant amount of Roman Catholic scholarship on Mary in early Christianity, much of it coming toward the end of the so-called "Marian Century" of 1850–1950. Nevertheless, these works frequently show a strong tendency toward dogmatic readings of the evidence that seek to align early Christian history with modern Roman Catholic doctrine, and occasionally they are also overly optimistic about how quickly veneration of the Virgin Mary took hold within ancient Christianity. While such perspectives have obvious value in a Roman Catholic context, they hold limited use for understanding the development of early Christianity and Mary's place therein. Thus, it would appear that a history of early Marian piety still remains to be written.[3]

I wish that I could promise that this book will answer all of our questions about the origins of devotion to the Virgin, but unfortunately the limitations of the evidence preclude such an outcome, a fact that no doubt is itself largely to blame for the relative neglect of this subject. Instead, what I hope to offer is a new approach to this topic that will contribute to a better understanding of how Mary emerged as a focus of Christian devotion. There is certainly much more to be said about Mary in early Christianity than can be contained in this single volume, and no doubt additional sources relevant to early Marian piety will continue to emerge. But one of the main goals of this book is to assemble the scattered and often overlooked evidence for early Marian piety, from the beginnings of Christianity up to and including the events of the Council of Ephesus (431), the Third Ecumenical Council, where Mary was famously proclaimed as "Theotokos," that is, the one who gave birth to God. Since there is practically no evidence of any Christian devotion to Mary prior to 150 CE (or, for that matter, to any other figure besides Jesus), as a practical matter this study will focus primarily on the period from the latter half of the second century to the first half of the fifth.

The reasons for selecting this chronological limit are fairly obvious: the Council of Ephesus is widely recognized as a watershed event in the history of Marian piety. In fact, the explosion of devotion to the Virgin in this council's aftermath was so significant that much previous scholarship has credited the council and its decisions with giving rise to the cult of the Virgin almost single-handedly.[4] Some scholars would even postpone the emergence of Marian veneration later still, locating its genesis only after the Council of Chalcedon in 451.[5] It is now increasingly clear, however, that devotion to the Virgin and even her cultic veneration had begun well before the Council of Ephesus had even convened. And there is significant evidence that the controversies of the Third Council were themselves at least partly fueled by an already vibrant devotion to Mary in Constantinople and elsewhere in the Roman Empire. So while Nestorius's Christological views, which were the main focus of this council, were certainly upsetting to his more learned theological opponents, it was his refusal to call Mary "Theotokos" that seems to have turned the tide of popular opinion against him. And although questions remain as to just how much Marian piety may have determined debates of this council and their outcome, there can be little doubt that widespread devotion to the Virgin played an important role in the broader conversation.

However one may estimate the relation between Marian piety and the events of the Council of Ephesus, there can be no question that devotion to the Virgin intensified considerably and spread widely following the council's decisions. As Brian Daley aptly observes, during the middle of the fifth century "the figure of Mary emerged like a comet in Christian devotion and liturgical celebration throughout the world."[6] Scholars of early Christianity have long struggled to comprehend this dramatic explosion of Marian piety after Ephesus, particularly in light of the apparent paucity of evidence for devotion to the Virgin in the previous centuries. Most Christian sources from the first four centuries in fact have surprisingly little to say about Mary. Early proto-orthodox writers enlist her motherhood of Jesus as a guarantee of his humanity; her virginal conception is a sign of his exalted status; her obedience at the Annunciation rectifies the disobedience of Eve, making Mary a "New Eve" for the New Adam; and her persistence in virginity is a model for other virgins. There is, however, little interest in Mary in her own right and almost no evidence of Marian cult before the middle of the fourth century. Such relative silence is indeed difficult to reconcile with the thriving Marian piety that we suddenly find in the fifth century, particularly in the eastern Mediterranean world.

Despite the limitations of the early evidence and the conviction of much earlier scholarship, the notion that the abstruse theological debates over Nestorius's Christology at the Third Council could somehow have generated the cult of the Virgin with such apparent velocity seems, frankly, rather preposterous. While the council's outcome and its proclamation of Mary as Theotokos obviously catalyzed the growth and spread of Marian cult, there also can be little question that veneration of Mary had already begun to establish itself before the events of Ephesus. The difficulty, however, lies in finding clear evidence of devotion to Mary during the first four centuries that can offer a meaningful precedent capable of explaining the eruption of Marian piety that took place in the middle of the fifth century. Although such evidence is surprisingly scarce when compared with Mary's prominence in the later Christian tradition, it is nonetheless sufficient to sketch a history of early Christian devotion to Mary.

There are in fact many traces of incipient Marian piety from the pre-Ephesian period, a number of which are by now well known, but these are scattered and often faint, making it difficult to judge their overall significance as witnesses to emergent devotion to the Virgin. One of the most famous of these is of course the *Protevangelium of James*, a late second-century biography of Mary that tells the story of her youth from her own conception through the Nativity of Christ. The *Protevangelium* reveals a surprisingly developed interest in the Virgin as a significant figure in her own right as well as early devotion to her unique holiness, although there is admittedly no evidence yet of any cultic veneration. Nevertheless, the remarkably advanced Marian piety of the *Protevangelium* stands at a considerable distance from the widespread devotion to Mary that would follow in the fifth century, and it is not at all clear what happened in between. As Averil Cameron observes, "The *Protevangelion* seems so developed for its date, and yet in a sense so isolated. It needs to be set in the broader context of apocryphal writings of a similar period."[7] In essence, this is what I aim to achieve in this volume, by bridging the *Protevangelium* with the Marian veneration of the fifth and later centuries through other sources from the second, third, and fourth centuries.

In order to accomplish this, one must examine a wide range of sources, including a number of long-overlooked and recently discovered texts, as well as other more familiar witnesses to early Marian piety. In particular, the apocryphal literature of early Christianity, that is, its extracanonical gospels and other related texts, offers a significant if largely neglected witness to early Christian interest in

Mary.[8] These extrabiblical writings, and especially the early Dormition and Assumption apocrypha, present much clearer evidence of devotion to the Virgin than one finds in the writings of the church fathers. Indeed, it would appear that a focus largely on patristic sources is at least partly responsible for leading earlier scholars to the conclusion that Marian veneration was largely unknown in the early church. For whatever reason, Marian piety seems to register more clearly in apocryphal and also liturgical texts than in theological or moral treatises. Why it is more visible in these contexts than in the writings of the early Christian intellectuals and bishops that we name the church fathers is admittedly not entirely clear, although it is worth noting that the church fathers generally have rather little to say regarding any kind of early Christian ritual practices.[9] Yet at the same time, the prominence of Marian piety in certain early Christian apocryphal writings is perhaps a sign that Marian piety first developed in milieux outside the purview of the "orthodox" church authorities, in heterodox and other theologically marginal communities. The sharply heterodox nature of some of these texts would appear to confirm such a hypothesis, and occasionally these sources reveal understandings of Mary that are decidedly different from those related by the church fathers: some early Christians, for instance, remembered the Virgin Mary as a learned teacher of the divine mysteries. In any case, as we shall see, these texts afford clear evidence that Marian veneration had come into existence already by the fourth century at the latest, even if the church fathers in the main seem to have kept their distance from this practice prior to the fifth century.

Scholarly response to the sparse state of our evidence for devotion to Mary during the early centuries has varied a great deal, although generally it has followed one of two directions, usually according to confessional orientation. Such a sectarian divide certainly comes as no great surprise, particularly given Mary's often volatile status in the history of Protestant and Catholic debate, where her veneration has long posed one of the major theological boundaries dividing these Christian communities. And despite the convergence of much Catholic, Protestant, and secular scholarship on Christian origins over the past several decades, as Beverly Roberts Gaventa observes, "the differences between Catholic and Protestant perspectives on Mary remain significant."[10]

Although one hesitates to generalize about something as diverse as modern Roman Catholicism, there has been a tendency in much Catholic scholarship, as noted already, to maximize the somewhat limited evidence of early Marian piety.[11] One of the most common solutions to this problem is to find ways of reading modern Mariological dogmas back into the writings of the New Testament and the early church fathers. Such an approach finds passages from early Christian literature that seem reminiscent of modern Catholic doctrines, and despite the clear absence of such beliefs from early Christian literature when read on its own terms and the obvious contextual difficulties of these readings, on this basis it is often alleged that the Marian dogmas of modern Catholicism also belonged to the ancient church.[12] While such an interpretive move is perhaps entirely appropriate within the context of Catholic dogmatics, where confidence in the eternal truth of the church's teaching effectively requires such readings of the early evidence,[13] these apologetic exercises fail to shed any historical light on the actual emergence of Marian piety.

On the Protestant side, other than general neglect the tendency has been to emphasize the dearth of evidence and on this basis to refuse the existence of any significant devotion to the Virgin prior to the middle of the fifth century: the Council of Ephesus is thus often adduced as the sole and sufficient cause for what amounts to an essentially medieval cult of the Virgin. In this way the early church can be made into a largely Mary-free zone that is well suited to Protestantism's rejection of the elaborate and intense devotion to Mary that characterizes its parent faith. Recent decades, it is true, have seen some renewed Protestant interest in Mary, no doubt much of it inspired by broader academic and theological concerns with women's history and gender. By and large such studies tend to focus primarily on exegesis of Mary's appearances in the New Testament, as one might expect, rather than on Marian doctrine or veneration.[14] It is also worth noting that this narrative of Mary's relatively late arrival on the scene also appears in a "post-Protestant" guise in certain more secular accounts taking a similar approach, and unfortunately here as in much earlier Protestant scholarship, a sort of anti-Catholicism occasionally can stand fairly close to the surface.[15]

Not surprisingly, these confessional dynamics have done little to foster critical study of early Marian piety. Happily, however, it would appear as if this gap is now beginning to narrow, as many Protestant theologians have begun to grapple with the fact that their acceptance of the first four councils makes Marian devotion somewhat difficult to ignore, while Catholic scholarship has shown an increasing willingness to embrace historical critical scholarship, particularly since the Second Vatican Council.[16] Nevertheless, the fact remains that outside of Catholic circles, little consideration has been given so far to the possibility that Christians may have begun significant veneration of the Virgin Mary prior to the Council of Ephesus; likewise, much (but certainly not all) of the earlier work by Catholic scholars is essentially apologetic or dogmatic in nature and thus of very limited historical value. And so it would seem that in many respects investigation of the early development of Marian piety has only just begun, and above all it will be essential now to look beyond the Council of Ephesus in order to discover its roots.

Setting Some Parameters

Before proceeding any further, however, it will be useful to define with more precision some of our terminology as well as to describe certain limitations of this study. Firstly, we should clarify some of the language that we shall use to refer to the various kinds of reverence that the early Christians had for the Virgin. The terms "piety" and "devotion" will be used in the most general sense to describe the full range of religious interests that the early Christians showed toward the Virgin as a figure in her own right, including celebrations of her unique holiness and purity or her supernatural qualities, such as we find for instance already in the second-century *Protevangelium of James*, or her status as a learned master of the cosmic mysteries, as we find in certain other texts. As a broader category, Marian piety or devotion may of course also include prayers to the Virgin or ritual acts performed in her honor, but in our usage these terms do not necessarily indicate the presence of such observances. Instead, devotion and piety will also be used in the absence of any liturgical practices to describe the most general kinds of early Christian reverence for Mary.

The terms "veneration" and "cult," however, will be reserved for instances in which some sort of liturgical component is involved, including not only ceremonies and annual commemorations but also petitions for the Virgin's intercession, which seem to form the basis for these more formal and elaborate ritual expressions of Marian piety. In other words, "veneration" or "cult" signals some sort of action on the part of Mary's devotees to express their reverence for her holiness and sacred power.[17] It should also be clear that the meaning of "cult" in this context has nothing to do with the word's contemporary usage in reference to certain new religious movements that exert a high level of control over believers' lives, occasionally leading to exploitation and abuse.[18] Rather, the term "cult," which derives from the Latin *cultus*, has long been used in traditional Christianity to refer to the practices involved in the veneration of individual saints, so that one can equally speak of the cult of Saint Jude or Saint Anne. As for "veneration," this word reflects a fairly conventional translation of the Greek words *proskynesis* and *doulia*, both of which came to be used as designations for the acts of reverence that are appropriately offered to saints and other creatures (such as kings, for instance). This more limited form of "worship" has traditionally been distinguished sharply from the true worship, known in Greek as *latreia*, that is properly offered to God alone.[19] Accordingly, we will generally avoid use of the term "worship" in reference to ritual acts of devotion offered to Mary and other saints, in order to avoid any confusion with the type of worship that the Christian faith reserves for God alone. Instead, we will designate such commemorations and prayers for intercession to Mary and the saints more precisely under the category of "veneration."

With a focus squarely on early Marian piety and veneration, then, this book will pay considerably less attention to the development of Marian doctrine, or Mariology, in the ancient church. Of course, it is impossible to completely sever these two topics, inasmuch as Mary's mounting significance in early Christian theological discourse was often closely linked to the growth and expansion of her cult. Nevertheless, as noted above, Mary's role in early Christian doctrine has been relatively well studied, at least in comparison with early Marian piety. Inasmuch as modern Roman Catholic scholarship has shown a particular concern with this topic, one may consult any number of Catholic studies on the history of Mariological doctrines, although again, these often must be used with some caution, particularly for the early centuries. From a more theologically neutral perspective, Hilda Graef's *Mary: A History of Doctrine and Devotion* and Brian Reynolds's excellent recent study *Gateway to Heaven* both offer comprehensive and insightful surveys of Mary's developing role in patristic thought. So in order to keep this volume to a manageable size, and also to avoid duplicating their fine work, I would refer readers who are interested especially in early Marian doctrine to either of these two volumes. Thus, while we will not entirely neglect the development of Marian doctrine in the ancient church, we will treat it only briefly and primarily in relation to parallel developments within early Marian piety.

It may surprise some readers (and possibly delight others) to learn that this book will refrain from offering explanations of early Marian piety that locate its genesis primarily in some larger cultural influence external to the Christian tradition. In my opinion, much current scholarship on the origins of Marian devotion suffers from a crisis of both overexplanation and insufficient information. Numerous studies have been published that would purport to explain devotion to the Virgin Mary as a result of some foreign impulse that has intruded upon the Christian faith or as something fully comprehensible only in light of some modern intellectual discourse that reveals the peculiar logic underlying such reverence for Mary. Indeed, works that take such an approach are often among the studies most cited by non-specialists, particularly because they appear to operate outside of the confessional interests that govern other more theologically oriented works. Nevertheless, it is hard not to see such approaches as a kind of extension of the more avowedly Protestant view of Marian cult as something grafted onto the Christian tradition only at a rather late stage. As a result, Marian piety is effectively made out to be something so exotic, so discordant with the fabric of the Christian faith that external influences must be identified in order to understand its very existence. Whether it be ancient goddess traditions, psychoanalysis, the "eternal feminine," or the anthropology of sacrifice, many scholars presume that something else must explain why and how the early Christians turned to Mary in prayer and veneration.[20]

To be sure, there is nothing inherently wrong with such perspectives in their own right, and all are immensely valuable for understanding the many facets of Marian devotion and its origins. Feminist critiques of Mary's overwhelmingly patriarchal representation are particularly needed and welcome. But the problem here is, as Leena Mari Peltomaa rightly observes, that this abundance of explanation has in fact prevented us from recognizing that we actually lack a historical reconstruction of the rise of the cult of the Virgin.[21] So much emphasis on discovering the skeleton key that unlocks the mystery of Christian devotion to Mary has left us without an account of Marian piety that describes how the basic principles undergirding these influential beliefs and practices actually arose from a logic that was native to the early Christian tradition itself. Instead, devotion to the Virgin is presented as something largely anomalous to the Christian tradition, a historical oddity that requires some sort of dramatic explanation for its genesis. By comparison, for instance, it is hard to imagine a similar urgency being given to discovering why so many early Christians were devoted to Saint Thecla or Saint Mary of Magdala: something peculiar seems to be at work in many of these approaches to the development of Marian piety.

Of all these different options, the goddess explanation has certainly proven to be the most popular, and so perhaps it warrants some direct attention. On the one hand, there is no denying that Mary's representation and veneration have been deeply colored by the influence of earlier traditions derived from the worship of various goddesses in the ancient Mediterranean world. Yet, on the other hand, these similarities are often superficial in nature, and they can frequently distract from more fundamental differences at both the conceptual and practical levels, as is also true more generally in the early Christian cult of the saints. For instance, Mary was a human being whose primary role is to intercede on behalf of other human beings with God: is this anything like the cultic worship of Isis or Artemis?[22] Moreover, it is a profound mistake to imagine that such parallels should somehow explain the origins of the cult of Mary and likewise reveal it as something exogenous to the Christian tradition.[23] The simple truth of the matter is that a great deal of traditional Christian faith and practice reflects earlier precedents from the Greco-Roman world, not only in the case of the veneration of saints more generally, but in other areas as well, such as the Eucharist and the celebration of Christmas. So much of early Christian culture was deeply imprinted by Hellenistic precedents that one must wonder why the influence of goddess traditions on Marian piety should somehow be singled out, as it often has been.[24] And as scholars have increasingly come to recognize, the Christian/pagan dichotomy that underlies such explanations is largely a false one, particularly in late antiquity.[25]

Moreover, Jonathan Z. Smith and Peter Brown have both drawn attention to the fact that such appeals to the "pagan" origin of certain Christian beliefs and practices, and particularly the veneration of saints, derive largely from Protestant invectives against Roman Catholicism or Enlightenment critiques of "vulgar" religious practices.[26] Of course, such misuse does not mean that the comparative history of religions should be entirely abandoned—far from it! Rather, we must instead be aware that this approach is not always ideologically neutral and may often reflect various sorts of inherent bias. And in the case of early Marian piety, it is often hard to miss such undertones: Protestant writers have often emphasized the influence of ancient goddess traditions in order to make devotion to Mary appear as something alien to the Christian tradition, framing the rise of

Marian cult in terms of her gradual "deification" rather than as a rather ordinary element of late ancient piety.[27] So while parallels between ancient goddess traditions and early Marian piety of course remain significant for the historian of religion, they simply do not explain the emergence of Christian devotion to Mary and likewise should not be allowed to control its interpretation in the way that one finds in much previous scholarship.[28] Instead, one is inclined instead to agree in this matter with Averil Cameron, who rightly concludes of Marian veneration that "no religious development of such importance can be explained in simple or monocausal terms. ... Pagan syncretism may have played a part, but in my view it was a minor one; competition would be a better model."[29]

Marian Devotion in the Context of the Cult of the Saints

Rather than looking for some external cause or explanation, then, the present study seeks to understand the origins of Marian piety primarily on terms drawn from within the Christian tradition itself. Devotion to Mary was a product of early Christian culture that grew naturally out of its concerns with Christology and virginity and, most especially, the practice of venerating the saints. There is simply no need to find some sort of outside influence that is responsible for Christian veneration of the Virgin Mary: it was implicit in the patterns of early Christian discourse. Of course, there is no question that precedents from ancient Mediterranean goddess traditions and insights from modern social sciences can offer important perspectives for studying the history of Marian devotion. Yet at the same time it seems absolutely essential to understand Christian veneration of Mary as something that arose from within the Christian tradition itself. The cult of the Virgin must have had powerful resonance with other central elements of early Christian discourse and practice for it to achieve the remarkable success that it did. And this becomes most evident as we begin to situate the emergence of devotion to Mary within the broader context of emergent Christian devotion to the saints. For that is how the cult of the Virgin should be understood in late antiquity: as simply one variation—albeit a remarkable one—of the nascent cult of the saints. Her veneration and intercession were not different in kind from that of other saints, but rather in quality.

Admittedly, Mary quickly emerged even in this period as a saint whose petitions and influence with her son surpassed that of other potential advocates. Likewise, we can see that already in late antiquity the Virgin had begun to acquire some of the accolades and attributes that would ultimately lead to her elevation above the rest of the company of the saints as a sort of "super-saint," especially in the late medieval and modern West. Indeed, in these later periods Mary sometimes came to be regarded as almost superhuman and was elevated dangerously close to an equal footing with her son. Nevertheless, I will not attempt here to account for these later developments in the medieval and modern West, since these elements are largely foreign to Mary's veneration in late antiquity, and moreover one can consult a number of fine studies on these aspects of medieval and early modern Marian piety.[30] Yet at the same time it would appear that this exaltation of Mary in later western Christianity is at least partly responsible for many of the over-determined explanations of Marian piety mentioned previously. Focus on these later developments has occasionally distorted scholarly perceptions of early Marian piety, thereby inspiring the search for a more dramatic cause for her cult.[31] While the near apotheosis of Mary in some quarters of the Roman Catholic tradition may perhaps warrant the identification of some extraordinary catalyst (although I remain skeptical), such later developments will not concern us as we try to understand the beginnings of Christian devotion to Mary. Instead, we need to dial things back a bit from the medieval Mary in order to better understand her role in ancient Christian faith and practice. At this early stage she was effectively a saint among other saints who was revered for her exceptional purity and holiness as well as her intimacy with her son, a more modest status that she retains, more or less, in much of the Christian East up until the present day.

Averil Cameron was seemingly the first to propose that the origins of Marian veneration are best understood when placed within the broader context of the emerging cult of the saints, and the present study owes a great debt to her pioneering work in this area, which must form a basis for any further investigation of this topic. Yet even she has recently maintained that it is "only after the Council of Ephesus and the recognition of her title as Theotokos in 431 CE that we find the real development of the cult of the Virgin which was to find expression in the sixth century in particular in the establishment of Marian feasts ... [and] stories of her appearances and of miracles performed by her."[32] Likewise, Cameron frequently remarks in her many publications on early devotion to Mary that the cult of the Virgin developed much more slowly than did the cult of other early saints, usually citing the cult of Saint Thecla as the main point of reference. Although she first proposed this comparison in 1978, its repetition by Cameron as well as others after her have made it into something of scholarly consensus.[33] In many respects Thecla presents an ideal figure for such comparison. Cameron goes a bit far in suggesting that Thecla was "more popular and influential in early Christianity than the Virgin Mary,"[34] yet it seems safe to say that this missionary companion of Paul was the only female figure in early Christianity whose popularity could possibly rival that of Jesus's mother.[35] Nevertheless, the evidence for early devotion to Mary actually compares quite favorably with that for Thecla, and in many instances it is much better.

16

In making her case for the priority of Thecla's cult, Cameron points especially to the famous itinerary of an early Christian pilgrim named Egeria, who in 384 visited a shrine of Saint Thecla on the southern coast of Turkey, near the city of Seleucia (modern Silifke): there, according to the late second-century apocryphal *Acts of Paul and Thecla*, she completed her life. In addition, Cameron notes that Thecla's depiction in visual art and on pilgrimage souvenirs, as well as the existence of a fifth-century *Life and Miracles* collection, offer clear indications of an active cult. For good measure, she also cites for comparison the veneration of Saint Menas in Egypt, and Saint Artemius and Saints Cosmas and Damian in Constantinople, all of whom, she maintains, had a clearly visible cult in this era. By contrast, Cameron posits that "in the case of the Virgin, the kind of evidence that is plentiful for the cult of Thecla from the fourth and fifth centuries tends not to be found until the late sixth or seventh centuries," that is, roughly two hundred years later![36]

Despite the frequent assertion of Marian veneration's tardy arrival by Cameron and other scholars as well, the truth of the matter is that on the whole the evidence for the cult of the Virgin is not significantly later, particularly if one looks beyond the environs of Constantinople. In fact, one of the main limitations of Cameron's otherwise fine work on this topic is its geographic focus on the culture of the imperial capital. Nevertheless, as has long been well known, the earliest shrines to the Virgin were established not in Constantinople, but in the Jerusalem area already by the first decades of the fifth century, if not even earlier. Admittedly, this is some forty years after we first learn of Thecla's shrine in Seleucia, but one certainly has to wonder: are several decades really evidence that Mary's cult was late on the scene or is this difference simply a matter of serendipity? Specialists on the early Jerusalem liturgies would tend to suggest the latter, and several scholars have proposed that in all probability Jerusalem's shrines and its annual feast of Mary likely go back at least to the later fourth century. And not only that, but around the same time that we find the first clear evidence for these Jerusalem shrines, the early fifth century, the church of Santa Maria Maggiore was just being completed in Rome, even as the Third Ecumenical Council itself was meeting in 431 at a church in Ephesus dedicated to the Virgin Mary![37]

In terms of literary production, the *Protevangelium of James* certainly offers a worthy rival to the *Acts of Paul and Thecla*, and judging from this basis, the Christians of the later second century seem to have held at least as much interest in the mother of Jesus as in this companion of Paul. And Mary certainly can best Thecla in this arena as we move into later centuries: an account of Mary's life and miracles can easily be dated to the fourth century—at least a century before we find the *Life and Miracles of Thecla* mentioned by Cameron, and in all probability another similar Marian narrative dates to the third century, if not even earlier. Moreover, both of these writings bear witness to the practice of intercessory prayer to the Virgin, and the fourth-century narrative additionally reveals a highly developed cult of the Virgin with three annual feasts in her honor. In terms of literary evidence, then, the cult of the Virgin actually fares better than the cult of Saint Thecla. Likewise, Thecla has no advantage with regard to material culture. Although early representations of Mary are somewhat rare, the same is true for Thecla, and the evidence for Marian piety in early church decoration and pilgrimage art is certainly comparable to that for Thecla.

As for Menas, Artemius, and Cosmas and Damian, Cameron's other points of comparison, only the first can claim evidence of a cult earlier than the Virgin. The first church dedicated to Cosmas and Damian in Constantinople is in fact from the middle of the fifth century, and the shrine of Artemius was dedicated only in the sixth century (while his life and miracles belong to the seventh).[38] Menas, however, it is true, was venerated in Egypt as early as the first decades of the fourth century.[39] But Menas was a martyr (as were Artemius and Cosmas and Damian for that matter), and it is a well-known fact that the cult of the martyrs preceded the cult of the saints: accordingly, one would expect his veneration to have begun prior to Mary's, since she was not a martyr. The veneration of saints who had not died as martyrs only began around the middle of the fourth century, once the persecutions came to an end.[40] Thecla too was regarded as a martyr, even if the earliest account of her life in the *Acts of Paul and Thecla* omits this detail. Thus, one should not be entirely surprised to find that the martyr Thecla may have become the focus of organized cult a little earlier than the Virgin Mary: given the history of the cult of Christian martyrs and saints, this would be expected. And yet, the evidence for early veneration of Mary compares rather favorably with Thecla's record and in some regards even exceeds it. On the whole, then, the evidence for early Marian veneration is really not as bad as we have frequently been led to believe, particularly when we measure her against other non-martyr saints: once again, perhaps the problem lies not so much with the evidence itself but rather with heightened expectations generated by the Virgin's exaltation in centuries to come.

It is perhaps a bit peculiar, however, that we find evidence of an active cult of the Virgin well before we have clear confirmation of a shrine dedicated to her. Typically, a saint's shrine was fundamental in the emergence of a cult, particularly in the case of the martyrs. The cult of the martyrs began at the graveside, where early Christians would gather to commemorate their local martyrs and seek their prayers on the anniversary of their death. The saint's grave and his or her relics provided the main locus for offering intercessory prayers and other ritual activities. With the conversion of Constantine in the early fourth century, it became possible to build churches on these sites, and as non-martyrs were soon added to the ranks of the saints, their graves and remains also were graced with increasingly grand sanctuaries and facilities for pilgrims. At these shrines the saints remained uniquely present and available to petitioners, who would often travel great distances to experience the holiness of such places and bring their prayers directly before these trusted advocates. Nevertheless, Mary was not a martyr and thus did not have an obvious spot for a shrine, such as one could discover for Peter or Paul or Thecla. Yet even more problematic was the fact that Mary had not left behind any bodily remains (a quality that she shares with Thecla), or at least so it came to be believed, particularly in those settings where her veneration was first beginning to take hold.

With no martyrdom and no relics, it would appear that a shrine was not as important to the emergence of the cult of the Virgin as it was for other saints, and the evidence would seem to suggest that her veneration may have initially emerged in the absence of a specific cultic center. There were of course other possible locations for a shrine besides the grave, and one of the earliest centers of Marian cult developed at an alternative site for the Nativity of Christ midway between Jerusalem and Bethlehem. Yet shortly thereafter the Virgin's empty tomb in the Garden of Gethsemane also emerged as a locus of her special veneration, and as the cult of the Virgin rapidly expanded and took hold of the Christian world during the fifth century, this church quickly took pride of place as the foremost Marian shrine. Like so many other saints, then, Mary's cult ultimately came to focus on her tomb, empty though it was. And in the absence of bodily relics, items of her clothing would eventually serve to evoke her holy presence within her shrines, especially in Constantinople. But with that, we stand at the end of our story; now, we must back up and start at the beginning.

Before we do, however, it is perhaps worth considering why it should matter that Marian devotion began in the early Christian period rather than only during the early middle ages: what difference does it make, after all, if Marian piety is earlier or later than the cult of Thecla? It matters for a number of reasons. Obviously the question of when Marian piety began is important enough to have generated a fairly entrenched narrative of its late onset. But more specifically, a better understanding of Marian piety's emergence will help to illuminate a number of specific elements within the development of early Christianity, as the following chapters will in part make clear. It matters, for instance, for how we understand the history of women and gender in early Christianity; it matters for how we understand the rise of asceticism. It matters for how we understand the early cult of the saints, of which Marian veneration is a significant component, even if it has often been left largely out of the conversation in studies of this topic.[41] The early history of Marian piety no doubt also matters in ways that we have yet to recognize. But most of all it matters for how we understand the history of Marian devotion itself and the Virgin Mary's representation within the history of Christianity—no small topic.

Innumerable studies of the Virgin Mary in medieval Christianity, both Byzantine and Western, operate with a presumption that Marian piety really began—or at least its most important elements did—only during that particular period in which the study's author holds the most interest and expertise. One routinely finds claims that the cult of the Virgin did not truly begin until the sixth, or the seventh, or the eighth century, or that certain elements only emerged in the ninth or the tenth.[42] In the West there is a strong consensus that Marian devotion really got going only in the high middle ages, beginning in the late eleventh and twelfth centuries with the invention of "affective piety."[43] Yet this occidentalist view almost completely ignores the long history of Mary's veneration in the Christian East before this time. To a certain extent these errors are excusable, in large part because the early history of Marian piety has been so neglected by scholars of early Christianity. But going forward we will want to rethink the development of later Marian devotion in light of a better understanding of Mary's place in early Christian piety. Thus it will be important for scholars of early Christianity to look forward with an eye toward connecting early and medieval Marian devotion, as I myself have often tried to do,[44] and likewise for western medievalists and Byzantinists to look backward toward the same end. Only thus can we come to a more comprehensive and contextualized understanding of the history of Marian devotion and its place within the broader history of Christianity.

The Structure of this Book

The chapter following this introduction will consider the evidence of Marian piety from the first two Christian centuries. We will begin inevitably with the New Testament, although we will not dwell there very long, given Mary's rather limited depiction within it. After briefly considering some intriguing perspectives on Mary's role in the process of salvation from some writings of the second-century fathers, we will quickly come to early Christian apocrypha, and especially the *Protevangelium of James*, which will be the main focus of this chapter. As noted already above, this early Christian biography of the young Virgin shows a remarkably developed interest in Mary for its era. Although it affords no evidence of any cult, the *Protevangelium* attests to a surprisingly advanced piety centered on Mary's exceptional purity and holiness already by the later second century. The difficulty, however, as others have noted, is to somehow connect this encomium of Mary's unique virtues with the later developments of her cult in the fourth century. In many respects the *Protevangelium* seems out of place with the other voices of second- and third-century Christianity, which generally do not share its high regard for Mary: its intense reverence for the Virgin shines like some isolated beacon in what otherwise appears to be a Marian "dark age" to either side.

Chapter 2, then, will navigate the difficult course of the third century, where evidence of Marian piety is seemingly scarce, and the early church fathers are not always as kind to the Virgin Mary as they would be in later centuries. As we will see, however, this period is not as barren of Marian devotion as many others have often assumed. Admittedly, there is nothing like the *Protevangelium*, and the church fathers of this era can be surprisingly laconic when it comes to Mary. Nevertheless, toward the end of this century we find the remarkable *Sub tuum praesidium* papyrus, a fragment of a prayer invoking Mary's intercessions that was written around the turn of the fourth century in Egypt. Moreover, if we look beyond the writings of the church fathers from this period, we find that Mary figures prominently in a number of early Christian apocryphal texts, often in some unexpected ways. In contrast to the *Protevangelium* and the church fathers, many of these writings exalt Mary not for her virginity and purity, but instead they revere her as an especially learned master of the cosmic mysteries. It is a rather different image of Mary from what we find in more "orthodox" sources.

Two apocryphal texts from the third and fourth centuries are exceptional, however, and their interest in the Virgin Mary and her veneration merits special attention. The writings in question are the earliest surviving accounts of the end of Mary's life, that is, her Dormition and Assumption. Although these texts have been largely ignored by scholars of early Christianity until the present, it is no exaggeration to say that they are equal in importance to the

Protevangelium for understanding Mary's significance in the early Christian tradition and the rise of her cult. Accordingly, each of these two apocrypha will be the focus of its own chapter. The first of these two early Marian narratives is a work often known in scholarly literature by its Latin title, the *Liber Requiei Mariae*, although we will use instead the English translation, the *Book of Mary's Repose*. The entire work survives only in a translation into Classical Ethiopic (Ge'ez), which seems to have been made sometime during late antiquity, probably not long after the conversion of Ethiopia, but there are also substantial early fragments in Syriac as well as in Old Georgian. No doubt this narrative's preservation in these less-known languages in part explains why it has been so long overlooked.

The Greek original of the *Book of Mary's Repose* dates most likely to the third century, although it is possible that it may be even earlier. In comparison with the *Protevangelium*, this apocryphon is less fixated on Mary's purity and holiness, and it presents her instead as a much more active figure, who possesses superior knowledge of the Christian faith and is revered by the apostles and other members of the Christian community. The story itself, which relates her glorious departure from this world and the miraculous transfer of her body to Paradise, is unmistakably designed to highlight Mary's uniquely exalted status among the followers of Christ. Yet the text also is strikingly heterodox, in sharp contrast to the stalwartly orthodox *Protevangelium*: Jesus is identified as a manifestation of the "Great Cherub of Light," for instance, and the text is riddled with concepts and vocabulary that would be more at home in a Gnostic Christian text. Indeed, the theological peculiarities of this ancient apocryphon alone should warrant it broader consideration within the study of early Christianity than it has yet received.

Perhaps most noteworthy for our purposes, however, is the evidence that the *Book of Mary's Repose* provides for nascent Marian veneration, already by the third century it would seem. Particularly in its conclusion, as Mary tours the places of the damned alongside the apostles, the power of her intercessions on behalf of sinners is made known. For this reason Enrico Norelli has recently proposed that the traditions of Mary's Dormition and Assumption first emerged during the second century in order to add validation to an existing practice of intercessory prayer to the Virgin: it is an intriguing hypothesis that certainly merits further reflection.[45] Yet it is also worth noting here that this earliest evidence for the veneration of Mary appears to come from a markedly heterodox theological milieu. This could suggest, as noted briefly above, that the cult of the Virgin had its origins somewhere outside of the proto-orthodox stream of early Christianity, a point that also could explain the relative silence of many early orthodox fathers concerning Mary.

The fourth chapter focuses on the second of these two important early Dormition narratives, the *Six Books Dormition Apocryphon*, so-called on account of its division into six separate books. Although this text is best preserved in several Syriac manuscripts of the fifth and sixth centuries, the Greek original and its traditions date almost certainly to the middle of the fourth century, if not perhaps even earlier. As much is indicated especially by their apparent connection with a group of fourth-century Christians known as "Kollyridians," whom Epiphanius of Salamis, a fourth-century bishop from Cyprus, condemns for their excessive devotion to the Virgin Mary. Most significantly, the *Six Books Dormition Apocryphon* provides compelling evidence for an early cult of the Virgin nearly a century before the events of the Council of Ephesus. It reveals a remarkably advanced level of Marian veneration, including, in addition to frequent inter-cessory prayers offered to the Virgin, now also organized cult, annual feasts, miracles ascribed to the Virgin, and even Marian apparitions. Judging from this Dormition narrative, there seems to be little question that the cult of the Virgin had already attained a high degree of complexity by the middle of the fourth century, at least in some settings. Yet, once again, it is seemingly noteworthy that also in this instance emergent Marian veneration is associated with an allegedly marginal group that was regarded as heretical by at least one contemporary church father. Even though, as we will see, there is absolutely nothing at all heterodox about the *Six Books Dormition Apocryphon*, or seemingly even the related group that was opposed by Epiphanius, his condemnation of Marian piety as theologically transgressive and subversive also suggests some intriguing possibilities regarding an "extra-orthodox" origin for Marian veneration.

Chapter 5 will examine other evidence for Marian devotion in the fourth and early fifth centuries, including, in addition to the writings of the church fathers, also nonliterary evidence for the cult of the Virgin, which begins to appear in significant quantities during the later fourth century. Admittedly, there is not as much evidence of this sort as one might like, but in this case devotion to Mary again compares favorably with other early saints. Representations of the Virgin in art are largely absent during the first few centuries, which is hardly a surprise given that almost no Christian art survives from before the third century, and depictions of the saints are quite rare until the fourth century. The only possible exceptions would be certain representations in the Roman catacombs, but the interpretation of these images is often difficult and subject to considerable debate. Still, there is a strong possibility that we find there depictions of Mary in a funerary context dating from the third century. Much more certain are the depictions of Mary as an *orans* on gold glass from fourth-century Rome, which together with a number of other early objects from before the Council of Ephesus show evidence of early Marian piety. Nevertheless, it is really only in the fifth century that we begin to find representations of Mary in art in any significant numbers, which again is fairly typical of other saints.

Even more important, however, is the evidence for early Marian piety that we find in liturgical sources. This is another area where we lack much evidence for the first few centuries of Christianity, but Mary is surprisingly well represented in some of the earliest witnesses to Christian worship. We know of liturgical feasts commemorating the Virgin in several major urban centers during the late fourth and early fifth centuries. Jerusalem emerges as the most significant of these, not in the least because its early liturgies are especially well documented and it is also the site of two of the earliest and most important Marian shrines. Among the most remarkable service books to survive from the ancient Jerusalem church is surely the recently published *Jerusalem Georgian Chantbook*, a work extant only in Old Georgian that preserves a large corpus of hymns from the late fourth and early fifth centuries. In this collection we find ample evidence that Mary's intercessions were regularly sought during the Sunday worship of the Jerusalem church in the period prior to the Council of Ephesus, along with a substantial corpus of Marian hymnography dating most likely to the early fifth century. In this respect, the evidence for early Marian veneration considerably exceeds what we find for the liturgical cult of most other early Christian saints.

Finally, this study will conclude with an analysis of the controversies surrounding the Council of Ephesus. In recent decades, scholars have increasingly recognized that devotion to Mary seems to have played a significant role in both the run-up to this council and even its outcome and was not merely a by-product of its decisions. Rather, there was already in Constantinople and seemingly in Egypt and Jerusalem as well an existing practice of Marian veneration. Accordingly, when Nestorius refused Mary the title of Theotokos, in the eyes of many he showed himself to be an opponent of the Virgin and her veneration. Even if he had merely wished to make a point of

Christology by questioning this title, he perhaps unwittingly stumbled into a circumstance in which he found himself on the wrong side of increasingly popular devotion to the Virgin Mary. The affairs leading up to the council show that Nestorius's opponents seem to have played this piety against him in orchestrating his downfall, particularly in Constantinople. Moreover, certain events reported to have transpired in the council's aftermath further suggest that an already vibrant Marian piety played a significant role in the council's decisions and their reception. A number of studies have additionally argued that the Empress Pulcheria herself played an instrumental role in establishing the cult of the Virgin in Constantinople during the early fifth century, and, furthermore, that she personally worked to engineer Nestorius's downfall on account of his hostility both toward her and toward Marian piety. More recent scholarship has cast some doubt on the extent of Pulcheria's involvement in both the promotion of the early cult of the Virgin and Nestorius's demise. It is admittedly true that some of these previous studies made use of some questionable sources, but on the whole the evidence that both Pulcheria and Marian piety played a significant role in fomenting the opposition to Nestorius is quite solid. Recent efforts to marginalize her from this controversy or even to argue that she actually supported Nestorius are simply not persuasive in light of substantial evidence to the contrary.

Therefore, despite an apparent consensus that Marian piety was relatively late in developing, the evidence for early Christian devotion to Mary is not nearly as meager as has often been maintained. To be sure, it is less abundant than one initially might expect given Mary's enormous importance in later Christian faith and practice. But when considered within the context of the emerging cult of the saints and in comparison with evidence for the veneration of other early Christian saints, particularly those who were not martyrs, the cult of the Virgin fares reasonably well. It is long past time, then, that Marian devotion should be recognized for its importance in the early history of Christianity, alongside the veneration of other holy men and women from this period. While one will find in this era a piety that is certainly much less extravagant than the medieval or modern cult of the Virgin, it is essential that we recognize the role that Marian piety played within formative Christianity. Perhaps now we can also leave behind the persistent need to explain the cult of the Virgin as an intrusion of pagan goddess worship or through some other foreign impulse, recovering instead an understanding of Marian piety as something that developed organically from within the early Christian tradition itself, emerging, at least initially, as simply one popular variant within the nascent cult of the saints.

And as for the Council of Ephesus, what happened there, it would appear, is not the beginnings of the cult of the Virgin, as many have assumed, but rather the embrace and promotion of an already existing set of practices by the empire and the Imperial Church. These political developments bear the responsibility for the explosion of Marian piety that ensued across the Roman Empire. This merger, the fusion of Marian piety with the Christian empire and its church, dramatically transformed the Virgin Mary's image and her veneration so that she quickly emerged as the patroness of the Roman (or Byzantine) Empire and its capital Constantinople. But that would be a story for another book.

CHAPTER ONE

A Virgin Unspotted: Devotion to Mary in the First Two Centuries

Mary in the New Testament

IN LIGHT OF THE prominence to which Mary would later rise in the Christian tradition, it is perhaps a bit surprising how little she figures in the New Testament and other early Christian literature from the first century or so.[1] For instance, Mary is almost invisible in the earliest Christian writings that we possess, the letters of Paul. Paul mentions Mary just once and in the vaguest possible terms: without naming her, he remarks that "God sent his Son, born of a woman" in his letter to the Galatians (4.4), written sometime in the early 50s CE. Here, Mary is little more than a biological fact, albeit an important one that guarantees the humanity of Christ for Paul and thus the reality of the Incarnation. But Mary herself has no broader significance and is not sufficiently important to merit even a name, let alone any interest in the details of her life or person.

Mary does not fare much better in the earliest Christian gospel, the Gospel according to Mark, which was written sometime around 70 CE. The author of Mark at least knows Mary's name, which on one occasion he provides, identifying Jesus as "the carpenter, the son of Mary" (6.3). This passage, however, makes no mention of any father, although it does name four brothers, "James and Joses and Judas and Simon," and further indicates that Jesus also had sisters. Jesus' mother appears a second time in this gospel, although without her name, in a passage that seems to indicate some sort of conflict or at least tension between Jesus and the members of his family. According to Mark 3.20–35, Jesus' family once tried "to seize him," because "the people were saying, 'He is beside himself.'" Then, when his mother and brothers later asked to see him, he responded, "Who are my mother and my brothers?" continuing to explain that his true mother and brothers are his disciples, those who do the will of God.[2] While the precise meaning of this reported encounter between Jesus and his family is certainly open to some interpretation, its significance for charting the development of early Marian piety is quite clear. Mark's gospel shows little interest in Jesus' mother beyond her biological and genealogical role, and it portrays her as an outsider to his movement who on one occasion tried to seize him, along with other members of his family, because the people believed him to be mad.[3]

As for the "historical" Mary of Nazareth who lies behind these earliest memories of Christian origins, unfortunately we can say little more about her than Paul and Mark report: that she was Jesus' mother. Indeed, from this perspective she is even more lost to us than her son, obscured by layers of early Christian "kerygma," that is, the effort to proclaim the message of faith in Christ and hope in his promise of salvation. Presumably the historical Mary was a Jewish peasant from Galilee who happened to give birth to a son whose prophetic mission would impact the world for centuries to come and inspire faith in millions and even billions of people. Yet what role—if any—Mary may have played in her son's ministry remains something of a mystery. Some evidence from the gospel traditions, as we have just seen, suggests that Jesus was possibly estranged from the members of his family, including his mother, perhaps over the very issue of his prophetic teachings and his claim to work wonders. Nevertheless, other traditions indicate Mary's active involvement not only in her son's public ministry but also in the larger economy of salvation that his followers came to believe was accomplished through his life and death. Not long after Mark's gospel was written, other gospel traditions preserve memories of Mary as a much more significant figure in the beginnings of Christianity. Although New Testament scholarship on the whole has tended to discount the possibility that Mary was involved in her son's mission and the formation of the early Christian church, the matter is certainly more complicated than such scholarly neglect might suggest. And whatever the historical reality of her relations with her son and his ministry may have been, these gospel traditions about Mary, particularly from the gospels of Luke and John, laid the foundations for early Christian devotion to the Virgin Mary.

The Gospel according to Matthew adds considerably to Mark's rather meager representation of Jesus' mother, even if its portrait is still rather minimal. Matthew's gospel, which was most likely written sometime between 80 and 90, begins with an account of Jesus' birth, and as one would expect, Mary figures significantly in this Nativity story (1.18–2.23). Yet Matthew also introduces Jesus' father, Joseph, who we quickly learn was not Jesus' actual father or even Mary's husband. According to Matthew, the two were merely betrothed when Mary miraculously conceived, without intercourse and while remaining a virgin. Although Joseph was initially skeptical (quite understandably) of Mary's claims, he was reassured in a dream that Mary's pregnancy was indeed of divine origin, in fulfillment of Isaiah's prophecy, "Behold, the virgin shall conceive and bear a son" (Matt 1.23; Isa 7.14). Thus already by the 80s, if not perhaps even earlier, many Christians had come to believe that Mary conceived and gave birth as a virgin. The main purpose of this belief was undoubtedly to highlight Jesus' divine paternity, but at the same time this doctrine also marks the inception of Christian devotion to Mary, since the miraculous preservation of Mary's virginity and her bodily purity quickly emerged as foundational elements of Marian piety both in early Christianity and in the centuries to come (and in the Islamic tradition as well, for that matter). Matthew then completes his Nativity account with traditions about the visit of the Magi and the Holy Family's flight into Egypt. Yet Mary's role in both of these episodes is largely incidental, and neither story played an especially significant role in the formation of early Marian devotion, at least as they are related in this gospel. But unquestionably the main achievement of Matthew's gospel with regard to Marian piety was its introduction of Mary's virginity, a point that became a cornerstone of Christian reverence for the mother of Jesus.[4]

The Gospel according to John, which was written roughly a decade or so after Matthew (most likely between 90 and 100), brings considerably more attention to Mary and her role in the beginnings of Christianity than its predecessors. Unlike Matthew and Luke, John's gospel lacks an account of Christ's Nativity and begins instead with theological reflections on the nature of Christ as a manifestation of the divine *Logos* or "Word" of God. Yet despite the apparent lack of interest in Christ's human birth, his mother figures prominently in John's gospel, where she is directly involved in her son's ministry and mission. Most notably, Mary is present for the wedding at Cana, which in this gospel inaugurates Jesus's public ministry, and it is primarily at her urging that Jesus performs his first miracle there by turning water into wine (2.1–11). It is true that there is some indication of tension in their conversation, for instance, when Jesus responds to her request, "Woman, what concern is that to you and to me?" (2.4). Nevertheless, as Elisabeth Schüssler Fiorenza notes, this story was seemingly taken from an earlier written source that was used by John known as the "signs source." In its original form, Schüssler Fiorenza suggests, the episode most likely portrayed Mary as in fact having a prominent role in the beginnings of Christ's ministry. The apparent tension between mother and son, she concludes, was probably introduced by the evangelist, who was uncomfortable with having Mary play such a pivotal role at this moment.[5] Yet in the end, Christ does what his mother asks of him, so that the overall effect of this incident is to connect Mary of Nazareth with the beginning of her son's public ministry. John's Mary thus is not estranged from her son's prophetic mission, but to the contrary she actively encourages it. Moreover, this episode laid important foundations for the subsequent development of Marian piety. The later tradition would especially recall this incident as evidence of the influence that Mary could have over her son, even when he was not entirely willing: such maternal persuasion was essential to belief in the special powers of Mary's intercessions with her son.[6]

Apparently, Mary's involvement in her son's ministry was not limited to the events at Cana in John's gospel. When Jesus departs from Cana for Capernaum, his mother is named as the first of his companions, along with his brothers and his disciples (2.12). The clear implication would seem to be that Mary continued on with Jesus and his other followers and was actively involved in his ministry. Oddly, however, Mary is largely absent from the Fourth Gospel after this point, and she does not reappear until near its end. Nevertheless, when she does appear again, it is at a highly significant moment: she is present among the women standing at the foot of the Cross (19.25–27). There her son takes the opportunity to address her directly from the cross, famously entrusting her into the care of his "beloved disciple," a figure who is traditionally identified with John and the author of this gospel.

Mary is thus present at both the beginning and the end of Jesus's ministry, a depiction that would seem to suggest that she had been his disciple from start to finish. She was likewise at the end of her life a companion of her son's most trusted disciple, this "beloved disciple" to whom the Fourth Gospel is attributed. No less important is the special concern that Jesus shows here for his mother's well-being. This too would inform later ideas of his special attentiveness to her concerns and his willingness to heed her pleas with him. So in the gospel of John, Mary appears as a faithful disciple of her son who inaugurates his ministry, an associate of his most beloved and trusted companion, and one whose petitions and needs warrant special concern from her son.[7] With this we certainly have come a long way from Mary's near invisibility in Paul and Mark and are headed steadily in the direction of her emergence as the most important and revered female figure of the Christian tradition.

Yet surely the richest and most influential portrait of Mary in the New Testament is found in the Gospel according to Luke. The gospel of Luke is roughly contemporary with Matthew and John, and by most estimates it dates to sometime between 80 and 100, although there are some scholars who would place it early in the second century. Like Matthew, Luke begins with a Nativity account, which empha- sizes Mary's virginal conception in even more dramatic fashion through the story of the Annunciation (1.26–38). In contrast to Matthew's terse notice that Mary "was found to be with child by the Holy Spirit" (1.18), Luke describes the angel Gabriel's unexpected appearance to Mary, who is surprised and skeptical to learn that she will conceive a son, since she is a virgin. After Gabriel further explains that she will miraculously conceive through the overshadowing of the Holy Spirit and the power of the Most High, Mary gives her consent, replying "Here am I, the servant of the Lord; let it be with me according to your word" (1.38).

Mary's story then continues as she travels to visit her cousin Elizabeth, who also has miraculously conceived a son, namely, John the Baptist. When they meet, Elizabeth greets Mary by crying out, "Blessed are you among women. . . . And blessed is she who believed that there would be a fulfillment of what was spoken to her by the Lord" (1.42, 45). Mary responds with the Magnificat, a canticle also known as the "Song of Mary," which would appear to be the earliest extant Marian hymn (1.46–55). Here, Mary speaks what amounts to "a pastiche of texts taken from the Old Testament," drawing especially on the prayer of Hannah from 1 Samuel (2.1–10).[8] The hymn offers praise to God, but also seeks to explain the tremendous events that had recently come to pass. Her words allusively relate God's actions in her own life back to prophetic motifs from the Old Testament, while at the same time looking forward to events that will soon transpire in Luke's gospel. Thus, she positions herself at the axis between the two covenants, associating her condition both with God's faithfulness toward Israel in the past and also with the fulfillment of God's promises that will come to pass through her divinely conceived son.[9]

In these episodes Luke's gospel offers the most developed reflection on Mary and her role in the beginnings of Christianity in the New Testament. Here, Mary is the first to hear and receive the gospel message of salvation from the angel Gabriel, to which she responds with faith, saying, "Let it be with me according to your word." Thus, Luke presents Mary as the first faithful disciple of her son and also as one who is "blessed among women" and will be called blessed by all generations. Then in the Magnificat, which completes this sequence, Mary speaks prophetically, recalling the promises of the prophets and foretelling the themes of her son's preaching. Such representation of Mary as the model of belief and discipleship in Luke certainly forms a sharp contrast with the silence of Paul and Mark.

Mary, of course, is also present for the events of the Nativity, and eight days later she goes up to the Temple in Jerusalem with Joseph and her infant son for purification (2.21–38). In this scene, commonly known as the Presentation in the Temple, the Holy Family encounters a prophet named Simeon. After praising God, Simeon addresses Mary, explaining the significance of her newborn son and also warning that "a sword will pierce your own soul too," a passage that later generations would often interpret in light of Mary's travails at the Crucifixion. Luke's narrative then abruptly leaps ahead twelve years, with the story of the young boy Jesus teaching in the Temple (2.41–52). As Jesus' parents begin their return to Nazareth from Jerusalem following the Passover feast, they suddenly realize that their son has somehow been left behind. After searching the city of Jerusalem frantically, they eventually find him teaching among the elders in the Temple. Mary initially upbraids her son, asking why he treated her and Joseph like this. Jesus offers an explanation, but Mary and Joseph fail to understand. It is another odd moment of tension between Jesus and his family, and his mother in particular, which is made all the more strange by the evangelist's remark that "His mother treasured all these things in her heart." This comment, which echoes a similar statement at the conclusion of the Nativity, could seem to suggest Mary's intimate knowledge of her son and her unique understanding of his divine nature.[10]

From this point onward Mary recedes largely into the background for the remainder of Luke's gospel, appearing again during her son's ministry only in the Synoptic tradition of Jesus' encounter with his mother and brothers (Luke 8.19–21). Even more than Matthew, Luke softens the tensions between Jesus and his family in Mark's account. Not only does Luke, like Matthew, omit the report that Jesus' family was seeking to restrain him because he was deranged, but he further has Jesus respond to the news that his mother and brothers wished to see him by proclaiming: "My mother and my brothers—these are the ones who hear the word of God and do it." There is no suggestion here that Mary is an outsider to Jesus's ministry, but to the contrary, she stands among those who heed the word of God.[11]

This characterization helps to clarify a specifically Lukan tradition that appears in Luke 11.27–28, where a woman from the crowd says to Jesus, "Blessed is the womb that bore you, and the breasts that you sucked," to which Jesus responds, "Blessed rather are those who hear the word of God and keep it!" Walter Delius strangely interpreted this passage as a "protest against efforts to promote the veneration of Mary," a rather odd conclusion that would seem to presume that such a practice had already begun to take hold during the first century of Christianity.[12] Other interpreters, mainly Protestant, have similarly understood this passage as somehow reflecting negatively on Mary, particularly by reading it together with Mark 3.31–35, where there seems to be some tension between Jesus and his family. Nevertheless, as John McGuckin notes, given that this passage occurs uniquely in Luke's gospel, there is no reason to subordinate it to this Markan material. One should instead read it in light of the first chapter of Luke, where Mary is named blessed, and hears and heeds the word of God at the Annunciation, as well as Jesus' declaration that his mother is among those "who hear the word of God and do it." When viewed from this perspective, Jesus' words are not so much a correction as a clarification. As McGuckin explains, here "Mary (as biological Mother) is not contrasted with the 'person of faith,' but rather highlighted as a person of faith: that is, she was able to suckle the child precisely because she was the obedient disciple who gave her *fiat* ['may it be so'] to God despite the danger in which it enveloped her."[13] Mary, then, is not inferior, but as in Luke 8.21, she is the one who hears the word and keeps it.

Despite Mary's absence from much of Luke's gospel, she suddenly reappears—albeit only briefly—in the second part of Luke's two-volume history of Christian origins, the Acts of the Apostles. There, Mary the mother of Jesus is named as present among Jesus' closest disciples in the Upper Room for the founding of the Christian church (Acts 1.14), only to completely vanish again thereafter. It is not clear what role she might have played on this momentous occasion, as she is merely mentioned, and why she was remembered as a participant in this reconstitution of Jesus' community is uncertain. Perhaps because she had such a prominent role at the beginning of Luke's gospel and was pivotal in setting in motion the divine plan that would be accomplished through her son, her presence in Acts marks a kind of narrative and theological symmetry, so that she is also present for the formation of the community of the saved and the inauguration of this second stage in the divine plan for salvation. The fact that she does not otherwise figure in the events of Acts certainly could suggest that her presence in this scene was largely inspired by such literary interests. Then again, as Gaventa notes, many of Jesus' followers quickly fade from the scene in Acts, including, for instance, Matthias who is chosen to replace Judas. Luke's history of the early church focuses instead largely on two figures, Peter and Paul. In any case, Mary's appearance in the Upper Room at the beginning of Acts solidifies Luke's characterization of her as one of Jesus' disciples.[14]

Mary's representation in the writings of the New Testament is thus diverse, as one would only expect, given the theological diversity of the corpus itself. Yet the chronology of these documents could invite certain conclusions about the evolving status of Mary within earliest Christianity. Her virtual absence from Paul's letters and the reports of family strife in Mark might suggest to some that Mary played no meaningful role in her son's movement and was in fact of little significance for the first Christians. Then only toward the end of the first century did she suddenly become of interest, as reflected in Matthew, Luke, and John, whose reports of Mary's involvement in her son's mission and ministry should accordingly be understood as little more than pious, theological embellishments of earlier traditions. Certainly, some scholars of the New Testament have drawn such conclusions from the evidence.[15] Nevertheless, as attractive as this developmental narrative may appear on the surface, there is, it would seem, somewhat more to the story, and the data are actually more complicated than this strictly chronological reading might suggest. Indeed, as other scholars have suggested, these different representations of Mary possibly reflect divergent attitudes toward the influence of the members of Jesus' family and the Jerusalem community in earliest Christianity.

The tensions between Paul and James the brother of Jesus within the early community are well known, and Paul himself even refers directly to his differences with James in his letter to the Galatians (1.13–2.14). By the time of Paul's conversion (ca. 34), it would seem, James had already emerged as the leader of the Jerusalem community, having reached some level of authority and influence over Peter and others of the apostles who had previously followed his "brother," Jesus of Nazareth. While there has been some debate over the centuries as to whether or not James was actually a son of Mary, there is no question that in some way he was a close family relation of Jesus. Both James and Peter were of sufficient stature in the early Christian community that Paul traveled to Jerusalem to meet with them concerning his mission to the gentiles just three years after his conversion. According to Paul, they were both supportive and endorsed his mission. Then fourteen years later he traveled back to

Jerusalem and met with the leaders of the community there, including James, Peter, and now John. Paul reports that on this occasion he laid out for them the message that he was preaching to the gentiles, which allowed them to become Christian without following the observances of the Jewish Law. Paul indicates that they again authorized his program, asking only that he would remember the poor. But later on, Paul found himself in a confrontation with Peter at Antioch, precisely over issues related to the gentiles and their observance of the Law. Peter, under the influence of certain people sent by James, began to refuse to eat with the gentiles "for fear of the circumcision faction," which would seem to be James and those who recognized his authority and the authority of the Jerusalem community. It is not clear how these events should be reconciled with Paul's earlier reports that James, Peter, and others in Jerusalem had approved and authorized his mission. But there is no mistaking that by the early 50s a rift had emerged between Paul and the leadership of the Jerusalem community, including James in particular.

This ideological struggle between Paul and his co-workers on the one hand, and a "circumcision party" led by James the brother of Jesus in Jerusalem on the other, has long provided an important lens through which to view the formation of earliest Christianity, particularly since the influential work of F. C. Baur and the Tübingen school in the mid-nineteenth century.[16] And while one should perhaps be somewhat careful about drawing the boundaries between "gentile" and "Jewish" Christianity too sharply in the middle of the first century, there is little question that by the time Paul was writing his surviving letters, he was engaged in some sort of conflict with Jesus' brother James and the faction that he led from Jerusalem over the issue of gentile circumcision and observance of the Law. Paul thus seems to have struggled against the influence that Jesus' relatives had within the nascent Christian movement, and so perhaps it is largely for this reason that he has so little to say about Jesus' mother, beyond the fact that she existed.[17]

Interestingly enough, this same division in the early Christian community can also explain Mary's near absence from Mark's gospel, as well as its portrayed tension between Jesus and his mother and other members of his family. Many New Testament scholars have identified the gospel of Mark as a work standing squarely within the Pauline theological trajectory,[18] and so not surprisingly we can find in Mark traces of antagonism toward the Jerusalem church and the leadership of Jesus's relatives. It is, of course, well known that Mark generally gives an unfavorable portrait of the Twelve, and their depiction has often been taken to indicate suspicion of their authority within the early communities that produced this gospel. Yet it would also appear that Mark's negative depiction of the relationship between Jesus and his family serves a similar interest. It shows that his brothers and his mother did not truly understand Jesus and his mission during his lifetime, and they were not among those who followed him from Galilee to Jerusalem. Consequently, any claims by his family to have special authority within the early community are severely undermined by their portrayal in Mark's gospel. And although Mark's location within the Pauline trajectory has been argued primarily on the basis of other, more theological criteria, it should be clear that this tradition of conflict and estrangement between Jesus and his family also serves the Pauline agenda of vindicating the mission to the gentiles against the critiques coming from James and presumably other members of Jesus' family in Jerusalem.[19]

Thus there is good reason to suspect that these traditions of tension between Jesus and his mother and brothers during his ministry are in fact a product of Markan redaction rather than an older memory of Jesus' actual estrangement from his family. It is true that the gospel of John similarly reports that Jesus's brothers did not believe in him (7.5), although, most importantly for our purposes, there is no mention of his mother in this context.[20] Perhaps we have here an echo of the Markan tradition in John, or possibly some but not all of his relatives did not believe in his mission and teachings: admittedly it is not entirely clear how to reconcile this verse with the interpretation proposed above. But we may conclude rather tentatively that Mary's absence from certain New Testament writings and her occasional portrayal as an outsider or even an opponent to her son's ministry possibly reflect the sectarian interests of Pauline Christianity. Therefore, one cannot simply assume that the Markan tradition of estrangement between Jesus and Mary at the time of his ministry reflects a primitive or authentic tradition in comparison with Mary's more positive portrayals in the other more recent gospels.[21] Instead, this memory was perhaps generated by theological interests common to Pauline Christianity and the gospel of Mark that aimed to marginalize and undermine the relatives of Jesus, rather than telling us something about the historical Jesus and his family's relation to his ministry.

Mary after the New Testament: The New Eve

The belief in Mary's virginal conception that figures so prominently in Matthew and Luke was quick to catch on, and a similar profession of Mary's exceptional status and her unique role in the economy of salvation also appears in the *Ascension of Isaiah*, an early Christian apocryphal text dating most likely from the beginning of the second century. The *Ascension of Isaiah* relates a tradition of Mary's virginal conception and birth that has some strong affinities with Matthew's account (11.2–14).[22] Nonetheless, as Enrico Norelli has argued, one should not simply assume that the *Ascension of Isaiah* has drawn these traditions from Matthew, as some older scholarship suggests; rather, both sources appear to have drawn independently on earlier traditions and biblical motifs in order to fashion different but related memories of Jesus' birth.[23] Also from around the same time are the letters of Ignatius of Antioch (ca. 35–107), which frequently profess belief in Mary's virginal conception and birthing. Indeed, for Ignatius, Mary's virginity seems to have become a cornerstone of the Christian faith, and he often proclaims it in language that resembles creedal formulations.[24] Likewise, the *Odes of Solomon*, a collection of early Christian hymns dating most likely from the middle of the second century, also maintain Mary's conception and giving birth while remaining a virgin. Yet the *Odes* add to this the idea that she brought forth her son without experiencing any pain, a doctrine that would soon become a prominent theme in Marian piety. Likewise the *Odes* describe Mary as "a mother with great mercies," noting additionally that "she loved with redemption, and protected with kindness."[25] Such characterizations could seem to identify Mary as the powerful intercessor and protector of the Christian faithful that we find expressed more clearly in the centuries to come. Nevertheless, it is questionable whether these passages should be interpreted thus in such an early text. Also from the mid-second century is the *Infancy Gospel of Thomas*, which tells a number of rather surprising tales from Jesus' childhood. But here Mary is mentioned only a few times and in passing, and without any notice regarding her virginity.[26]

The notion of Mary's virginity would receive further theological development during the course of the second century, first at the hands of Justin Martyr (ca. 100–165) and later by Irenaeus of Lyons (d. 202), both of whom wove from this doctrine a portrait of Mary as the New Eve, whose chastity and obedience undid the original Eve's primordial immorality and disobedience. With these two thinkers we see the first significant moves toward developing Mary as a figure who plays a role in her own right within the drama of human salvation, albeit in a fashion that powerfully reinscribes patriarchal ideas of female virtue as chaste and submissive. Justin was a philosopher who converted to Christianity and laid down some of the fundamental principles of what would ultimately come to be defined as "orthodox" Christianity. Only a few of his writings survive, one of which, the *Dialogue with Trypho*, is a literary dialogue in which Justin answers the objections of a fictionalized Jewish opponent. Here, Justin mounts a spirited defense of Mary's virginal conception and birthing against Jewish accusations to the contrary, focusing especially on the question of whether the woman foretold in Isaiah 7.14 is in fact a "virgin" or more simply a "young girl."[27] Justin also moves in some new theological directions in identifying Mary's response to God at the Annunciation as a pivotal moment in the process of salvation. Mary's willing participation in God's divine plan enables the destruction of sin and death that was unleashed by Eve's disobedience.[28] While there is no indication of any emergent devotion to the Virgin in Justin's writings, his reflections on her active role in the process of salvation elevate her status significantly within the discourse of Christian theology.

Irenaeus, writing toward the end of the second century, develops this idea of Mary as the New Eve further still. Although he is perhaps most well known as a staunch opponent of heresy, who wrote voluminously against other Christians for their "deviant" beliefs and practices in his *Against Heresies*, in a more positive sense Irenaeus was also one of the great architects of what would eventually become the orthodox Christian faith. Indeed, many of the most basic principles of Christian orthodoxy owe their formulation to Irenaeus's efforts to define and defend what he believed to be the truth in the face of stiff competition from Gnostic and other early varieties of Christianity. One of the most central ideas in Irenaeus's exposition of the Christian faith is his notion of the recapitulation of the human race, that is, the renewal and perfection of humanity through God's incarnation in Jesus of Nazareth, an idea that he develops from Paul and the Pauline tradition. Christ is the new Adam who repairs the damage done to humankind through the first Adam's disobedience: through his incarnation and life on earth Christ renews the human race and makes it possible for it to regain its former glory. Not surprisingly, Irenaeus is quick to draw Mary into this scheme, so that she becomes a new Eve for the new Adam. In an extended comparison between the two women, he draws out many of the same points previously expounded by Justin, explaining for instance how Mary's virginal obedience undoes the disobedience of the virgin Eve. Nonetheless, Irenaeus presses this logic further still, so that he even identifies Mary as "the cause of salvation" who "rescues" the human race from its bondage to death. Through her obedience, he explains, Mary makes possible not only her own salvation but also that of all of God's creation.[29] While Christ himself is the salvation of human-kind, Mary herself is for Irenaeus, as Brian Reynolds writes, "a fixed point, on whom the whole history of salvation depends."[30]

Irenaeus also describes Mary in one instance as "the advocate of the virgin Eve," a peculiar expression that some Roman Catholic scholarship has interpreted as expressing already the root idea of Mary as "the great intercessor for all mankind."[31] The passage certainly could seem to suggest as much, and potentially it may offer early evidence of incipient veneration of the Virgin Mary within Irenaeus's community. When read alongside the high praise for Mary evidenced in the *Odes of Solomon*, one might be tempted to speculate that she had already emerged as an effective mediator with her son in early Christian piety. Nevertheless, the fact that Marian intercession is not mentioned anywhere else in this text, and likewise is not attested in any other context for some time to come, suggests rather strongly that this language should instead be understood as somehow metaphorical. For Irenaeus, then, as for Justin, Mary seems to be a figure primarily of dogmatic rather than devotional concern. While he breaks important new ground in attributing to Mary a pivotal role in the economy of salvation in her own right, even going so far as to name her "the cause of salvation," his writings ultimately afford little if any evidence of emergent Marian piety.

The First Marian Biography: The *Protevangelium of James*

The first visible shoots of early Christian devotion to Mary emerge from a late second-century biography of the Virgin in Greek known by the problematic and somewhat misleading title of the *Protevangelium of James*. No surviving manuscript so names this early Christian writing, and the title seemingly owes its existence to its first editor, Guillaume Postel, who in 1552 published the text in a Latin translation as the *Protevangelium Iacobi*.[32] The narrative's attribution to James is fairly common in the manuscript tradition, where the text passes under a wide range of titles. Nevertheless, the earliest surviving manuscript, from the early fourth century, identifies this text as "the Birth of Mary, the Apocalypse of James," and its most recent editor has argued that only the first part, "the Birth of Mary," has any likelihood of being original.[33] Ideally, then, we should probably rename this apocryphon "the *Birth of Mary*," but the title *Protevangelium of James* has by now obtained such wide currency that any attempt to change it would likely only introduce further confusion. Therefore, simply for the sake of convenience we will retain this unwieldy and inaccurate title.

Perhaps the most problematic element of this now conventional title is its suggestion that this writing is in some sense a gospel, which would seem to imply that its concern is primarily with the life and ministry of Jesus, which in fact it is not. Instead, the *Protevangelium* is a biography of Mary from the time of her own miraculous conception until she gave birth to Jesus, which concludes with some related traditions about the fate of John the Baptist and his parents during Herod's massacre of the innocents. Admittedly, the prefix "proto-" does seem to identify the work as some kind of "pre-gospel," but any associations that this apocryphal text has with the gospel genre are minimal.[34] More importantly, however, this title distracts readers from the narrative's real content: the miraculous life of Mary and her supernatural qualities prior to the birth of her son. No less problematic is the related classification of this text by modern scholarship among the "Infancy Gospels" of early Christianity, as seen in numerous collections of Christian apocrypha and the often-used English title, the "Infancy Gospel of James."[35] Identification with this genre again seems to suggest that we have here a text concerned primarily with the life of the young boy Jesus, which simply is not the case. It is true that the events of Christ's birth are related in the final third of the apocryphon, but nothing further is mentioned about his early childhood, and the focus is otherwise squarely on his mother Mary. Indeed, one has to wonder how this early biography of the Virgin, originally entitled the *Birth of Mary*, came to be classified as an Infancy Gospel in the first place.[36] Quite probably early editors of the Christian apocryphal writings found the *Protevangelium*'s intense interest in glorifying the Virgin to be so incongruous with their views on Mary's place in the early church that they did not know what else to make of it. Whatever the cause, there is little justification for placing this biography of Mary among the Infancy Gospels of Jesus, and one would certainly hope that future scholarship will correct this error and recognize the *Protevangelium* for what it really is: a Marian apocryphon and not an apocryphal Infancy Gospel.

Yet to a certain extent, one also has to wonder whether the designation of this text as an apocryphon is altogether appropriate. It is true, of course, that the *Protevangelium* is an extracanonical text that treats events and characters from the biblical tradition, which certainly fits the definition of a Christian apocryphon.[37] But at the same time the influence of this particular narrative on the subsequent Christian tradition is so vast that it must also be regarded in a certain sense as "quasicanonical." For instance, the *Protevangelium*'s account of Christ's Nativity has determined the representation of this event in Eastern Christian art even to this day, so that his birth is depicted in a remote cave, as in the *Protevangelium*, rather than in a stable in the city of Bethlehem, as in the canonical gospels. Indeed, it would appear that the earliest celebrations of the Nativity in the Jerusalem region were probably commemorated not in nearby Bethlehem, but instead at a site halfway between Jerusalem and Bethlehem along the roadside, where, according to the *Protevangelium*, Mary gave birth to her son Jesus.[38] More importantly for the present purposes, however, the *Protevangelium*'s account of Mary's parentage, her own conception and birth, her wondrous childhood in the Temple, and the birth of her divine son quickly became the "canonical" account of Mary's early life, establishing the basis for innumerable apocryphal, hagiographical, and liturgical texts in the ages to come. The *Protevangelium* was itself frequently employed as a liturgical reading, especially for the feast of Mary's Nativity, but also for the feasts of the Presentation, of Joachim and Anna, Mary's Conception, the Slaughter of the Holy Innocents, and even for Christmas. Largely for this reason, the *Protevangelium* was frequently copied during the Middle Ages, so that it survives today in at least 140 Greek manuscripts and another 169 in Church Slavonic.[39]

Yet, despite such widespread popularity in the Christian East, this early Christian apocryphon was not as successful in the West, where it was condemned as heretical around the year 500 in the so-called "Gelasian Decree."[40] Nevertheless, even in the West the *Protevangelium*'s traditions were enormously influential, largely through their reuse in later Latin apocrypha. Although we know that a Latin version of the *Protevangelium* existed in the Middle Ages, it is attested only by a few fragments and its influence on other early Irish apocrypha.[41] Instead, the *Protevangelium*'s traditions became widely diffused primarily through the highly popular *Gospel of Ps.-Matthew* and its later derivative, the *Book of the Nativity of Mary*, each of which survives in well over a hundred manuscripts.[42] Although these early medieval reworkings of the *Protevangelium* both served to bring its Nativity traditions into greater harmony with the canonical gospels, the bulk of the *Protevangelium*'s account of Mary's childhood and childbearing remains intact. And so, thanks primarily to these two texts, which also were frequently used as liturgical readings, the *Protevangelium*'s traditions about the Virgin would permeate western Christendom as well.

Such a highly influential text certainly ought to be regarded as more than just an apocryphon, at least in the sense that many have commonly come to think of this category of literature, that is, as failed or rejected scriptures. The *Protevanglium* certainly was not a failure nor were its traditions rejected. Its influence on the later Christian tradition was considerable to say the least, and without a doubt it easily surpassed that of certain other writings that were included in the biblical canon (such as, for instance, the Apocalypse of John, which was widely regarded as non-canonical in the Christian East during the Middle Ages).[43] The same is equally true of many other Marian apocrypha, especially including some of the early Dormition narratives, to which we will turn in chapters to come. The profound influence that these Marian writings had on later Christian culture and their use in worship as liturgical readings belies their classification among the spurned scriptures of ancient Christianity. To the contrary, their traditions were received with a certain amount of authority, and they laid the textual foundation for Marian devotion in both the East and the West. Like a number of other apocrypha, then, the *Protevangelium* should not be conceived so much as a failed rival to scriptural authority, once intended for inclusion within the biblical canon, but rather as a valued supplement to the scriptures that belongs more properly within the category of church Tradition, along with other sorts of non-biblical texts that were regarded as authoritative.[44]

In terms of content, the *Protevangelium* begins with the Virgin Mary's parents, who we learn were named Joachim and Anna. Because they were childless and seemingly unable to conceive, Joachim finds himself marginalized by other members of the community, and so he withdraws into the wilderness for forty days and forty nights to fast and pray in hopes that God will somehow bless him with a child. Anna too is distressed, and she also prays to God that she might miraculously conceive as Sarah had done long ago. When an angel appears to Anna with the promise that she will conceive, she vows to dedicate the child to God. Likewise, an angel speaks to Joachim in the wilderness, informing him, "Go down from here; behold, your wife Anna has become pregnant," seemingly, one should note, in Joachim's absence.[45] Their child, Mary, is born after six, seven, eight, or nine months; there is significant variation on this point in the manuscript tradition. From the time that she begins to walk at six months old, Mary is kept in a state of purity in her bedroom, where she is attended by "the undefiled daughters of the Hebrews." Then, when she turns three, Anna fulfills her promise and takes Mary to the Temple where she will live, consecrated to God and fed by the hand of an angel. When she reaches twelve, however, the priests realize that she can no longer remain in the Temple, since she will soon begin to menstruate and thus become a source of impurity.[46] An angel appears to the high priest, instructing him to assemble the widowers, so that the Lord will give a sign indicating who should become Mary's guardian. The widowers all receive rods, and when Joseph's turns into a dove, he is entrusted with Mary, whom he somewhat reluctantly takes into his home.

One day while she is out drawing water, an angel appears and addresses Mary, who quickly flees in terror. After she returns home, the angel appears again and informs her that she will miraculously conceive a child whose father will be God. As in Luke's gospel, Mary consents, and soon goes to visit her kinswoman Elizabeth. Mary remains three months with Elizabeth and then returns home, where she secludes herself from other members of her community. When Joseph eventually sees that she is six months pregnant, he is alarmed and frightened of the consequences that he will face for not having guarded her virginity while she was under his care. Mary insists that she is still a virgin, despite her condition, and Joseph deliberates how he should handle this delicate situation, ultimately resolving, as in Matthew, to send her away quietly. That night, however, an angel comes to Joseph in a dream, explaining the child's divine origin and putting his concerns to rest. Soon thereafter, other members of the community discover Mary's pregnancy, and Mary and Joseph are both publicly accused. They are both forced to drink the "water of the Lord's conviction,"[47] an ordeal known from the Hebrew Bible (Num 5) and rabbinic literature that is usually reserved for women who were accused of adultery. When they pass the test, the priest declares them both vindicated by God.

The events of the Nativity then follow, as Joseph and Mary set out together for Bethlehem to register for the census. Before they actually reach Bethlehem, however, the child is ready to come forth at the "third milestone," roughly halfway between Jerusalem and Bethlehem. There Mary has a vision of two peoples, "one weeping and lamenting and one rejoicing and exulting,"[48] and Joseph finds a cave in the desert where she can give birth. Leaving Mary in the care of his sons, Joseph sets out to find a Jewish midwife, and while underway, he relates in the first person a miraculous stoppage of time, which is undoubtedly meant to indicate the moment when Jesus was born. Joseph then locates a midwife and persuades her to return with him to the cave. When they reach the cave, they find it covered by a cloud, and then when the cloud recedes, they see an unbearably bright light before finally beholding the newborn child with his mother Mary. The midwife soon withdraws and meets another woman named Salome, who refuses to believe her report that a virgin has given birth. Instead, Salome insists on inspecting Mary's condition for herself, and when she inserts her finger to test Mary's virginity, her hand is consumed by fire. Not surprisingly, she immediately repents, and an angel appears, telling her if she touches the child with her hand it will be healed. After she has done so, her hand is restored, and she departs with a warning from the angel not to tell anyone what she had seen. The visit of the three wise men follows, along with a brief mention of Herod's slaughter of the innocents. The narrative then concludes with a set of traditions about John the Baptist and his family during Herod's massacre. John and his mother Elizabeth are temporarily swallowed up into a mountain to protect them from Herod's rage, while Herod's officers interrogate and murder John's father Zacharias in the Temple in an effort to find his young son, whom Herod believes to be the future king who threatens his rule. It is a bit of a peculiar conclusion for a biography of Mary, and some scholars have suggested that this final section regarding John and his family may be a later addition, but the current consensus tends to favor a more unified view of the text as it has been received, even if its author may have drawn on earlier sources.[49]

The *Protevangelium* and the Beginnings of Marian Piety

Not only did the *Protevangelium of James* lay crucial foundations for future devotion to the Virgin Mary, but the apocryphon is itself evidence of an emergent reverence for Mary already in the later second century. To be sure, there is no indication of any cult or prayer offered to Mary in the *Protevangelium*, but in the broader sense defined in the Introduction, this first Marian biography unquestionably marks the beginnings of Marian piety in ancient Christianity. Although there is some debate regarding the purpose of the *Protevangelium*, most scholars are agreed that its aim is first and foremost to glorify the Virgin Mary. Admittedly, there are also clear apologetic interests at work in the *Protevangelium*, and some scholars have emphasized these more than others.[50] In particular, the narrative seems partly designed to answer the kind of "slanders" against the Virgin Mary that we find in Celsus (an early "pagan" opponent of Christianity) and the early rabbinic tradition, which allege that Mary was no virgin but was instead a poor woman who conceived her son out of wedlock with a Roman soldier. In response, the *Protevangelium* underscores the wealth of Mary's parents and her remarkable purity from childhood. Not only was she a virgin at the time she conceived, but she even remained a virgin after giving birth, as Salome's foolish inspection dramatically demonstrates. Nevertheless, at the same time the *Protevangelium* goes well beyond what is necessary to answer such accusations in praising Mary's character and extolling her supernatural qualities, so that it is difficult to see apology as the primary motive for this work. While the author may have wanted to defend Mary against such calumnies, clearly there was an even greater interest in expounding her unique holiness and her pivotal role in the drama of Christian salvation. As Mary Foskett concludes, "Praise of Mary—rather than the need to defend her—drives this early Christian narrative."[51]

Likewise, the *Protevangelium* is not a work primarily about Christology, even if by necessity it does address certain Christological issues. Christ's birth from a virgin is, of course, an important sign of his divine origin in early Christian literature, as already noted, and for obvious reasons this theme figures prominently in this earliest biography of his mother. Yet, throughout most of the narrative (excepting the final few sections), the focus rests squarely on Mary rather than her son: even at the moment of Christ's birth, Mary and her marvelous virginity remain the center of attention.[52] If one merely wanted to demonstrate the reality of Christ's virgin birth, it would hardly be necessary or even very efficient to do so by producing a full narrative of his mother's birth and childhood. As Norelli notes, one could effectively accomplish the same end by focusing the story instead on Joseph rather than Mary. One finds just such a narrative, for instance, in the now lost Latin "special source," a second-century Infancy Gospel known primarily from its use in later Latin and Irish apocrypha, and to a certain extent the *Ascension of Isaiah*, which also similarly focuses on Joseph.[53] Accordingly, the *Protevangelium*'s keen interest in Mary's exceptional holiness cannot be ascribed simply to Christological concerns about the Virgin Birth; rather, it must be seen as a deliberate choice to focus on Mary as a figure of great significance for the Christian faith in her own right. Indeed, as Beverly Roberts Gaventa observes, "a reader who knew only the Protevangelium might reasonably conclude that Mary is the holy figure and that Jesus's holiness derives from hers."[54]

The *Protevangelium* imbues Mary throughout with what Gaventa names "sacred purity," a quality that she distinguishes from notions of moral and ritual purity but instead defines as indicating her complete immersion within the sacred.[55] In other words, Mary is portrayed as possessing a unique holiness that distinguishes her from other human beings, not in the sense of her observance of personal piety, but rather as one who embodied the sacred itself in her own person. From the very start the *Protevangelium* underscores Mary's extraordinary holiness at every turn. Her miraculous conception and birth offer an early sign of her supernatural qualities and invest her, like her son, with a divine origin. It seems that Mary's parents, Joachim and Anna, had reached a relatively advanced age without being able to conceive a child, and only when they petitioned God with prayer and fasting was Anna able to conceive. The wondrous nature of Mary's conception is heightened by the fact that her mother seems to have conceived without intercourse, as Mary would herself conceive years later. Although there is no indication that Anna was a virgin—and it seems in fact that the couple had been trying to have a child—Mary was apparently conceived in Joachim's absence through divine intervention. According to the *Protevangelium*, Joachim had departed for the wilderness and had been there for some time when Anna had a vision indicating that she would give birth. That this sequence is no mere coincidence is made plain by the angels who appeared to Anna. They inform her that an angel had also appeared to Joachim while he was still in the wilderness, telling him that his wife "has become pregnant" (*Protev* 4.3) so that it seems to have happened in his absence through miraculous divine intervention. When Joachim then returns from the wilderness, Anna rushes to greet him, informing him herself, "I who was once childless have become pregnant" (*Protev* 4.9).

There is, however, one should note, some significant variation in the manuscript tradition for both of the key passages, so that many versions instead have the future form, "will become pregnant," thus placing the event in the future, after Joachim's return from the wilderness. Some scholars have preferred this reading, in which case Mary's conception would have taken place through sexual intercourse, albeit still miraculously, given Joachim and Anna's inability to conceive previously. Nevertheless, most scholars have preferred the perfect tense reading here, including the text's most recent editor. There are in fact several reasons for following this variant to the conclusion that the *Protevangelium* originally portrayed Mary's conception as occurring in the absence of sexual intercourse. In the first place, this is the reading found in our oldest manuscript, which dates to the late third or early fourth century. Moreover, the past tense here reflects the more difficult reading of the two, in the sense that it disrupts the expected sequence of the narrative. As a general rule, text critics tend to prefer such difficult readings, on the principle that the easier variant is more likely to have been introduced to the text by a later copyist as correction than vice versa. Perhaps most important, however, is the fact that Mary's miraculous conception without inter-course fits so well with the *Protevangelium*'s persistent emphasis on Mary's sacred purity. Her divine conception in the absence of sexual intercourse aligns perfectly with her portrayal as the very embodi-ment of holiness. And so, despite some measure of scholarly debate on the issue, it seems most likely that the *Protevangelium* originally described Mary's miraculous conception as having occurred while her father was far away in the desert.[56]

Nevertheless, this tradition certainly does not warrant the conclu-sion that the *Protevangelium* advances the doctrine of Mary's Immaculate Conception, as some Roman Catholic scholars have proposed.[57] The dogma of the Immaculate Conception teaches that Mary was conceived in her mother's womb without Original Sin, the *macula originalis*. Yet the idea of Original Sin as it developed in Western Christianity is difficult to place before Augustine, and since there was no clear notion of Original Sin in the later second century, it is very difficult to imagine the *Protevangelium* as indicating that Mary was conceived without it. It is true that the absence of sexual intercourse at her conception fits well with later Augustinian reflec-tion on the relation between sexuality and the transmission of Original Sin, but to read a second-century text in such terms is entirely anach-ronistic. Therefore, it would appear that while Mary was miraculously conceived without the intercourse of her parents, in no sense can one say on the basis of the *Protevangelium* that Christians of the second century believed either in her virginal or Immaculate Conception.

If Mary's miraculous conception offers an important sign of emergent reverence for Christ's mother and a belief in her extraordinary nature, the same can equally be said of her birth, which also was exceptional. As noted already, there is some significant variation in the manuscript tradition concerning the timing of Mary's birth, with different manuscripts indicating that she was born in the sixth, seventh, eighth, or ninth month after her conception (*Protev* 5.5). Earlier editors seem to have preferred the nine-month reading, presumably since this would seem to be the most biologically correct. Nevertheless, once again our earliest manuscript, which was only discovered in the mid-twentieth century, reports that Anna gave birth to Mary in the seventh month.[58] Also, this and other variants indicating a shorter gestation period offer more difficult readings, since they contradict the natural order of childbirth. Precisely for this very reason the tradition of Mary's birth after seven months is likely to be primitive. Moreover, in the ancient Mediterranean world, a birth after only seven months was considered the sign of a great person, so that Mary's premature birth in the *Protevangelium* is not some sort of ignorant mistake but yet another indication of her miraculous origin and her unique holiness. In early Judaism, for instance, other remarkable individuals, such as Samuel, Isaac, Moses, and Jesus, were said to have been born after only seven months. The classical tradition similarly regarded a birth after seven months as highly auspicious, and in both contexts a seven-months birth generally followed a divine or miraculous conception. The tradition of Mary's birth after just seven months is thus no misunderstanding of biology but rather further evidence of belief in her elevated stature that corresponds with the tradition of her conception in the absence of sexual intercourse.[59]

When Mary began to walk after six months, her mother vowed that she would not walk on the earth again until she had been delivered to the Temple, as Anna had promised the Lord in her prayer. She turns Mary's bedroom into a "sanctuary," where she is attended by "undefiled daughters of the Hebrews." On her first birthday, the priests come and bless Mary with "the ultimate blessing, which cannot be surpassed," proclaiming that "because of her" the Lord will bring redemption to Israel.[60] On her second birthday, Joachim and Anna decide to wait a year before delivering Mary to the Temple, and when she turns three, they bring her to the priests in the company of the undefiled daughters of the Hebrews. The priests rejoice, and Mary dances before the altar and is showered with favor by the Lord. While in the Temple, she is fed, like the prophet Elijah before her, from the hand of an angel: even her food is otherworldly, and she is served by the Lord's own attendants. Mary's connection with the Temple and the priests is a persistent theme of the narrative, which serves to inscribe her within the sacred space of the Temple itself. Although the typology of Mary as the Temple of the Lord would not develop into its mature form for several more centuries, clearly the *Protevangelium* envisions Mary as a physical embodiment of holiness much in the same way that the Temple served as an unmatched locus of divine sanctity on earth. She is herself, as Foskett observes, in some sense a "sacred object dedicated to the Lord."[61]

Upon turning twelve years old, Mary had to leave the Temple, because she would soon begin to menstruate, and so she was entrusted into Joseph's care. From this point we move into territory that overlaps significantly with the canonical gospels. The Annunciation and the Visitation follow, and despite some unique twists, the scenes have many similarities with Luke's gospel. Likewise, Joseph's doubts concerning Mary are allayed by a dream, but the priests subject them both to the trial of water, which, of course, they pass, affirming both Mary's virginity and again her close association with the Temple. Then, on the way to the Nativity, Mary suddenly has a vision before she gives birth: she sees two peoples, one weeping and lamenting, and the other rejoicing and celebrating. The meaning of this vision is not entirely certain, and it is not explained in the *Protevangelium*, but it would appear to predict the response to her son's ministry: some will accept him and enter into joy; others will reject him at their peril. In this way Mary assumes the prophetic role given to Simeon in Luke's gospel, so that she foretells her son as one "destined for the falling and rising of many in Israel."[62] When Mary gives birth in the cave and Joseph returns with a midwife, the midwife is amazed, and departing she informs a certain Salome that this day a virgin had given birth. Salome, however, is skeptical and will put Mary to the test herself. When she physically inspects Mary, her hand instantly withers, as if she had just inappropriately touched a sacred object. Although Salome is soon healed by holding the infant Jesus, the episode makes clear not only Mary's virginity but also the inviolable sanctity of her person. From this point on, Mary admittedly recedes somewhat into the background, but so too does her son. The visit of the Magi follows, and then the slaughter of the innocents, which quickly yields to the concluding traditions of John the Baptist and his family that strangely complete this early biography of Mary.

The *Protevangelium*, therefore, does much more than merely fill out the missing details of Mary's life prior to the canonical gospels. Rather, it portrays her as the epitome of sacred purity, as perfect holiness embodied in a human being. From the outset, her miraculous conception and birth alert readers to her extraordinary nature. Her consecration by the priests with a blessing surpassing all other blessings and a childhood spent dwelling in the Temple align her with the unique sanctity of the House of God itself. This Mary is no ordinary human being who merely consents to bear the Son of God, as in Luke's gospel. She is instead a numinous being, exalted and revered as the personification of God's transcendent holiness. Despite the absence of any cultic veneration or prayer to the Virgin, the *Protevangelium* attests to an emergent piety focused on Mary's person and her singular importance for the Christian tradition. Here, Mary is not just blessed among women but is truly exceptional among humankind. Nevertheless, this viewpoint seemingly remained an isolated one during the later second century and even into the third. It is not known where the *Protevangelium* was composed, and Egypt, Syria, and Asia Minor have all been suggested as possibilities. Nor do we know anything about the community that produced this text, and so it is difficult to provide any meaningful context for the Marian devotion evidenced in this early biography. The *Protevangelium* stands out significantly amid the diversity of second-century Christianity, particularly for the high esteem it has for the Virgin. Without this text we would have little reason to suspect that Mary had already emerged as a figure of great religious significance for Christians in this era. Yet, by the same token, the *Protevangelium*'s Marian piety poses a puzzling anomaly that is difficult to relate not only to other elements of second-century Christianity but also to later developments in Marian devotion. What happened between the *Protevangelium* and the emergence of the cult of the Virgin in the fourth century admittedly remains something of a mystery. While the following chapters will shed some significant light on the progress of Marian devotion during this period, the *Protevangelium* still raises perhaps as many questions as it answers.

Conclusions

With the important exception of the *Protevangelium*, then, Christianity in the first two centuries does not offer much evidence of devotion to the Virgin Mary. The New Testament writings in general are rather laconic when it comes to Mary, but they are so also with regard to the other members of Jesus' family. The main Marian theme that emerges during the first hundred years of Christianity is a belief that Mary conceived while remaining a virgin, although it is true that many of the earliest Christian writings show little interest either in Christ's mother or in the manner by which he was conceived. Moreover, Mary's virginity initially seems to have been a doctrine primarily about her son Jesus: it was a sign of his divine origin rather than any indication of her special holiness. Yet with Luke's gospel we witness the first interest in Mary's contribution to the process of salvation. To be sure, her virginal conception remains linked with her son's exalted status rather than her own. But Luke presents Mary as the first to hear and believe the promise of redemption through her son. Her faithful consent to the divine plan was essential to its realization, and so Luke proclaims her blessed among women and by all future generations.

By the time we come to Justin and Irenaeus in the middle of the second century, both Mary and her virginity have begun to assume a more prominent role in the economy of salvation, so that she becomes the New Eve, whose chaste obedience is the antidote to Eve's seduction by the serpent. Irenaeus even goes so far as to call Mary the "cause of salvation" and the "advocate" of Eve. Yet the *Protevangelium of James* is certainly the high-water mark of Marian piety during the first two centuries of Christianity. The *Protevangelium* elaborates the doctrine of Mary's virginity with new force, so that she is Joseph's ward and never his wife, and she remains a virgin even after giving birth. Moreover, Mary's virginity is no longer simply a token of her son's divine parentage, but rather it has become an emblem of her own sacred purity. In the *Protevangelium* Mary is revered as the embodiment of holiness, whose own miraculous conception signals her exalted status from the very beginning of her life. There is unfortunately little from the second or third century that can be compared with the intense devotion to Mary that we witness in the *Protevangelium*, making it difficult to situate its precocious Marian piety more broadly within the development of Christian faith and practice. Yet, as we will see in the chapters that follow, there is nonetheless significant evidence of a mounting interest in Mary and her importance for the Christian faith during the third century, much of it coming from some unexpected and previously overlooked sources.

CHAPTER TWO

Mother of God and Mother of Mysteries: The Third Century

IN MANY RESPECTS THE third century shows little progress in the development of Marian devotion. In this era it is certainly true of the church fathers, who do not advance much beyond the Marian doctrines developed by their predecessors from the second century. In some cases, we find surprisingly negative assessments of Mary and her role in the formative Christian community as well as questions about whether she remained a virgin after giving birth. Nevertheless, at the same time we find toward the end of this century some of the first clear evidence of intercessory prayer directed to the Virgin, in the form of a papyrus fragment that preserves an early form of a well-known Marian prayer. Moreover, if we look beyond the writings of the church fathers to the apocryphal literature of this period, we find a great deal of interest in Mary, albeit of a somewhat different nature from what we might expect in view of the later tradition. It seems that many early Christians revered Mary not so much for her virginity and sacred purity as for her intimate and unequaled knowledge of her son's esoteric teachings. While the "proto-orthodox" Christians of this age increasingly focused their faith on the hope of salvation through the Crucifixion and Resurrection of Jesus, other

Christians believed that their salvation would come through secret, cryptic teachings that Jesus had brought into this world from the heavenly realm. In some instances we find that Jesus' mother was highly esteemed for her profound knowledge of these saving doctrines. One can readily imagine how such an idea would have arisen: after all, who would have known this divine savior more completely than his own mother, who raised him up from a child? Several early Christian apocrypha remember Mary in this way, including the earliest narrative of Mary's Dormition and Assumption, the *Book of Mary's Repose*. This third-century text, however, is of such great significance for understanding early Christian devotion to Mary that we will treat it separately in the following chapter, despite its important connections with some of the writings considered in this chapter.

Mary and the Church Fathers of the Third Century

Among the most influential church fathers of the early third century was a North African Christian named Tertullian (c. 160–c. 225), who converted to Christianity sometime around the end of the second century. Tertullian of Carthage was the first major Christian thinker to write in Latin, and accordingly his influence on the subsequent Christian tradition in the West is considerable. Nevertheless, toward the end of his life he embraced a heterodox group known as the Montanists, to which he was attracted largely by their moral rigor, it would seem, but in most respects he remained doctrinally orthodox. When it comes to the Virgin Mary, however, Tertullian is perhaps most remarkable for the somewhat lower esteem he holds for the mother of Jesus, at least in comparison with other contemporary proto-orthodox writers.[1] On the one hand, Tertullian vigorously defends Mary's virginal conception, which by this time had become an established dogma for those Christians who, like Tertullian, maintained the unique authority of the four gospels now in the New Testament canon. He also adopts the Eve–Mary typology advanced by Justin and Irenaeus before him, although with somewhat more restraint than the latter: there is no notion that Mary is the "cause of salvation" or an advocate for Eve.[2] Yet, on the other hand, Tertullian explicitly rejects the idea of Mary's virginity *in partu*, that is, that she remained a virgin after giving birth. Likewise, he also insists that Mary eventually married her betrothed, Joseph, and conceived children by him, as evidenced by Jesus' brothers and sisters.[3] Most striking, however, is Tertullian's assertion that Jesus rejected his mother, which he argues on the basis of Mark's report of conflict between Jesus and his family (Mark 3.21–35), and also Jesus' response to the woman who proclaimed "blessed is the womb that bore you" (Luke 11.27–28). Not only was Mary not among Jesus' followers during the time of his ministry, but on one occasion Tertullian even equates her with the unbelieving Jews![4] Clearly, in Tertullian we meet the opposite end of the spectrum from the *Protevangelium*, and no other early church father takes such a low view of the Virgin Mary, with the possible exception of John Chrysostom, whom we will meet later in chapter 5.

Elsewhere in northern Africa, in Alexandria, we find a very different attitude toward Mary reflected in the writings of the two principal church fathers of early Egyptian Christianity, Clement of Alexandria (c. 150–c. 215) and Origen of Alexandria (184/185–253/254).[5] Clement in particular is an intriguing figure, who often seems close to Gnostic and other esoteric strains of Christianity that were prominent in Alexandria during his time, and the fact that much of his work was not preserved certainly raises some questions as to just how "orthodox" Clement actually was. His views of the Virgin Mary, however, are much closer to the *Protevangelium*, which he seems to know and cite with approval, than they are to his Carthaginian contemporary Tertullian. Clement's only reference to Mary, at least in what survives of his works, occurs in a single passage from his *Stromateis* or *Miscellanies*. There, he refers to the persistence of Mary's virginity *in partu*, alluding to the story of the midwife from the *Protevangelium* as confirmation of her condition after giving birth.[6] Origen's views on the subject are much harder to pin down, since he seems to say different things about the state of Mary's virginity. In his homilies on Luke he denies Mary's virginity *in partu*, but in his homilies on Leviticus he affirms it.[7] Since both of these works survive only in Latin, there is some question as to whether the difference may have been introduced by one of Origen's translators. Nevertheless, in his commentary on Matthew, which does survive in Greek, Origen seems to indicate that she retained her virginity, although unfortunately the passage is not entirely clear on this point.[8]

Whatever his views on the physical state of Mary's virginity after giving birth may have been, Origen believed that Mary remained sexually chaste throughout her life and never had relations with Joseph. As Jesus had inaugurated a tradition of virginity for men, so had Mary for women.[9] Yet Origen did not think that Mary was entirely without fault. At the crucifixion she fell prey to doubt, along with Jesus' other followers, so that she too stood in need of redemption by her son. This was the meaning, Origen explained, of Simeon's prophecy that a sword would pierce Mary's soul: it was stricken with uncertainty and confusion rather than filled with faith as she watched her son dying on the cross.[10] There is also some suggestion that Origen may have been the first writer to use the term Theotokos, that is, "the one who gave birth to God," to describe Mary.[11] This information comes to us only in a later report from the fifth-century church historian Socrates, who says that Origen first used the term for Mary in his commentary on Romans. Unfortunately, however, the Greek original of this commentary has not survived, and the Latin translation does not use this title. Complicating matters further are two Greek fragments of a commentary on Luke attributed to Origen where Mary is called the Theotokos, although the authenticity of these fragments is disputed. Therefore, while there is a strong possibility that Origen may have begun to use this title for the Virgin Mary already in the early third century, we cannot be certain. Only at the end of the third and the beginning of the fourth century does such usage become established, at which point it begins to become increasingly common.

As for the church fathers of the later third century, they show surprisingly little interest in Mary and add almost nothing to the development of Marian doctrine. The reasons for this collective indifference are not entirely clear, but their inattention perfectly exemplifies the general patristic neglect of Mary during the early centuries. Perhaps this silence is also a reflection of the fact that we do not have very much Greek patristic literature from the later third century in the first place. In any case, if we are to try to connect the intense early Marian piety of the *Protevangelium* with later developments in the cult of the Virgin, we will have to look elsewhere. Fortunately, however, in the midst of this apparent drought of Marian devotion, a remarkable scrap of papyrus suddenly emerges from Egypt to provide some of the earliest evidence of Marian veneration, in the form of an intercessory prayer offered to the Virgin.

The *Sub Tuum Praesidium* Papyrus and the Beginnings of Marian Veneration

In 1917 the John Rylands Library in Manchester, which houses one of the world's most important collections of ancient papyri, added to its inventory a small fragment containing a prayer in Greek to the Virgin Mary that seems to date from the end of the third century. The fragment, number 470 in the collection, was published only in 1938, and very soon thereafter specialists on early Christian liturgy recognized its text as an early form of a familiar prayer to the Virgin that is known also in the ancient Greek, Latin, and Coptic liturgies and is still in use today.[12] The papyrus is normally named for the first line of the hymn, in Latin *Sub tuum praesidium*, and in English, "Beneath your protection." In its present state the text is badly damaged and highly fragmented, and the complete hymn is known only through restoration. In its reconstructed state, the text is as follows: "We take refuge beneath the protection of your compassion, Theotokos. Do not disregard our prayers in troubling times, but deliver us from danger, O only pure and blessed one."[13] Obviously, this prayer is directed toward Mary, who is named here Theotokos, and it seeks her intercessions. As such, it seemingly offers early evidence that Marian cult had indeed begun to emerge by the later third century. The reverse side of the papyrus is blank, leading its first editor to conclude that it must have been intended for private use. More recently, Hans Förster has deduced from photographic reproductions of the papyrus that it had been folded, leading him to conclude that it had possibly been used as an amulet.[14]

The *Sub tuum praesidium* papyrus indicates, then, that at least some Christians in Egypt had begun to pray to the Virgin Mary and ask for her intercessions already by the end of the third century. The use of the text in an amulet would certainly be consistent with such a practice and seems to demonstrate that, by this time, Marian veneration had begun to take on multiple forms. Nevertheless, the use of the first-person plural suggests that the text was designed and presumably used for a congregational setting. The appearance of such a text on this papyrus and possibly in an amulet at a time when the church fathers are frustratingly silent regarding devotion to the Virgin could suggest that Marian piety initially emerged within a more popular and less culturally elite context. Our other major source of early evidence for devotion to Mary might similarly invite such a conclusion. The *Protevangelium* is unquestionably a more accessible text than most of the writings produced by the early church fathers, and like many other Christian apocrypha it possibly reached a broad range of readers and listeners, and was perhaps even used liturgically in some early communities.[15] Indeed, as others have noted before me, there is a very real possibility that the *lex orandi* of early Christianity, that is, its patterns of worship and piety, developed an interest in the Virgin Mary before she fully affected the *lex credendi* of the early Christians, that is, their doctrinal beliefs. As much would certainly explain the disconnect between the early church fathers' lack of concern with Mary and the evidence of early devotion that we find in the *Protevangelium* and in this papyrus.[16] The possibility of such a difference between what was happening in "popular" piety and in the increasingly rarefied world of early Christian theology is definitely something that we will want to keep in mind.

There has been some question, one should note, regarding the date of this papyrus. In its initial publication, the editors dated the document to the fourth century. Nevertheless, at the same time they also note that their paleography expert was unwilling to place it any later than the third century on the basis of its writing style. Despite the evidence of the handwriting, then, which is a standard method for dating papyri, the editors conclude that the text must instead belong to the fourth century, since "it is almost incredible that a prayer addressed directly to the Virgin in these terms could be written in the third century."[17] Likewise, the prayer's use of the term Theotokos for Mary does not fit with the third century, they maintain, because this title was not in use before the beginning of the fourth century. Therefore, on the basis of these presumptions about the development of Marian piety, the editors decided to look past the evidence of the handwriting and date the papyrus to at least a century later than its paleography indicated.

Since its publication, a number of scholars (and particularly Catholic scholars) have opted to date the papyrus following its paleography to the third century, while some others have continued to prefer a fourth-century date.[18] It is true that in some ways this evidence of prayer to the Virgin and the use of the title Theotokos might fit better with the fourth century than with the third, but one certainly should not exclude out of hand the possibility that both practices, as well as this papyrus, date as early as the third century. As we have just noted, there is significant evidence to suggest that Origen had begun to call Mary the Theotokos as early as the first half of the third century. While there is admittedly some debate about the sources in question, the tendency of scholarship has been to recognize Origen as the first writer to use the term.[19] Moreover, there is an early Eucharistic prayer, the so-called "anaphora of Egyptian Basil," that specifically invokes the Virgin's intercession in the context of other saints, apostles, martyrs, and the like. This prayer, which liturgists date to the early fourth century, invokes the congregation to commemorate "especially at all times the holy and glorious Mary, the Theotokos; and by her prayers have mercy on us all."[20] Accordingly, it is not too difficult to imagine that a similar prayer, such as we find on the *Sub tuum praesidium* papyrus, could have been produced only a little earlier in Egypt, perhaps in the later third century. Moreover, as we will see in the next chapter, the earliest narrative of the Virgin Mary's Dormition, the *Book of Mary's Repose*, appears to offer evidence of belief in the powers of Mary's intercessions already in the third century.

There is, then, good reason to suspect that a prayer to the Theotokos might have been in circulation in Egypt already during the third century, and thus it seems unwise to disregard the evidence of the handwriting in favor of a prejudice against the possibility that Marian veneration may have begun to develop so early in some quarters. Otto Stegmüller identifies a number of other documents with strong similarities to the handwriting on this papyrus, and these date from either the later third or the beginning of the fourth century.[21] In light of this evidence, and the initial suggestion that the paleography reflects handwriting from the third century, the end of the third century seems to be a likely date for the production of this document, although one certainly should not rule out the possibility that it might be even slightly earlier.

Particularly interesting in Stegmüller's study, however, are his comparisons between the *Sub tuum praesidium* prayer and certain hymnic prayers from the apocryphal *Acts of Thomas*, a text composed at the beginning of the third century. Although Stegmüller does not propose that these apocryphal traditions are the source of this early Marian prayer, he does note that the "compassionate mother" of the *Acts of Thomas*, who is a figure in the heavenly realm, seems reminiscent of Christ's mother in the *Sub tuum praesidium*, whose protecting compassion is sought. The fact that the *Sub tuum praesidium* prayer asks Mary to deliver the petitioners herself, without any mention of her intercessions or of the Father or the Son, leads him to conclude that this prayer may have been linked with heterodox groups within early Christianity. While that is not the only possible interpretation of this language, it certainly does invite some intriguing speculations. Stegmüller further suggests a connection with Gnostic Christianity on the basis of the *Acts of Thomas*, although to be sure, few scholars today would identify this text as Gnostic, even though it is often quite heterodox.[22] Yet Stegmüller's proposal that this prayer might be associated with early Christian esoteric traditions and apocryphal literature is especially enticing, particularly in light of the apocryphal traditions about Mary to which we now turn.

Jesus' Gnostic Mother: Mary as Teacher of Sacred Mysteries

In 1945 an important collection of early Christian texts was discovered in Upper Egypt near the village of Nag Hammadi. It was a discovery of incredible significance for our understanding of early Christianity, far more significant, for instance, than the Dead Sea Scrolls, which were unearthed just three years later, even if the Dead Sea Scrolls have received a great deal more publicity.[23] In total, this cache of texts, commonly known as the Nag Hammadi Library, amounts to thirteen codices containing fifty-two different texts, all written in Coptic, the majority of which were previously unknown. Moreover, these new gospels, letters, and apocalypses are for the most part quite heterodox, and many show considerable affinity with an early Christian group that was previously known primarily from the accounts of their proto-orthodox opponents: the Gnostic Christians. Although there has been some debate in recent years as to whether one may continue to use the term Gnostic to refer to certain elements within early Christianity, the designation remains viable, albeit in more limited and specific usage than was once the case.[24] Nevertheless, perhaps now more than before, scholars have come to recognize that this collection of texts is not strictly Gnostic, but instead reflects a much broader range of doctrinal diversity within early Christianity than we had previously been able to recognize.

One of the most intriguing features of these new texts is the prominence that they often give to female figures, in both the mortal and the heavenly realms, at least in comparison with most other early Christian literature. Initially, scholars embraced these more inclusive traditions with great enthusiasm, hoping that they might offer a model for a less patriarchal form of Christianity in the present. Nevertheless, before very long they began to recognize that despite the important roles given to women and other female beings in these texts, many of the patriarchal assumptions of the ancient Mediterranean world remained operative in the early Christian communities that produced this literature.[25] There can be no mistaking, however, that women are represented more prominently in many of these texts than they are in contemporary proto-orthodox sources, and they frequently appear as leaders within the early Christian movement who work alongside the male apostles as equals. Without a doubt, the most significant of these women is Mary, who appears in a number of different writings from the Nag Hammadi collection as well as in several other related apocrypha preserved primarily, like the Nag Hammadi texts, in Coptic. Indeed, some of these writings, including the *Gospel of Mary* and the *Pistis Sophia*, had been known already for half of a century or more before the Nag Hammadi texts were discovered.

Over the past several decades, a scholarly consensus has remained contentedly assured that this Mary represents Mary of Magdala, one of the followers of Jesus who is known from the canonical gospels. Nevertheless, the fact of the matter is that this woman is rarely identified in these texts with any further precision beyond the name Mary; only occasionally is she identified specifically as the Magdalene or the Nazarene. Moreover, in those instances where Mary is named as the Magdalene in a particular text, Mary the mother of Jesus is also specifically indicated in the same text, so that the identity of any unspecified Mary remains highly questionable in these writings as well. Although the hermeneutic instability of this Mary's identity was exposed well over a decade ago, scholars working on these texts have been reluctant to acknowledge the problems with their assumptions about this character, as well as to consider how ancient Christian interpreters—rather than modern scholars—might have understood this Mary. There is often such unquestioned confidence that this Mary simply *is* the Magdalene that more complex issues regarding the nature of interpretation and the instability of meaning and language have been largely ignored in this instance. The reason for this is fairly obvious: part of the interest in unearthing Mary of Magdala as a leader within the early Christian movement seems to lie in finding evidence from the beginnings of Christianity that would support women's ecclesiastical leadership in the present. While I am entirely sympathetic to this contemporary aim, I cannot agree with how these texts have often been interpreted to this end. Moreover, I would suggest that women's liturgical leadership does not require such evidence from early Christian apocrypha to support it. Rather, such a practice should be adopted, in my opinion, on the basis of other principles, such as justice and equality, and not by looking to the authority of the period of origins as normative.[26]

Mary in the *Gospel of Mary*

Perhaps the single most important of these apocryphal Mary texts is the *Gospel of Mary*, in which, not surprisingly, Mary figures prominently. Admittedly, this text is usually dated to the late second century rather than the third, but its possible relation with many of the other apocryphal texts mentioning Mary finds its placement more naturally in this chapter than in the previous one. Often the title of this gospel is given, quite misleadingly, as the *Gospel of Mary Magdalene*, and in fact most scholars have maintained with inexplicable confidence that its protagonist is Mary of Magdala. Yet the truth of the matter is, nowhere in any of the three copies of this document that we possess is Mary identified as Mary of Magdala—or Mary of

Nazareth, for that matter: she is just Mary, without further qualification. The specificity encountered in many modern translations has been introduced by the hand of modern scholars. For many years this Mary's identity rested largely on unfounded assumptions about this gospel's use of the names *Mariam* and *Mariamme* for its main character, both of which are alternative spellings of Mary. There was long a belief that the forms *Mariam* and *Mariamme* were used exclusively for the Magdalene, while the mother of Jesus is always called *Maria*. Nevertheless, such alleged precision is demonstrably false, and the names are used interchangeably for both women: in fact, one could argue that both *Mariam* and *Mariamme* are used more frequently for Mary of Nazareth than for Mary of Magdala in early Christian literature.[27] Moreover, in the canonical gospels Mary of Magdala is usually identified by her town of origin, in order to distinguish her from Mary (of Nazareth), for whom this is not the case.[28] Therefore, it is completely unclear which Mary is in fact represented in this gospel, and in addition to the Magdalene and the Nazarene, Mary of Bethany has also been suggested as a possible identity for this figure. For this reason alone, as well as for others that will soon become apparent, this apocryphal Marian gospel is entirely relevant to our investigation of early Christian devotion to Mary.

The *Gospel of Mary* is a fairly short text, and much of it is missing, which only compounds the problems of its interpretation. Of an original nineteen folios, only nine have survived in the Coptic version, which preserves this early Christian apocryphon most completely. The gospel begins in the middle of a conversation between Jesus and his disciples. He speaks initially with Peter, largely about the relation between matter and the spirit. When he has finished, the Savior commissions his disciples to go forth and preach, after which he departs. The disciples are then worried whether they are actually up to the task. Mary intervenes and begins to reassure them, and Peter says to Mary, "Sister, we know that the Savior loved you more than the rest of women. Tell us the words of the Savior which you remember—which you know (but) we do not, nor have we heard them." Mary responds, promising that "What is hidden from you, I will proclaim to you," and she begins to relate a vision of the Savior and her dialogue with him, but after about eight lines the text suddenly breaks off, again in midsentence.[29] When the gospel resumes, after several missing folios, we find Mary continuing to reveal what the Savior had taught her, in a discourse on the ascent of the soul as it seeks to pass by the guardians of the heavenly realms.

When she has finished, there is a confrontation, as some of the disciples question what Mary has just said. Andrew says to the others, "Say what you (wish to) say about what she has said. I at least do not believe that the Savior said this. For certainly these teachings are strange ideas." Peter echoes his brother, adding "Did he really speak with a woman without our knowledge (and) not openly? Are we to turn about and all listen to her? Did he prefer her to us?" Mary tearfully responds, "My brother Peter, what do you think? Do you think that I thought this up myself in my heart, or that I am lying about the Savior?" Levi quickly comes to her defense, answering Peter, "Peter, you have always been hot-tempered. Now I see you contending against the woman like the adversaries. But if the Savior made her worthy, who are you indeed to reject her? Surely the Savior knows her very well. That is why he loved her more than us. Rather let us be ashamed and put on the perfect humanity and acquire it for ourselves as he commanded us, and preach the gospel, not laying down any other rule or other law beyond what the Savior said."[30] Levi has the last word, and thereafter, we are told, the apostles begin to go forth to preach and teach.

The *Gospel of Mary*'s final account of dissension among Christ's early followers over Mary's teaching is exceptionally valuable for the light it sheds on certain controversies within earliest Christianity, including especially the question of women's leadership within these early communities. The *Gospel of Mary* obviously supports this practice, which it first exemplifies and then defends, using Levi to directly answer Andrew's and Peter's objections. Andrew and Peter no doubt are meant to represent those, particularly proto-orthodox, Christians who were increasingly opposed to women's authority as teachers and liturgical leaders. Mary's discourse, and that of the Savior before her, position this gospel somewhere within the orbit of Gnostic Christianity, even if it is not, in the most technical sense, a Gnostic text. Accordingly, this text seems to comport with other evidence suggesting that women were more accepted as teachers and religious leaders in communities that valued esoteric knowledge as a vehicle for salvation.[31] And so we have here in the *Gospel of Mary* a representation of Mary as a leader among the earliest disciples and apostles of Christ, who is revered—by some at least—for her unique command of the secret mysteries of the universe, knowledge of which is essential for salvation. She is, moreover, beloved by the Savior more than other women and even the rest of the disciples, indicating a special relationship between this Mary and Jesus.

Of course, the *Gospel of Mary* fails utterly to tell us just who this Mary is. It is certainly possible that she could be identified with the Magdalene, as most previous scholarship has assumed. Yet it is no less likely that this Mary is Mary of Nazareth, the mother of Jesus, and in light of some of the representations of Mary of Nazareth that we find in certain other apocrypha, and in the earliest Dormition narrative especially, there is every reason to expect that we might find Jesus' mother depicted as a learned master of the cosmic mysteries, as Mary is in this gospel. Now that the fiction of an identification based on the form of her name has been exposed, the question of this Mary's identity has become far more complicated than previously recognized. And regardless of whomever the original "author" may have had in mind when writing this gospel (which surely we can never know), we must also grapple with the question of how this Mary would have been interpreted by readers and hearers of this text in the second and third centuries. Undoubtedly there were Christians who would have understood this Mary to be the mother of Jesus no less than the Magdalene.

Marys in the Canonical Gospels and the Gospel of Mary

Scholars who continue to maintain that this Mary is the Magdalene generally do so on the basis of appeals to Mary of Magdala's depiction in the canonical gospels as well as through comparison with a carefully constructed and fixed canon of other apocryphal texts—particularly in Coptic—that could seem to support this interpretation. Mary of Magdala's prominence in the canonical gospels certainly could speak in favor of her identification with this Mary. There is no question that Mary of Magdala must have been an important figure in Jesus' movement, and one would imagine that her significance might have been even greater than the gospel narratives remember.[32] Luke (but only Luke) names her among Jesus' followers during the time of his ministry and further adds that she, along with two other women, were supporting the movement financially (Luke 8.2–3). Three of the four gospels identify her as one of the women present at the Crucifixion, and in Matthew and Mark she serves as a witness to Jesus' burial. In the Synoptics, Mary Magdalene goes with other women to the tomb on Sunday morning, and they are the first to find it empty and announce this to the apostles. But in John's gospel, this honor belongs to Mary of Magdala alone, and shortly after she discovers the empty tomb, the risen Christ appears to her first of all and tells her to preach the good news of his resurrection to his followers. This Johannine tradition of Mary Magdalene as *apostola apostolorum*, "the apostle of the apostles," is particularly important, since her privilege of being the first to behold and speak with the resurrected Savior could suggest her identification with the Mary of the *Gospel of Mary*, who relates a dialogue that she had with the risen Christ. Likewise, the apostles' skepticism at Mary of Magdala's report in Luke and the longer ending of Mark compares favorably with the conflict between Mary and certain apostles in the *Gospel of Mary*.

At the same time we would do well to remember that Mary of Nazareth is herself quite prominent in several of the New Testament gospels, and there are certainly reasons to conclude on the basis of her representation there that she also could be the Mary of the *Gospel of Mary*. As we have just seen in the previous chapter, not only do the writings of the New Testament describe Mary of Nazareth's participation in events of her son's ministry and passion, but she is also identified as having been present in the company of the apostles for the beginnings of the Christian church in Acts. Of course, there is the tension between Christ and "his own," and then with his mother and brothers in Mark 3.20–35, but as we noted, this representation may have more to do with divisions and rivalries within the early Christian community than with any actual conflict between Jesus and the members of his family. And even if one were convinced that the historical Jesus was in fact estranged from his mother and his family, that would not decide this particular question, since the probabilities of historical-critical scholarship hold only limited relevance for determining this Mary's identity. Rather, the aggregate of the gospel traditions inherited by the early Christians is paramount in this instance, rather than one single passage set against the others. This pre-critical composite was the image of Mary of Nazareth that would have influenced the production and interpretation of stories about Mary in subsequent Christian literature. It is true that Mark 3.20–35 presents an episode in which Christ distinguishes the members of his "eschatological family" from his biological family, suggesting his mother's separation from his ministry. But looking at the totality of the canonical gospel traditions, as they were (more or less) received by Christians of the second and third centuries, we see that Luke and John explicitly include Mary of Nazareth within Christ's "eschatological family," while Matthew softens Mark's exclusion.[33] Consequently, for the present purpose, Mark 3.20–35 must be interpreted in light of these "facts," instead of against them, yielding an image of Mary of Nazareth in early Christian memory as one who was supportive of and occasionally a participant in her son's earthly ministry.

Luke's gospel in particular (the only gospel to mention the Magdalene during the period of Jesus' ministry) portrays Mary of Nazareth as one of her son's disciples and as a prophet.[34] From the start, it develops the Virgin's role in the Incarnation and emphasizes her willing participation in the process. Luke thus presents her not only as a member of Christ's eschatological family, but even as a model of discipleship, who at the Annunciation is the first to hear and receive the word of God. Luke portrays Mary of Nazareth as being "first and foremost a disciple of Jesus, ... but also a prophet," who in the Magnificat recalls the words of the prophets and foretells the themes of her son's preaching.[35] No less importantly, Luke's second volume, the Acts of the Apostles, describes Mary of Nazareth's involvement in the nascent church. Here, Luke notes her presence among the apostles in the "upper room," and although she is not specifically identified as a leader, she is singled out among the other women present. The clear implication would seem to be that, after Christ's resurrection and ascension, Mary of Nazareth played a role in the formation of the Christian church (or at least, was reputed to have) and was in the company of the apostles as they began to preach the gospel, as a "founding mother" of the Jerusalem community.[36] Luke's presentation of Mary of Nazareth thus certainly would favor her identification with the main character of the *Gospel of Mary*. While Mary Magdalene is remembered as a participant in Jesus' public ministry and in the events of the Passion and Resurrection, there is no similar witness that she stood among the apostles after the Resurrection and Ascension and participated in the initial formation of the Christian church, as is the case with Mary of Nazareth in Acts.

Also indicative of Mary of Nazareth's significance are her appearances in the gospel of John, the very gospel that also presents some of the strongest evidence for the Magdalene's importance in earliest Christianity. The first of these occurs at the wedding of Cana, an event that in John's gospel inaugurates Jesus's public ministry. Here, not only is Mary of Nazareth present, but she persuades her son to perform his first miracle. As this episode concludes, John indicates that she continues on with Jesus and his disciples to Capernaum, appearing to remain actively involved in his ministry. It would seem then that Mary of Nazareth can rival the Magdalene's participation in Jesus's Galilean ministry, at least as she is portrayed in the Fourth Gospel.

John's gospel also remembers Mary of Nazareth to have been, like the Magdalene, an important participant in the events of the Passion. While her absence from this scene in the Synoptic accounts is certainly important for historical-critical study, the early Christian tradition frequently harmonized these divergent accounts, identifying Mary of Nazareth with one of the various "other Marys" mentioned in the Synoptic accounts.[37] But, in John, Mary stands beneath the cross, together with several other women, including Mary Magdalene, and the beloved disciple, whom later tradition would identify with John. From the cross, Jesus addresses both his mother and the beloved disciple, entrusting her to his care, an action which, as one group of modern interpreters explains, "points to the future, the era of the disciples who will come after Jesus," thereby signaling her importance in this next phase of her son's mission. By thus becoming the mother of the beloved disciple, who is "the disciple *par excellence*" in John's gospel, Mary of Nazareth "becomes herself a model of belief and discipleship." And at the episode's conclusion, the gospel explains that Mary lived with the beloved disciple from that moment on.[38] Since this figure was undoubtedly an important leader in the early church (again, traditionally, John), one might well imagine from this that Mary of Nazareth accompanied the beloved disciple as he spread the gospel, so that she was actively involved in the beginnings of the Christian church. Certainly later generations of Christians did not hesitate to draw this conclusion, and such a memory of Mary compares favorably with Mary's depiction in the *Gospel of Mary*.[39]

Therefore while the tension between Jesus and his family in Mark 3.20–35 could suggest his mother's estrangement from his ministry, the portraits of Mary in Luke and John present her instead as actively involved in his prophetic mission from start to finish: from before he was even conceived into the beginnings of the early church. One must recognize that the early church, unlike the modern critic, was not prone to reading with suspicion, ferreting out dissonances: rather, it read with fidelity, searching for consonance. Within such a hermeneutic, Mary of Nazareth's faith at the Annunciation, her involvement at the wedding in Cana, her presence at the cross, her association with the beloved disciple, and her appearance among the apostles for the beginnings of the church in the Upper Room, undoubtedly would have invited the early Christians to remember her as someone who had been instrumental in the beginnings of the Christian faith.

Moreover, who would have been better positioned to know what Jesus had taught than his mother, who had been with him from his birth through to his death? Jesus' mother also seems to be an excellent candidate for any Mary who is said to have been beloved by Jesus more than other women or his disciples. All in all, based on the traditions of the New Testament, Mary of Nazareth compares much more favorably with the star of the *Gospel of Mary* than most scholars have previously thought (or wanted) to consider.

Mary and the Risen Lord: John 20:1–18

In many respects, then, Mary of Nazareth's representation in the New Testament easily rivals that of the Magdalene, despite some important differences in their portrayals. Nevertheless, many scholars have maintained that Mary of Magdala's role as *apostola apostolorum* at the end of John's gospel strongly tips the balance in her favor when seeking to identify the *Gospel of Mary*'s protagonist. Only Mary of Magdala, and not the mother of Jesus, could be said to have seen and spoken with the risen Christ.[40] There is, however, one should perhaps note, some dispute regarding the historicity of this account, inasmuch as the various gospel accounts of these events are contradictory and Paul reports that the risen Christ first appeared to Peter and then the Twelve.[41] But once again, whether or not this particular tradition can survive the scrutiny of historical criticism is not really relevant to the question at hand: what matters instead is that Christians in the second and third centuries believed that the risen Christ had appeared to Mary. Even so, despite the confidence that many scholars have placed in this tradition's ability to decide which Mary appears in the *Gospel of Mary* and a number of other similar apocrypha, during the second and third centuries, when most of these texts were written, this tradition itself underwent some significant interpretative changes. At stake was nothing less than the very identity of this first witness to the resurrection.

John's gospel names this woman simply as Mary until the very end of the scene, when suddenly we learn that it is Mary Magdalene who informs the apostles that she has seen the Lord. Nevertheless, despite the final specificity of John's gospel, this Mary's identity quickly began to shift toward Jesus' mother already by the second century, particularly in Syria.[42] Such a change certainly complicates any simple notion that this passage from John can somehow decisively resolve the issue of Mary's identity. If anything, the tendency toward replacing Mary of Magdala with Mary of Nazareth in this role might suggest instead that texts produced during this era tend to present the mother of Jesus rather than the Magdalene as the risen Christ's privileged interlocutor. Although some uncertainty surrounds the origins of this tradition in which Christ first appears to his mother instead of the Magdalene, it almost certainly dates back at least as far as Tatian's *Diatessaron*, a work composed sometime between 150 and 180.[43] This early harmony of the four canonical gospels quickly displaced its sources to become the primary gospel text of the Syrian church during the third and fourth centuries, after which time it was itself only gradually supplanted by use of the four canonical gospels instead.[44] As a result of its displacement, no complete copy of the *Diatessaron* has survived,[45] and consequently its contents have to be determined indirectly, based largely on the testimony of several second- and third-hand witnesses. Only when a number of these converge can we obtain a high degree of certainty that a particular tradition was present in the *Diatessaron*, and in the case of the risen Christ's appearance to his mother, we are fortunate that the assemblage of witnesses to this tradition is extraordinarily reliable. Indeed, according to the established principles for reconstructing the contents of the *Diatessaron*, there can be little question that the gospel traditions of the early Syrian church portrayed Mary *of Nazareth* as the one to whom the risen Christ appeared and spoke. The fact that the Old Syriac version of the fourfold gospels and other Syrian witnesses from the third and fourth centuries contain the same reading leaves almost no doubt that prior to the fifth century, in Syria it was the mother of Jesus, rather than the Magdalene, who was the first to witness the resurrection and speak with the risen Christ.

The fact that this early tradition of Christ's appearance to his mother took hold especially in Syria rather than somewhere else is of paramount importance for how we interpret the *Gospel of Mary*. Specialists on early Christianity have often identified Syria as the birthplace of Gnostic Christianity, with Helmut Koester even going so far as to proclaim Syria "the Country of Origin of Christian Gnosticism."[46] And while this designation is certainly debatable, particularly since Egypt also presents a region of potential importance for the beginnings of Gnostic Christianity, almost all of those apocrypha featuring a Mary whom scholars identify with the Magdalene seem to have had their origin in Syria.[47] Since the texts in question, like the *Gospel of Mary*, specify Mary's identity only rarely and inconsistently, perhaps we should look to the traditions of early Syrian Christianity more broadly in order to decide the case. Given the early Syrian tradition's identification of Mary of Nazareth as playing a significant role in the events of the resurrection (at the Magdalene's expense), the mother of Jesus quickly emerges not only as a viable candidate, but indeed as a likely one. It is thus essential to recognize that these early Syrian gospel traditions would almost certainly have influenced the interpretation of these apocryphal traditions, if not also their composition. Accordingly, these traditions make for the rather likely prospect that Mary of Nazareth may have been, at least in the eyes of many early Christians, identified with the

Mary who appears in the *Gospel of Mary* and in other similar texts from this age as well.

Mary in Other Early Christian Apocrypha

The Gospel of Thomas, *the* Sophia of Jesus Christ, *and the* Dialogue of the Savior

The *Gospel of Thomas* is even earlier than the *Gospel of Mary*: without question it was composed before 150, and the most likely date seems to be sometime around 90–100, making it roughly contemporary with several of the canonical gospels, although some scholars think that *Thomas* is even earlier. The *Gospel of Thomas* is a "sayings" gospel, that is, it is a collection of Jesus' sayings without any narrative context, and in the final one of these sayings Mary appears, again in tension with Peter. "Let Mary leave us," Peter says, "for women are not worthy of life." Jesus answers, "I myself shall lead her in order to make her male, so that she too may become a living spirit resembling you males. For every woman who will make herself male will enter the kingdom of heaven."[48] The meaning of this passage is not at all clear, and several different explanations of what it means to make Mary male have been proposed. Mary here is admittedly not an expert in the sacred mysteries, as we find in other texts, although she is seemingly in the company of Jesus' disciples. Her identity is uncertain, as it was in the *Gospel of Mary*, and there is no indication as to whether she is the Magdalene or the Nazarene. Accordingly, Marvin Meyer advises that we should recognize that in the *Gospel of Thomas* "a 'universal Mary' is in mind, and that specific historical Marys are no longer clearly distinguished." Indeed, this would seem to be the preferred solution, given the absolute lack of any clarity from the text itself.[49] Even if this is not what the original authors of this tradition may have intended, undoubtedly various early Christian interpreters would have understood this Mary's identity differently. And this principle applies equally to other texts where we find ourselves also confronted with an otherwise unidentified Mary.

The *Sophia of Jesus Christ*, for instance, is another apocryphon where Mary appears in a similar role and again without any further specification. In this text, most likely from the second century, Mary twice questions the risen Savior, who has appeared to his disciples and is in dialogue with them.[50] Another text depicting Mary in conversation with the risen Christ is the *Dialogue of the Savior*, also from the second century. Here again, Mary stands in dialogue with the Lord, along with his other disciples, although in this instance she appears to be in complete harmony with the other disciples. Mary speaks frequently with the Savior, and in the course of the dialogue she emerges as one who possesses exceptional knowledge and understanding of the cosmic mysteries.[51] Yet, as in the *Sophia of Jesus Christ*, this Mary's identity is not further specified, and despite the frequent assertion that she is Mary of Magdala, the evidence for this is simply lacking. Rather, in both of these texts, as in the *Gospel of Mary* and the *Gospel of Thomas*, Mary is just as plausibly identified with the mother of Jesus, and again, one imagines that many early Christian readers and listeners would have understood this woman as representing Mary of Nazareth.[52]

The Gospel of Philip

Mary also appears in the *Gospel of Philip*, and in this text her identity is even more complex. Here both the Magdalene and the mother of Jesus are specifically identified at certain points in the text, while other passages refer only to a woman named Mary. The *Gospel of Philip* is seemingly an anthology of excerpts from other Gnostic (and more specifically Valentinian) Christian texts that dates most probably from the third century. In one key passage, the *Gospel of Philip* refers to several different Marys at the same time, seeming to conflate their identities: "There were three who always walked with the Lord: Mary, his mother and her sister and the Magdalene, the one who was called his companion. For Mary was his sister, his mother, and his companion."[53] On the basis of this passage a number of scholars have concluded that "Mary" in this gospel is best understood not as being a single figure, but rather as a conflation of several different historical women,[54] much as Meyer suggested of Mary in the *Gospel of Thomas*. Yet elsewhere in *Philip*, in a somewhat garbled section, Mary Magdalene is explicitly identified as "the companion of the [...]," and he "[... loved] her more than [all] the disciples [and used to] kiss her [often] on her [...]."[55] Perhaps more than any other, this passage has led scholars to the conclusion that Mary in the *Gospel of Philip* and therefore in many of these other texts is in fact the Magdalene and she alone.

To a certain extent this position is understandable, since in many of these Marian apocrypha Mary is described as the Savior's favorite. But at the same time there is no reason why this passage should uniquely control the interpretation of Mary in these other texts or even within the *Gospel of Philip*, particularly since it is itself an anthology of other writings. We certainly may not assume that this tradition regarding the Magdalene was known to the authors and audiences of these other texts. Moreover, in another section, the *Gospel of Philip* has some very interesting things to say about Jesus' mother that seem to align her instead with this apocryphal Mary. The passage begins by discussing her conception of Jesus: "Some said, 'Mary conceived by the Holy Spirit.' They are in error. They do not know what they are saying. When did a woman ever conceive by a woman? Mary is the virgin whom no power defiled." There can be little question which Mary the text has in view here, given the mention of her virginal conception. This Mary, we then learn, "is a great anathema to the Hebrews, who are the apostles and the apostolic men."[56] Although the exact meaning of this passage is admittedly somewhat elliptic, it would appear to refer to some sort of strife between Mary of Nazareth and the apostles, an image that resonates well with Mary's depiction in other apocrypha as standing in conflict with Peter and the other apostles. The *Gospel of Philip*, then, really does not resolve the question of who Mary is, as some scholars have imagined, but instead its traditions only throw into sharper relief the ambiguity of this woman's identity.

The Pistis Sophia

The same is no less true of yet another early apocryphon, the *Pistis Sophia*, a work written sometime during the third century. Here, as in the *Gospel of Philip*, both Mary of Magdala and Mary of Nazareth are at times specifically indicated, while in other instances Mary is named without any further clarification. Therefore Deirdre Good concludes that in this text Mary has a "composite identity," although for some peculiar reason she does not include Mary of Nazareth in this composite, focusing instead on Mary of Bethany and "other women in the Gospels."[57] The *Pistis Sophia* is a fairly lengthy text, in contrast to some of the others that we have considered thus far, and so its Marys appear both more often and at greater length. The format of the text is a revelation dialogue, in which the Savior is in extended conversation with several of his disciples, seemingly after the Resurrection. Mary quickly emerges as a prominent interlocutor, who speaks with Jesus more than any of the others do.

Mary first appears after a lengthy revelation by Christ, when she explains for the others the meaning of the hidden mysteries that he has just revealed. Following her interpretation, Jesus congratulates her, saying, "Well said, Maria. You are blessed among all women on earth."[58] Previous interpreters have inexplicably looked past this obvious Lukan epithet, presumably because they were so focused on the use of the name *Mariam* for this character elsewhere in the text, believing this to be a fail-safe identifier of the Magdalene. Nevertheless, the language here immediately brings to mind not Mary of Magdala but Mary of Nazareth, whom the Holy Spirit inspired Elizabeth to name "blessed among women" in Luke 1.42. This same Mary then continues to converse with the Savior, asking him several questions, with nothing at all to suggest that this Mary is anyone other than she whom he has named "blessed among women." After the Savior answers Mary's questions, he next reveals "the song of praise which the Pistis Sophia spoke in the first repentance, as she repented her sin," and then Mary once again offers an interpretation for the others. When she has finished, the Savior addresses her, "Well said, Mariam, thou blessed one, thou pleroma or thou all-blessed pleroma, who will be called blessed by all generations."[59] Here again, one cannot miss the obvious reference to Mary of Nazareth's words in Luke 1.48, "all generations will call me blessed," which unquestionably must have signaled to readers (or hearers) that this Mary is in fact the mother of Jesus and not the Magdalene. Such a description unambiguously aligns this Mary's identity with Mary of Nazareth.[60]

After Jesus gives another brief response, "Peter leapt forward and said to Jesus: 'My Lord, we are not able to suffer this woman who takes the opportunity from us and does not allow anyone of us to speak, but she speaks many times.'"[61] Undoubtedly this "insufferable" woman is the Mary who has only just recently finished speaking, Mary of Nazareth. So here again, we find conflict and tension between the mother of Jesus and the apostles, in this case Peter, just as in the *Gospel of Mary*. This same Mary then continues to speak throughout the rest of the *Pistis Sophia*'s first book, and she remains the Savior's primary interlocutor. Only toward the end of the first book is her identity more specifically indicated as "the mother of Jesus."[62] Yet the reason for this sudden clarity is quite obvious: immediately thereafter a second Mary is introduced to the dialogue, whom the text initially names "the other Mary," without any further clarification. Presumably this other Mary must be Mary of Magdala, and in fact later in the dialogue she is specifically identified as such.[63] Nevertheless, her introduction here as the "other" Mary only adds further confirmation that the Mary who has spoken thus far in the dialogue is indeed the mother of Jesus.

Despite the prominence of both Marys at the close of book 1, they strangely disappear from the conversations in the first part of book 2 of the *Pistis Sophia*. Eventually, "Mary" speaks up to explain her silence, complaining to Christ, "my mind is understanding at all times that I should come forward at any time and give the interpretation of the words which she [Pistis Sophia] spoke, but I am afraid of Peter, for he threatens me and he hates our race."[64] Seemingly this is the same Mary who drew Peter's ire in the first book, namely, Mary who is "blessed among women" and "will be called blessed by all generations." Nevertheless, later, in the second half of book 2, a "Mary" reappears among the Savior's primary interlocutors, only now she is explicitly named the Magdalene, and throughout the remainder of this book she is repeatedly identified as Mary of Magdala.[65] And so Mary of Magdala also appears in the *Pistis Sophia* as one learned in the mysteries of the universe and also as a favorite of the Savior.

A "Mary" appears again in books 3 and 4, and while book 3 twice specifies the presence of the Magdalene,[66] these two major sections of the text otherwise fail to indicate which of the two Marys is in fact speaking. Given Mary of Nazareth's prominence in book 1 and the simultaneous appearance of both Marys at the end of that book, it does not seem wise to follow Carl Schmidt (and many others) in identifying every unspecified Mary with the Magdalene. It is far more plausible, I think, to attribute the confused state of the text to the variety of different sources that it has drawn on, some of which understood "Mary" predominantly as the Virgin (book 1 especially) and others that saw in her the Magdalene (the second part of book 2 especially).[67] Such a view of this text strongly supports an understanding of this apocryphal Mary as a "composite figure" who combines in a single literary character the identities of both the Magdalene and the mother of Jesus. Yet, in any case, however one might ultimately resolve this dilemma, the *Pistis Sophia* unmistakably shows that Christians of the third century remembered the mother of Jesus as a learned master of the cosmic mysteries, who obtained these secrets directly from her son and interpreted them for her son's followers.

The Gospel (Questions) of Bartholomew

Finally, one finds a similar portrait of Jesus's mother in another contemporary apocryphon, the third-century *Gospel (Questions) of Bartholomew*, a text that, like these others, also places a high value on esoteric knowledge.[68] Here again we find Mary in dialogue with her son's followers, fielding their questions and explaining the sacred mysteries for them. The text begins with a revelation dialogue between Jesus and the disciples, in which Bartholomew is the main interlocutor. When Jesus then departs roughly one-third of the way through the text, the disciples turn in his absence to his mother. After some discussion among themselves, Bartholomew approaches her and asks on their behalf if she would tell them "how you conceived the incomprehensible, or how you carried him who cannot be carried or how you bore so much greatness." Mary initially declines to answer their question, because if she were to begin to tell them what they wanted to know, "fire will come out of my mouth and consume the whole earth." The apostles persist, however, and eventually Mary relents. She and Peter briefly dispute which of them should lead the others in prayer, but Mary yields and offers a prayer. When she finishes, she instructs several of the apostles to hold her, "so that, when I begin to speak, my limbs are not loosed." She begins to tell a story from her childhood in the temple, reminiscent in some respects of the *Protevangelium*: "one in the form of an angel" appeared to her, and after performing several miraculous signs he promised that "in three years I will send my word and you shall conceive my son, and through him the whole world shall be saved." Then, as quickly as he appeared, he vanished. But even as she was relating this story to the apostles, "fire came from her mouth, and the world was on the point of being burned up." Jesus immediately appeared to her and said, "Say no more, or today my whole creation will come to an end."[69]

The apostles then ask Jesus to see the places of torment, and the apocryphon continues with a visit to hell. When they return to the Mount of Olives, Jesus again appears, and Bartholomew asks to behold the devil himself. Jesus reluctantly acquiesces, and "Beliar" is raised up out of the earth, restrained by 660 angels who have bound him with fiery chains. The apostles are immediately overcome and fall down as dead. But Jesus revives them, and he invites Bartholomew to tread on the devil's neck. Bartholomew is initially afraid to do so, but as he summons his courage, he strangely invokes the Virgin Mary by acclaiming the wonder of her divine maternity in a prayer. "O womb more spacious than a city! O womb wider than the span of heaven! O womb that contained him whom the seven heavens do not contain. You contained him without pain and held in your bosom him who changed his being into the smallest of things. O womb that bore, concealed in (your) body, the Christ who has been made visible to many. O womb that became more spacious than the whole creation." It is an unusual prayer, given the circumstances: one might expect instead a more direct request for her aid and protection. Moreover, such invocation of Mary's womb as "wider than heaven" and having contained the uncontainable, the infinite God, is much more common in texts from the fourth and later centuries. Nevertheless, the prayer seems to be a part of the original third-century text, which makes for a very early witness to this aspect of Marian devotion.[70]

The *Gospel (Questions) of Bartholomew* thus presents Mary in two very different lights simultaneously. In the second section we find Mary portrayed as one who is learned in the sacred mysteries, whose teaching on esoteric topics the apostles actively seek out. Then later, when Bartholomew prepares to step on Satan's neck, he invokes the mystery of Mary's miraculous conception and birth of God. The former theme, Mary as teacher, fits well with her depiction in the other second- and third-century apocrypha that we have considered in this chapter, as well as with her portrayal in the earliest Dormition narrative, to which we will soon turn in the following chapter. But the elaborate praise of Mary's miraculous pregnancy seems to anticipate the more "orthodox" and familiar Marian piety that took shape especially in the early Byzantine period. The *Gospel (Questions) of Bartholomew* thus seems to intersect both with the early Christian traditions of Mary as a revered teacher who was an expert on the divine mysteries as well as with devotion to Mary because of her divine maternity. Although we have seen the roots of this latter form of piety already in the canonical gospels and the *Protevangelium*, in the years to come Mary's role as the Mother of God will increasingly emerge as the primary foundation of her veneration.

Conclusions

The church fathers of the third century provide disappointingly meagre evidence for the development of Marian devotion in this period. Tertullian offers a surprisingly negative assessment of Mary and her role in earliest Christianity, while Origen and Clement do not add much to what came before them. The church fathers of the later third century, for their part, are inexplicably reticent when it comes to Mary. Yet there is also the remarkable *Sub tuum praesidium* papyrus, which reveals that some Christians had already begun to pray to Mary and seek her intercessions by the end of the third century, if not perhaps even earlier. With this, we have some of the earliest evidence for the cult of the Virgin, which seems to have first taken hold, at least in some communities, even before the fourth century. Nonetheless, a very different image of Mary emerges from certain apocryphal writings of the late second and the third centuries. Here, we find Mary revered not for her divine maternity or her sacred purity, as in the church fathers and the *Protevangelium*, but instead as a privileged interlocutor of the Savior who has an authoritative knowledge of the saving cosmic mysteries. This Mary teaches and is occasionally in conflict with the other apostles, although in other texts they actively seek her sacred knowledge. It is perhaps an unfamiliar image of the mother of Jesus, but it is one that had significant currency within some of the theologically diverse Christian communities of the late second and third centuries. Here we also see some of the first evidence that could suggest a connection between reverence for Christ's mother and heterodox forms of early Christianity. Indeed, one wonders if perhaps Mary's association with varieties of early Christianity considered to be theologically deviant by the proto-orthodox could explain her relative neglect by the early church fathers, who were interested in little beyond her virginal conception and birth. But possibly Tertullian's insistence that Mary was not a follower of Christ during his lifetime is aimed to counter traditions such as we find in these apocrypha, where Mary is a highly esteemed teacher among the other apostles. Tertullian was certainly well informed about many of his theological opponents, although admittedly he does not draw such a direct connection himself.

I suspect that some readers of this book will continue to insist that in nearly all of the instances considered above, Mary is unquestionably to be identified as the Magdalene. This certainly is to be expected, given the force with which this interpretive orthodoxy has established itself. Nevertheless, despite the confidence about resolving this Mary's identity that many scholars continue to profess, the matter is actually much more complex than such certitude would appear to indicate. The truth of the matter is that we must reorient ourselves toward thinking of this Mary as an intertextual figure and thus recognize just how much Mary of Nazareth must have equally come to the minds of many ancient interpreters. It seems unlikely that we will ever be able to determine with any certainty which historical Mary stands behind these representations.[71] And it is by no means a given that the actions and characterizations ascribed to this apocryphal woman reflect those of an actual historical person from the beginnings of Christianity. Instead, it is far more likely that this Mary is a sort of mythological figure who, while she may typify the roles played by women in certain early Christian communities, does not represent a single specific woman, be she Mary of Magdala, Mary of Nazareth, or anyone else.[72] In some cases Mary of Nazareth is specifically identified in this role, as is the Magdalene. Therefore we must acknowledge that even as some early Christians may have understood this Mary as the Magdalene, so too would many Christians have understood her to be the mother of Jesus, even in instances where she is only named as Mary.

As such, this Mary is a literary character that draws into its composite many different women, including the Magdalene and the Nazarene especially, but perhaps Mary of Bethany should also be thrown into the mix. Mary is very much an intertextual figure in the sense that certain postmodern literary theorists have defined this term, an aspect that becomes even more clear once we dissolve the ideological illusion of a group of closely related "Gnostic" apocrypha that should be interpreted collectively and in relative isolation from other early Christian writings, as often has been the case.[73] This figure's representation in a particular text should not be closed off and limited by the bounds of a given text or even by the aggregate of apocryphal Mary traditions considered in this chapter. Like all texts, and ultimately all language, the apocryphal Mary is a figure woven from a variety of preexisting texts and discourses that have been reworked into a new combination. As other scholars have occasionally remarked, particularly in regard to the interpretation of the *Gospel of Philip*, this Mary's identity is not coherent or unified, but rather is a composite produced out of fragments from related cultural texts, images, and discourses.

Such a complex view of this apocryphal Mary's identity can best account for her multifaceted representation and should likewise caution us against weighting the perspectives of historical-critical New Testament scholarship too heavily in this case, particularly because we are interested primarily in how the early Christians would have understood these texts. Just because Mary of Magdala may perhaps appear to modern biblical scholars as a more likely participant in Jesus's ministry than his mother, we cannot assume that the producers and consumers of early Christian apocrypha in the second, third, and fourth centuries would somehow have shared this modern view. It is thus essential that we begin to examine these texts in relation to other early Christian writings that portray Mary of Nazareth in a similar fashion. Without a doubt, the most important of these texts is the earliest narrative of the Virgin Mary's Dormition and Assumption, to which we now turn in the next chapter. In this apocryphon, most likely also from the third century, we find Mary of Nazareth esteemed by the apostles for her knowledge of the sacred mysteries necessary for salvation, along with, no less importantly, some of the earliest evidence for the practice of Marian intercession, which seems to corroborate the date of the otherwise isolated *Sub tuum praesidium* papyrus.

CHAPTER THREE

Mother of the Great Cherub of Light:
The *Book of Mary's Repose*

THE ANCIENT TRADITIONS OF Mary's Dormition and Assumption offer one of the most important and yet underutilized sources for understanding the rise of Marian piety and cult within early Christianity. Part of the reason for their neglect is no doubt the sheer complexity of this literary corpus, which amounts to some forty different texts scattered across nine different ancient and medieval languages. For a long time the internal history and chronology of this tangle of narratives was only poorly understood, making it difficult to integrate their traditions more broadly with the history of early Christianity. Likewise, the preservation of the earliest and most important Dormition narratives in languages other than Greek and Latin undoubtedly discouraged many scholars from exploring these remarkable tales of the end of Mary's life. Nevertheless, the past fifty years have seen a steady stream of newly edited and translated Dormition narratives, and in recent decades the study of these traditions has advanced to the point where we have a much better understanding of their early history as well as reasonably accurate dates for the earliest versions.[1] Now that these foundations have been laid, the early Dormition narratives have a great deal to contribute to our knowledge of both early Marian piety and the diversity of early Christianity itself.

For the most part, the earliest Dormition traditions fall into one of two major groups, each of which reflects a distinctive narrative type. Although the earliest exemplars of both textual families first appear only in the later fifth century, it is clear that these traditions are considerably older. Only a handful of elements are common to both literary traditions, and so they appear to have developed independently from one another. These shared features are as follows: Mary dies at her house in Jerusalem; at least some of the apostles are present; Christ receives his mother's soul when it departs her body; Mary is transferred in body and/or soul to Paradise; and the Jews are portrayed as hostile to Mary. Yet beyond this slim core, the two narrative traditions diverge rather significantly, and, it is worth noting, there are also several minor textual traditions in addition to these two main groups. In this chapter and the next we will examine the earliest exemplars from each of these two main literary traditions, both of which are named for narrative elements distinctive to each textual family. This chapter will consider the earliest narrative from the so-called "Palm of the Tree of Life" traditions, or "Palm" traditions for short, so called on account of the prominence given to a branch taken from this mythical tree in narratives of this type. Of the two main literary traditions, this one appears to be the oldest, and it was also the only narrative type to circulate widely in the Christian West.[2]

The earliest known representative of this large and influential textual family is a writing known as the *Book of Mary's Repose*, a lengthy account of Mary's Dormition and Assumption that survives complete only in a translation into Classical Ethiopic (Ge'ez). Significant fragments also exist in Old Georgian and especially in Syriac (Christian Aramaic), where the same text is named the *Obsequies of the Virgin* (although we will stick with the *Book of Mary's*

Repose in order to avoid confusion).[3] Other important early witnesses to this textual tradition survive in Greek, Latin, Coptic, and Old Irish, but the earliest narratives in each of these languages have significantly revised the more ancient traditions that we find in the *Book of Mary's Repose*. Nevertheless, these more recent redactions are at the same time extremely valuable, not only for helping to reconstruct the contents of this oldest Dormition narrative, but also for their confirmation that the Ethiopic translation faithfully transmits a very early account of Mary's glorious departure from the world. This last point is of particular significance, since the complete Ethiopic version survives only in manuscripts copied during the fourteenth and fifteenth centuries: it is essential that we can confirm this translation's contents through comparison with other closely related, early witnesses to this narrative type.

The most important evidence for the antiquity of this text comes from its Syriac fragments, the oldest of which are from a manuscript that was written in the later fifth century. Since we know from comparison of the various early witnesses to this narrative type that it was originally written in Greek, this Syriac version is itself a translation, and the original thus must date even earlier, to the early fifth century at the absolute latest and most likely even earlier. Only a small portion of the text is extant in this ancient Syriac manuscript, which leaves significant questions regarding the bulk of its content: could some or even most of it have been added sometime between the fourth century and the fourteenth, the date of our earliest complete manuscript? Here is where the early versions in other languages are so important, and through their comparison with the *Book of Mary's Repose* and with one another, it is possible to confirm that the Ethiopic translation has very faithfully preserved the ancient Greek narrative that was its source.[4] Moreover, the language of the Ethiopic translation is itself extremely archaic, a feature that seems to indicate its production in the fifth or sixth century, perhaps not long after the conversion of Ethiopia to Christianity in the mid-fourth century.[5] By every measure, then, it would appear that this Ethiopic version reliably transmits a very early account of Mary's Dormition and Assumption that had been composed already by the fourth century and is most likely even earlier than that.[6]

As we turn to the contents of the *Book of Mary's Repose*, we find an unusual constellation of ideas that seems highly out of place in a text that would have been composed any later than the third century. Many of its key themes and features show strong affinities with heterodox and esoteric varieties of early Christianity, such as we saw in the texts considered in the last part of the previous chapter. Admittedly, dating on the basis of theological content is somewhat more speculative and subjective than the more definitive evidence afforded by the early manuscripts. Nevertheless, it is by no means uncommon to date texts on this basis, and the dating of many early Christian writings depends primarily on evaluation of the ideas that they contain and the age that these seem best to reflect. For instance, early Christian apocrypha and other anonymous or pseudonymous texts often must be dated in this manner, including a number of the Nag Hammadi writings considered in the preceding chapter. As we will see, the *Book of Mary's Repose* is centered around a number of ideas that had become highly aberrant by the fourth and later centuries and were quite foreign to the emergent discourse of Christian orthodoxy in this era. Accordingly, we can locate this text with some confidence to the third century, although the possibility of an even earlier origin, perhaps in the second century, should not be excluded.[7]

The nascent Marian piety reflected in this apocryphon is largely consistent with such an early date. Devotion to the Virgin is just an occasional theme of this ancient Marian biography, which reveals only the most basic elements of Marian veneration. Indeed, it is somewhat surprising just how much is absent from this narrative, which seems to be indicative of its early production. For instance, the apostles do not afford Mary any special reverence when they first greet her, nor are there any indications of a formal cult of the Virgin. Mary does not work any miracles, there are questions about her virginity, and she expresses doubts and a fear of dying because, according to her own words, she once sinned. Yet the *Book of Mary's Repose* unquestionably sees Mary's emergence as a figure of theological significance in her own right and not merely as some Christological annex. And perhaps most importantly, the *Book of Mary's Repose* bears early witness to belief in the power of Mary's intercessions, offering what is seemingly the earliest evidence of this practice.

Mary's Little Angel

The *Book of Mary's Repose* begins in a manner fairly typical of the Palm Dormition narratives, but before long we find ourselves in very unfamiliar territory, and some of its traditions prove to be completely baffling. In the opening scene Mary learns of her impending death from "a great angel" who appears to her and says, "Arise, Mary, and take this book, which he has given to you, he who established Paradise, and give it to the apostles, so that when they open it, they will read it before you; for on the third day, your body will die. For I will send all of the apostles to you, and they will prepare your body for burial."[8] So far, this great angel and his book are not especially out of the ordinary, although in most Palm narratives the angel presents Mary instead with the wondrous Palm branch for which this literary tradition is named.[9] As the narrative proceeds, we soon learn that both the angel and the book are quite exceptional in some unexpected ways. When the great angel completes his initial address, Mary asks to know his name, so that she will know what to tell the apostles. "Why do you ask me my name?" he replies. "For it is a great wonder to be heard. When I have come, I will tell you what my name is. Then tell the apostles in secret, so that they will tell no one. And they will know my authority and the power of my strength: not because of the book alone, but also because of my name, since it will be a source of great power. And it will be a revelation to all those in Jerusalem, and to those who believe, it will be revealed. Go then to the Mount of Olives, and you will hear my name, because I will not speak it to you in the midst of Jerusalem, lest the whole city be destroyed."[10]

The angel's response is significant for any number of reasons, but perhaps most important is its emphasis on the power of esoteric knowledge and sacred words, evident here in the concern over the great angel's name. The great angel agrees to reveal his name to Mary, and he also instructs her to share it with the apostles when they arrive: the name, he says, is a source of power and a revelation for all those who believe. But Mary must go outside of the city and ascend the Mount of Olives in order to learn this awesome name, since to speak it within Jerusalem would bring about the city's utter devastation. Such reverence for the power of sacred names is characteristic of the Jewish tradition, and accordingly many scholars have seen this theme, among others, as evidence of a connection between these traditions and early forms of "Jewish Christianity." Nevertheless, the category Jewish Christianity is so vague and fraught with problems that it turns out to be not very useful beyond its application to those Christian groups who continued a strict observance of the Law, in contrast to Pauline and other forms of early Christianity that rejected such practices. Since the *Book of Mary's Repose* gives no indication of any concern with maintaining the Jewish Law, its interest in the power of holy names is perhaps better compared instead with the extended discussion of this topic in the Gnostic *Gospel of Truth*. It is thus a theme that draws the *Book of Mary's Repose* more into the orbit of early Christian esotericism than early Judaism.[11]

As Mary ascends the Mount of Olives, the trees on the mountain incline to venerate the book in her hand. When she reaches the top, both Mary and the reader learn something surprising about this great angel's identity: Mary suddenly recognizes him as Jesus, her son. No one else, she concludes, could effect such a miracle. The great angel confirms that he is indeed Jesus, further explaining that "I am he who is in the trees and who is in the mountain." Here is the first indication that this earliest Dormition narrative adopts what is commonly known as an Angel Christology, that is, it understands Jesus to have been the earthly manifestation of a powerful angel. Although the proto-orthodox view of Jesus as an incarnation of God Godself would ultimately come to prevail at the ecumenical councils of the fourth century, the early Christians held a variety of opinions about how the special nature of Jesus Christ should be understood in relation to the one God of the Hebrew Bible, Yahweh. One attractive option was provided by the widespread speculation in early Judaism regarding powerful angels who attend God in heaven and manage the cosmos on God's behalf, often having semi-divine powers in their own right. For many Christians during the first few centuries, these mighty angels offered a ready model for understanding how Jesus could possess quasi-divine knowledge and power and yet still be distinguished from God the Father, to whom he prayed.[12] Jesus, they concluded, was the manifestation of one of these great angels, who revealed divine things within the mortal realm, just as we find in the *Book of Mary's Repose*. Although such Angel Christologies were fairly common during the first three centuries of Christianity, they are more or less unheard of after the beginning of the fourth century, and so this doctrine offers one of the clearest indications that this early Dormition narrative was likely composed before the end of the third century.[13]

A Dysfunctional Holy Family

As this Christ-angel continues his response to Mary on the Mount of Olives, his words soon become utterly cryptic. Presumably the text here invokes other esoteric traditions that were known to the early Christians who used it, but now these teachings have become lost to the ages, leaving this passage incomprehensible to modern readers. Before long, however, some measure of sense returns to the discourse, and the Christ-angel speaks with his mother at length in what amounts to an extended revelation dialogue. Their conversation focuses on four main topics, and not surprisingly the Christ-angel does most of the talking. Initially the angel addresses his mother's failure to understand his power, recalling a story from the Flight into Egypt that is perhaps better known from the seventh-century Latin *Gospel of Ps.-Matthew*.[14] The story appears here, however, in a rather different form that must be at least several hundred years older, and some of its differences are astonishing. The great angel asks his mother to recall the time when they were traveling together through the desert, and he, a young child, began to cry. Joseph grew annoyed by the noise and lashed out at Mary, ordering her to nurse the child in order to silence him. She does so, but eventually when they come upon some trees, Mary asks Joseph if it would be possible to find something for them to eat. At this point Joseph launches into a sudden tirade, in which he complains that he has been unfairly burdened with both Mary and a child who is not his own and he shockingly accuses her of failing to guard her virginity.

The Christ-angel recalls their conversation for his mother: "Then he rebuked you, saying, 'What can I do for you? Is it not enough for you that I became a stranger to my family on your account; why didn't you guard your virginity, so that you would [not] be found in this; and not only you, but I and my children too; now I live here with you,

107

and I do not even know what will happen to my seven children?'"[15] After Joseph explains that it is not possible for him or anyone else to reach the fruit high up in the tops of the trees, he returns to his bitter grievances against Mary. "I have been afflicted from all sides because of you, because I have left my country. And I am afflicted because I did not know the child that you have; I only know that he is not from me. But I have thought in my heart, perhaps I had intercourse with you while drunk, and that I am even worse because I had determined to protect [you]. And behold, now it has been made known that I was not negligent, because there were [only] five months when I received you in [my] custody. And behold, this child is more than five months."[16] This is pretty outrageous stuff: Joseph accuses the mother of Jesus of becoming pregnant because she failed to guard her virginity, and his initial thoughts were that he might have impregnated her himself by essentially raping her one night while drunk. Indeed, so shocking are Joseph's revelations that one might initially be tempted to suspect his words reflect some sort of misunderstanding by the Ethiopic trans-lator or some other sort of corruption of the text during its transmis-sion. Yet we are fortunate that this same section is extant also in an Old Georgian fragment, and this parallel version confirms the passage almost word for word as found in the Ethiopic.

Clearly, then, Joseph's rather unflattering thoughts regarding the parentage of Mary's son were a part of the original Greek text. And these harsh words against Mary, which could hardly be more different from the *Protevangelium*'s persistent emphasis on her sacred purity and virginity, are yet another important sign of the text's antiquity. Joseph's charge against Mary is surprisingly unmitigated, and he appears as truly believing that Mary had compromised her virginity in conceiving Jesus. Not only does he impugn Mary's character, but his own as well, as he seeks to reassure himself that the child is not his own. Apparently given to bouts of drunkenness, Joseph wonders if perhaps one night after having too much to drink he might have ravaged the young girl who had been given into his charge, but thankfully the child is too old, having been born just five months after he became Mary's guardian. Joseph further notes that he had deserted seven children of his own in order to care for Mary and her son. One wonders about their fate: have they been abandoned and left to fend for themselves? All in all, it is a vignette suggestive of a high level of dysfunction within Jesus' admittedly rather nontraditional family, and to my knowledge it is unique in early Christian literature for this unharmonious representation of the Holy Family. By the fourth century, such characterization of Mary and Joseph is almost unimaginable, since Mary had become highly revered for her Perpetual Virginity (as we will see in chapter 5), and Jerome also enlists Joseph as a model for male virginity, and so Mary and Joseph together serve as exemplars of marital continence.[17] Indeed, even in the third century it is somewhat difficult to imagine anyone writing so irreverently of the mother of Jesus and portraying such unqualified discord within the Holy Family.

In the end, however, Joseph abruptly moderates his outburst with a confession that "truly, he was not from your seed, but from the Holy Spirit. And he will not leave you hungry, but he will have mercy on you; he will provide for me, and he will remember that I am a sojourner, as you are a sojourner with me."[18] It is difficult to reconcile this conclusion with Joseph's rather forceful accusations against Mary that she had failed to preserve her virginity. His sudden change of heart is not explained, and one suspects that this final statement is the work of a later hand that felt the need to correct the text. Joseph's ultimate profession of Jesus's miraculous conception by the Holy Spirit serves both to mollify the jarring improprieties of his previous words and to harmonize the entire episode with the image of the Holy Family in later Christian piety as well as in the gospels. Indeed, one wonders how the original author(s) of this text would have understood Matthew 1.18–25, which relates the angel's visit to Joseph in a dream and Joseph's persuasion that Mary's child had been conceived miraculously by the Holy Spirit. Perhaps one must assume that Matthew's gospel was not an authoritative text within the early Christian community that originally produced this peculiar account of the Flight to Egypt. In any case, such an irreverent portrayal of Mary and Joseph stands sharply at odds with their representation in other early Christian sources, and this dissonance is yet another sign of this writing's antiquity. Other redactors would soften the episode even further. The Georgian version, for instance, eliminates Joseph's suspicions of himself and his corresponding admission of drunkenness, while in the seventh-century *Gospel of Ps.-Matthew*, Joseph is barely allowed to speak at all: when Mary expresses her hunger, he calmly notes that water seems to be their more pressing need, and with this minor marital disagreement, harmony is restored to the Holy Family.

The Secret Prayer of Ascent

As Mary and her son continue their conversation, the topic turns to Mary's forthcoming departure from the body.[19] The Christ-angel promises that he will come on the fourth day after her death to take her body to Paradise. Mary wants to know how all of this will happen, and she asks the Christ-angel what to expect. He tells her not to worry, promising that he will come to her himself with all the hosts of angels. Now, however, he has come to her in order to reveal certain secrets that are necessary for salvation, as he (somewhat oddly) explains: "For I have been sent to tell you, so that you will then give [what I tell you] to the apostles in secret, because this is hidden from those who seek it from Jesus the Saviour."[20] The main content of this revelation would appear to be a secret prayer that the dying must say so that their souls will be able to escape past the guardians of the cosmic spheres and return to God and the realm of spirit. Unfortunately, large sections of this discussion are highly opaque, and we lose the Georgian parallel at just this moment, adding to the difficulties of interpretation. Presumably, once again, we are dealing here with oblique references to other now lost esoteric traditions that informed the world view of this text's community, a problem that has possibly been compounded by the translator's failure to fully comprehend as well. Nevertheless, it is clear that the main thread of this section is a secret, salvific prayer that the Christ-angel entrusts to his mother, with instructions that she should teach it to the apostles.

The angel tells his mother that he received this prayer from the Father, and that without the prayer it is not possible for the soul to ascend. Apparently, not everyone is able to say this prayer (although the text is quite difficult here), and so Mary is instructed to "tell the apostles in secret, 'Do not reveal this.'" It must be kept secret, it would seem, from those who love the world and have not desired and kept the word of the Lord. The Christ-angel then further explains to Mary that "you will need to observe [the prayer] with every world. And even if a person has gained the whole world, and he has been abandoned to the beast with the body of a lion and the tail of a snake, what is his profit? . . . Truly it is thus, Mary; for it is not possible to pass by the beast with the body of a lion and the tail of a snake, so as to pass through every world. . . . The prayer, Mary, transcends your mother's [Eve's] nature, which prevails in every creature, on account of which there is death."[21]

The secret prayer thus seems to serve as a password that will enable the soul to pass through various "worlds" during its ascent after death. This is a relatively common theme in much early Christian esoteric literature, where saving knowledge is necessary for the soul to rise through the cosmic spheres and return to the realm of light and spirit. These cosmic spheres are frequently guarded by the "demiurge," the wicked creator of the material world, and his "rulers," who attempt to prevent the soul's escape and force it to return to the earth, where it will live and die again.[22] We have already seen such a world view, for instance, in Mary's teaching at the end of the *Gospel of Mary*, which offers an intriguing parallel to the *Book of Mary's Repose* on this point. Such an understanding of the universe and the process of salvation led many early Christian groups to offer their adherents secret knowledge of a very practical nature, consisting of passwords that would allow the soul to pass by these guardians during its ascent. By speaking the right words at the appropriate time and in the proper order, one could force these cosmic rulers to allow passage through the spheres and into the spiritual realm.[23] This secret prayer in the *Book of Mary's Repose* appears to have a similar function, a connection that is underscored by the description of the one who impedes ascent as a "beast with the head of a lion and the tail of a serpent." This description matches the frequent depiction of the creator and chief ruler of the cosmic powers, the demiurge, in Christian Gnostic texts as "lion-like" or "lion-faced," or, in the case of the *Apocryphon of John*, as a "lion-faced serpent."[24]

The section that follows also seems to point in the direction of Gnostic or at least esoteric Christianity, as the Christ-angel again alludes to other arcane traditions that explain the purpose of the prayer. Here, he seems to give a very compressed account of the Gnostic cosmological myth, which posits the creation of the material world by an imperfect, often malicious power, that is, the "demiurge" or, as he is known here, "the Ruler." The passage in question appears to describe the creation of Adam in terms that relate this event to the process of the soul's salvation from its imprisonment in the material world. "But on that day the body of Adam was in the glory that dwelled upon him, the body that sat lying on the earth, which he made with the Father, who was with him in counsel and participation. And this is that which was from the beginning and was even before the angels and the archangels, before the creation of the powers by me, until he sat and he was moved by the Ruler, when it was apparent that he could not arise. And God knew what was in the soul; and he rested and placed rest in his heart so that it would pray to him. And when the Father said this to Adam, he arose and was in the custody of the Father and the Son and the Holy Spirit until this day."[25] As it stands now, the passage is rather confusing, but it seems to reflect something very similar to Gnostic Christian beliefs about Adam's creation. According to the Gnostic creation myth, some sort of "power" from the spiritual realm accidentally became captured within the material realm, presenting the problem of how to restore this "spiritual power" to the "Pleroma" or "Fullness," as both ancient Gnostic texts and the *Book of Mary's Repose* name this divine, spiritual realm. A plan is then devised to effect the restoration of this spiritual power in the creation of humanity, and through the transfer of this power to the human race, it will ultimately be able to return to the Pleroma. In the first act of Adam's creation, then, according to this myth, the demiurge forms Adam's physical body, and sometimes his soul as well, but Adam remains motionless. Only when a spiritual component is added, consisting of the spiritual power from the transcendent realm, does Adam finally come to life. With this spirit now placed in Adam, his descendants will eventually restore this spiritual substance to the Pleroma, whence it came and where it belongs.[26]

The Christ-angel's revelations to his mother continue, as he explains that this mystery had previously been hidden from "the wise, and it is not even written in the Scriptures, so that the scribes would not see it and the ignorant would not hear it among their children."[27] Mary is seemingly the first person to whom he has entrusted these secrets, and she in turn is directed to share them with the apostles. The great angel then resumes discussion of the secret prayer, posing the rhetorical question, "Who are they who will say this with their heart and soul completely?" Answering his own question, the angel explains: "For before creation are those who boast before humanity, saying, 'We belong to God.' His memory arouses them as they seek recovery from their illness."[28] Here again we find some themes that are familiar from other early Christian esoteric writings. As just noted, many early Christians believed the human spirit to be a power that had fallen away from the spiritual realm and become imprisoned in the material realm, and more specifically, within humankind. According to many of these same esoteric traditions, however, this spirit is not present in all human beings, but only in certain people, a spiritual race, to whom the message of salvation is primarily addressed. This would seem to be the idea implied here in the *Book of Mary's Repose*, since only some of humanity is from "before creation" and may boast accordingly, "We belong to God." Because this spirit was originally from the spiritual world, which preexisted the physical universe, those who possess it truly are from before the creation of the material world, as the Christ-angel here describes them.[29] The language of remembrance and the notion of material existence as an "illness" are also reminiscent of other early Christian esoteric traditions. The present condition of humanity is frequently identified as a "sick" or "drunken" state into which the spiritual essence of humanity has fallen, losing all memory of its divine origin.[30] Only by regaining knowledge of one's divine origin can one be freed from the confines of the material world and return to the spiritual realm. This remembrance consists of the esoteric, saving knowledge that the Savior brings into the world, as seemingly described here in the *Book of Mary's Repose*.

In some previous publications I have argued on the basis of these and other passages from the *Book of Mary's Repose* that this writing bears evidence of contact with Gnostic Christianity, and so it should be interpreted especially within the context of this early Christian movement. In more recent publications, however, I have begun to back away from this claim, in part because the category of Gnostic Christianity has itself become so fraught in contemporary scholarship on early Christianity that its usage is not always very helpful. Moreover, I also have become increasingly convinced that it is perhaps best not to try to pin this text too closely to one particular kind of early Christianity or another, but instead to allow its genuinely peculiar mix of ideas to stand on its own.[31] The *Book of Mary's Repose* seems to reflect the beliefs of an almost unique early Christian group that believed in salvation through esoteric knowledge and seems to have embraced a creation myth with some striking similarities to the Gnostic myth. And in this text, Mary the mother of Jesus is the one who is entrusted with the hidden mysteries that will save humankind—or at least a part of it. It is a portrait of Mary that certainly calls to mind some of the texts examined in the previous chapter.

The Parable of the Wormy Trees and Jesus the Angel of Death

As Mary continues her conversation with the Christ-angel, he further explains that in addition to those who are "before creation" and can boast, "We belong to God," there are also those who make requests of God, but "God does not hear them, because the will of God is not among them."[32] A cryptic story then follows, which is presumably intended to explain the difference between these two peoples. The Christ-angel asks his mother to recall the time when a "thief ... was taken captive among the apostles," and he begged them to intercede with their master on behalf of himself and some others. When the apostles approached Jesus on the thief's behalf, he replied, "These are

115

the shepherds of the house of Israel, who are beseeching on behalf of the sheep, so that they will be pardoned and glorified before humanity. And they cannot sanctify themselves, because they exalt themselves like the strong. Did I not give them many signs?" The apostles still do not understand (nor, frankly, do I), and so Jesus inflicts a sort of "parable" on them in order to enlighten them further.

Jesus takes his apostles to a mountain and causes them to become hungry. When they complain of their hunger, Jesus commands that a grove of trees, full of fruit, should appear on the mountaintop. Jesus sends the apostles over to go and pick fruit from the trees, but they return empty-handed, explaining that when they reached the trees, they found no fruit on them. Jesus then persuades the apostles that they failed to see the fruit because the trees were too tall, promising them that if they go over again, he will cause the trees to bend so that the apostles can take their fruit. The apostles return from the trees a second time, again with no fruit, and, having become frustrated, they demand of Jesus, "What is this, a mockery?" Jesus then bids them to go to the trees a third time and sit underneath them. When the apostles do so, "immediately the trees released stinking worms." When the apostles now return to Jesus a third time, he offers an explanation, telling them to turn and look again at the trees. Then the apostles see that the trees have suddenly become human beings, who "stand and pray and are prostrate on their knees, while repenting," yet "there is no fruit to God in the repentance."[33] Although this "parable" is admittedly quite peculiar, it seems to elaborate on the previous distinction between those who belong to God and those whom God refuses to hear. As the parable's conclusion continues to explain, when those people symbolized by the trees attempt to ascend, "they are returned to the world," and God turns away from them. These would appear to be those who are not able to receive the saving, esoteric knowledge. Admittedly, however, why they are not able to receive it remains somewhat unclear; seemingly, their love of the material world is the thing that keeps them bound to it.

The Christ-angel reminds his mother to share all of these secrets with the apostles, so that they will reveal the mystery to those who believe. Then he suddenly switches topics, explaining that he wants to give his mother an example of "what power was given to me from God the Father when he sent me into the world to destroy sinners and to bless the just." He begins by telling her, "I am the third thing that was created, and I am not the Son; there is no one greater than me," and then adding "I am the one who destroyed every firstborn of Egypt because of the great evil that was in them."[34] Apparently this great angel who was manifest in Mary's son was also the same angel that brought death to the firstborn sons of the Egyptians just before the Exodus as well as the one who destroyed Sodom and Lot's wife. He brings this revelation dialogue with his mother to a close by recounting two extra-biblical traditions associated with the Exodus that are also known from early Rabbinic literature: the punishment of the Egyptians for the death of Rachael's unborn child when she is forced to work in place of her sick husband; and the story of the miraculous discovery of Joseph's bones and their return to the Holy Land with the fleeing Israelites.[35] In both instances, the Christ-angel explains, he was responsible for the outcome.[36] Finally, just before departing, the Christ-angel reveals his name to his mother, reminding her again to share it with the apostles: Adonai'el is his name, a variant of Adonai and also the name of a great angel who frequently appears in Gnostic and magical texts.[37]

Death and the Maiden: Mary's Funeral Preparations

Mary returns home with the book that the angel had given her, and she prays, blessing her son and thanking him for choosing her to be the one who was found worthy of receiving his mysteries. Her prayer is also preserved in the earliest Greek Dormition narrative, and there we can see even more clearly that it is larded with vocabulary resonant with early Christian esotericism, including references to the "Pleroma," the "bridal chamber," and the "hidden race," all common Gnostic technical terms.[38] Most peculiar in this respect is the use of the term *paralēmptōr*, a term meaning "one who receives."[39] It is an extremely rare word in Christian Greek, but one that is fairly common in Coptic Gnostic texts, where it generally is used, as seems to be the case here, as a technical term for heavenly powers that meet the soul at its separation from the body and guide it safely past the cosmic Ruler and his minions to the Pleroma.[40] Eventually Mary asks her son to come to her himself at her death as he promised, so that no other power will come upon her soul when it goes forth from the body. Mary's concerns here become clearer when, after she has finished praying, she assembles all of her family and friends in order to announce her impending death. After telling them that she will soon die, she explains for them what happens when the soul goes forth from the body. "For two angels come to a person, one of righteousness and one of wickedness, and they come with death. And when [death] acts on the soul that is going forth, the two angels come and admonish his body. And if he has good and righteous deeds, the angel of righteousness rejoices because of this, because there is no [sin] that was found upon him. And he calls his other angels, and they come to the soul. And they sing before it until [they reach] the place of all the righteous. Then the wicked angel weeps, because he did not find his part in him. And if there are evil deeds that are found in him, that one rejoices. And he takes seven other angels with him, and they take that soul and lead it away. The angel of righteousness weeps greatly."[41]

Mary's friends and neighbors are alarmed to learn of her fear that the wicked angel might come upon her soul when it departs the body.

If she, who is the "mother of the whole world" and the "mother of [the] Lord," is worried, what chance do they have of escaping its clutches? Mary begins to reassure them, and then, quite astonishingly, she confesses that she is afraid because she once sinned by not believing in God. While fleeing with Joseph and two of his children to Egypt (who seem to be absent in the previous account of this event), Mary heard the voice of the slaughtered infants crying out. She turned to see who was speaking, and when Joseph returned she said to him, "Let us go from this place, because I saw an infant who is not from this world." Then she looked again and recognized him as her son, who said to her, "Mary, my mother, every sin is imputed to you, because you have tasted the bitter as the sweet." Mary offers the following explanation, the meaning of which unfortunately is not very clear: "I did not believe, my brothers, that I had found so much glory, until I gave him birth, since I did not at all know the menstruation of women, because of him. Now, however, I understand. And all of this took place and everything was said to me and made known to me then on the road, as was his power."[42] Perhaps the passage is confused because the translator was alarmed by what he found in the original, or again, possibly there are some now-lost esoteric traditions that lie behind her explanation. In any case Mary's admission of her sin is yet another sign indicating the antiquity of this writing. It is difficult to imagine anyone writing this confession after Mary's sinlessness had emerged as an important focus of Marian doctrine and devotion. The idea that Mary could have sinned (as separate from the question of her Immaculate Conception in the Western church) seems to have belonged particularly to the late second and early third centuries, when it is voiced by Irenaeus and Tertullian. By the fourth century, agreement on her sinlessness had become fairly widespread.[43]

The next morning the apostles begin to arrive, and John is the first to knock on Mary's door. Initially John is overcome when he learns that Mary soon will die, but after she reassures him, she brings him into her inner chamber. There she teaches him the secret prayer of ascent that the Christ-angel had told her and asks him to teach it to the other apostles. Mary also brings forth the book that the great angel gave her, and she hands it to John, telling him, "My father John, take this book in which is the mystery. For when he was five years old, our master revealed all of creation to us, and he also put you, the twelve in it."[44] When they exit the chamber, the rest of the apostles also arrive, miraculously flown in on clouds to attend the Virgin's funeral. After they greet one another and offer prayers, they enter Mary's house to speak with her. Seeing them, she offers a prayer of thanksgiving to her son, "the Great Cherub of Light, who dwelt in my womb," praising him for fulfilling his promise to gather the apostles to her before her death. Once again we see here the Angel Christology that characterizes this text, as Mary identifies her son with the Great Cherub of Light, a title also present in the earliest Greek Dormition narrative. Just who or what exactly this Great Cherub of Light is admittedly is something of a mystery. So far the only other instance where I have found a similar title is on a Coptic amulet, which mentions "the Great Cherub of Fire (or Light)."[45] Another possibility is Ezekiel 28.14, where the king of Tyre is sometimes identified with the Cherub who walked among the stones of fire, although this passage is itself highly ambiguous. Often this figure is identified with Satan, which might seem a bit peculiar, yet given some of the oddities of this text, one should not rule out even this possibility: and after all, Lucifer means "the light bearer" (cf. Isa 14.12). Paul also says that Satan appears as "an angel of light" (2 Cor 11.14). In any case, what is quite clear here is that once again Christ is understood to have been the manifestation of a great angel, whom we now know to be the Great Cherub of Light.

At this point Peter suggests that someone should present a learned discourse as they wait through the night, and after Peter and Paul argue over who is more worthy to do so, Peter eventually yields and agrees to speak. Peter begins to explain the mysteries of death and the afterlife for the crowd that has gathered to keep vigil for Mary's death.[46] Yet most significantly for our purposes, before very long he invokes Mary's intercessory powers, exclaiming that "the light of our sister Mary's lamp fills the world and will not be extinguished until the end of days, so that those who have decided to be saved will receive assistance from her. And if they receive the image of light, they will receive her rest and her blessing."[47] Here is the first evidence in the text of belief in the power of Marian intercession, and while Peter does not explicitly pray for Mary's intercessions, the power of her assistance for those who wish to be saved is made plain. The fact that this passage appears almost identically in the earliest Greek version again ensures that it was undoubtedly in the original and is not a later addition.[48] Eventually, however, Peter begins to speak too openly about the sacred mysteries, and he is interrupted by a great light and a voice admonishing him not to disclose any secrets to the crowd, but to speak instead in terms that they can receive.[49] After acknowledging the authority of this divine intervention, Peter resumes with a lengthy tale of two servants, the gist of which is that it is better to remain a virgin than to marry.

Mary's Dormition

When Peter has finished and the sun rises, Mary goes forth from her house and says her prayer, presumably the secret prayer of ascent. She then returns within and lies down, and thus "she fulfilled the course of her life" with the apostles gathered around her. A sweet smell, "like the odor of Paradise," suddenly filled the room, and all those standing around fell asleep, "except only the virgins: he kept them from sleeping so that they would be witnesses of Mary's funeral and of her glory." Comparison of this episode across all of the earliest narratives from the Palm tradition indicates that originally these three women alone remained awake for the events of Mary's actual Dormition while the male apostles all slept right through it.[50] Christ then arrives on a cloud in the company of an innumerable multitude of angels and enters Mary's room, while the angels wait outside. Mary praises her son for fulfilling his promise, and he receives her soul in his hands before giving it over to Michael. The apostles behold her soul, which was "a perfect form, but its body was both male and female, and nevertheless one, being similar to every body and seven times white." The apostles are amazed by its pure whiteness, but Christ explains that all souls are thus until they are tainted by sin.[51] He then instructs them to place Mary's body in a tomb outside of the city, but before he departs, her body cries out to him, begging him not to forget it. Christ promises his mother's body, "I will not abandon you, pearl of my new treasure: by no means will I abandon you, the closed sanctuary of God! By no means will I abandon the one who is truly the guarantee!"[52]

The apostles begin to process out of the city with her body, and when the high priests hear the noise and singing of her funeral procession, they plot to "kill the apostles and burn the body of the one who bore the deceiver." The angels who were processing alongside of the Virgin's bier then attack the Jews and strike them with blindness, preventing their assault. One of the priests, however, is somehow able to lunge onto Mary's bier, and he grabs hold of it and tries to overturn it. Yet no sooner does he touch the bier than his hands are severed from his arms and left dangling from the bier. Immediately he cries out in torment and begs the apostles to help him, and they explain that if he believes in Christ, he will be healed.

The priest responds with a peculiar confession in which he admits that he and the other priests knew all along who Jesus was, but they opposed him in order to keep the lucrative commerce of the Temple flowing. Then he embraces Mary's holy body and professes faith in both her and her son, continuing to bless her "in his own language" for three hours and "prophesying and bringing forth testimonies from the 100 books of Moses." When he touches the bier again and prays, his hands are restored, and the apostles give him a leaf from the palm branch that they were carrying, so that with it he might heal those among his fellow Jews who are willing to believe and thus be cured of their blindness.[53] Thus, like the bodily relics of other saints and martyrs, Mary's remains effect the physical healing of her assailant, while a leaf from the palm branch, a contact relic, restores sight to those Jews who are willing to believe.

The apostles eventually reach the tomb and place Mary's body inside, leaving them to wait for several days until Christ returns for it as he promised. In the interim they begin to converse, and Paul asks Peter to reveal the cosmic mysteries to him: "Our father, you know that I am a neophyte and this is the beginning of my faith in Christ. For I did not meet the master, so that he could tell me the great and glorious mystery. But I have heard that he revealed it to you on the Mount of Olives. Now then, I beg you to reveal it to me too." Peter refuses, explaining that he is afraid that Paul might not be able to handle these mysteries, and so he suggests that they wait until Christ returns in order to see what he says. The text unfortunately becomes rather confused at this point, although soon Paul begins to relate an expanded version of a tradition that is also known from the *Testament of Solomon*.[54] When he finishes, the apostles agree with what he has said and try to persuade him to continue speaking, so that he would not press them further to reveal the sacred mysteries. Paul recognizes their unwillingness to reveal these secrets to him, and so he asks the other apostles to tell him instead what they preach and teach when they go forth to spread the gospel.[55]

Peter says that he teaches that "anyone who does not fast all of his days will not see God," and John says that "anyone who is not a virgin all of his days will not see God." Paul thinks that perhaps Peter and John are a bit strict because the former is a bishop and the latter is himself a virgin, and so he asks Andrew. Andrew replies that he preaches that "everyone who does not leave father and mother, and brothers and sisters, and children and houses, and everything that he has, and go forth after our Lord, he will not be able to see God." Paul is quite taken aback by their severity, and so the other apostles ask him what he preaches. Paul responds with a program of moderate asceticism, advocating marriage, almsgiving, and fasting only one or two days a week. The other apostles begin to murmur at this, when suddenly Christ reappears and vindicates Paul, rejecting the teachings of Peter, John, and Andrew as "destructive" and proclaiming "that you should receive [the teaching] of Paul. For I see that the whole world will be caught in Paul's net." As for the mysteries, Christ promises to share with Paul the heavenly mysteries, in contrast to the earthly ones that he has previously revealed to the others.[56]

In itself this episode is not particularly important for understanding the early history of Marian piety, but it is once again significant for determining the date of this text.[57] The *Book of Mary's Repose* seems to address here Christians who were questioning Paul's status as an apostle, but such opposition to Paul seems to have been largely confined to the second and third centuries.[58] Likewise, after the second century such ringing endorsements of marriage in the face of a call to celibacy become increasingly rare, and the third century saw instead the rise of a "moderate encratism," which, while not fully condemning marriage, could not allow its equality in comparison with the celibate life.[59] By the fourth century such ideas could lead to trouble, as the opposition to Helvidius and Jovinian reminds us.[60] Thus it is all the more striking to find such moderate views joined to this pivotal moment in the life of the Virgin, as her son arrives to retrieve her virginal body and takes the occasion to chastize the ascetic extremism of his disciples in favor of Paul's endorsement of marriage and moderation. In comparison with the Mariological and ascetic literature of the fourth century and later, it is nothing short of astonishing that the Virgin's life is used here as a platform for ideas of ascetic restraint, seemingly aimed at married householders rather than world-renouncing virgins. This unusual feature seems to indicate the text's production sometime before the image of Mary as the archetypal virgin became the norm, adding to the list of other anomalies that point toward an early date, most likely in the third century if not even earlier. Likewise, as Jean Gribomont observes in his brief study of this second apostolic council of Jerusalem, it would appear that the *Book of Mary's Repose* must have been composed prior to the establishment of monasticism in the fourth century, which essentially resolved the problems addressed here by creating two classes of Christians.[61]

The Assumption and Apocalypse of the Virgin

With Christ's return, the *Book of Mary's Repose* begins its apocalyptic conclusion, which is partly known also from the Syriac fragments and appears almost identically in the Irish recension of this apocryphon as well as in an early Latin précis.[62] While it is not altogether impossible that this apocalyptic tour of the other world was once a separate tradition from Mary's Dormition, there is at present consensus that this Marian apocalypse originated as a part of the *Book of Mary's Repose*.[63] This celestial journey begins as Christ commands that Mary's body should be taken on clouds to Paradise in the company of the apostles and thousands of angels. There her body is taken to the Tree of Life and reunited with her soul. The apostles then remind Christ that he had promised them while still on earth that they would be able to see the places of torment. Reluctantly he agrees, and what follows is a tour of the places of punishment that has some intriguing points of contact with the early medieval *Apocalypse of the Virgin* but also with the fourth-century *Apocalypse of Paul*. And most importantly, it seems that the *Apocalypse of Paul* depends on this section of the *Book of Mary's Repose*, adding further evidence of its relative antiquity.[64]

Again a cloud snatches up Mary and the apostles, and together with Michael and the Lord they travel to the place where the sun sets. At the Lord's command, the pit opens, revealing the torments of the damned. As the visitors draw near to the pit, the damned spot Michael and beg him to intercede on their behalf. Michael reassures the damned that God's angels are always interceding on behalf of all humanity and all creation. Then the angels of the waters, the winds, and the clouds intercede, followed by Michael himself, who begs the Lord to give the damned rest from their torments. Christ rebuffs Michael's request, asking him if he could possibly imagine that he loves these lost souls more than the one who gave them life and breath. Then a brief tour of Hell follows, in which Mary and the apostles witness various sufferings endured by the damned and learn their specific causes. When Mary and the apostles have finished their sightseeing, the damned plead with Mary for her assistance, crying out, "Mary, we beseech you, Mary, light and the mother of light; Mary, life and mother of the apostles; Mary, golden lamp, you who carry every righteous lamp; Mary, our master and the mother of our Master; Mary, our queen, beseech your son to give us a little rest." Others of the damned look to the apostles, calling out to Peter, Andrew, and John. The apostles, however, scorn their request, rejoining, "Where did you place our doctrine that we taught you?" at which the damned "were very ashamed and could not reply to the apostles." Yet in the end their pleas meet with some success, and Christ grants them three hours of respite every Sunday, "because of the tears of Michael, my holy apostles, and my mother Mary."[65] Here, then, is some very early evidence of Marian intercession, seemingly from the third century and perhaps even earlier than the *Sub tuum praesidium* papyrus, whose early dating it also can partly substantiate. With this we have the beginnings of the cult of the Virgin, albeit in a strikingly heterodox account of her Dormition and Assumption.

Prior to the publication of the *Book of Mary's Repose*, there was some question as to whether Mary's intercession for the damned may have been a late addition to the Irish and Latin versions of this text, inasmuch as the Syriac fragments are interrupted just before the tour of Hell begins.[66] Nevertheless, as Mary Clayton observes, the close parallels to the *Book of Mary's Repose* in other early texts assure us that "Mary's role as intercessor almost certainly goes back to the beginning of the [Dormition] tradition." Enrico Norelli likewise concludes that this intercessory excursion belonged to the earliest version of this apocryphon, and, as noted above, it appears to have directly influenced a similar episode in the *Apocalypse of Paul*.[67] But its antiquity is now definitively confirmed by a recently published Syriac fragment of the *Book of Mary's Repose* from the British Library: this late fifth-century palimpsest clearly describes Mary's intercession for the damned during her visit to Hell with the apostles.[68] It should be noted, however, that Mary's mediation here is not portrayed as uniquely powerful, as we will find in later texts, but instead her assistance is presented alongside of angelic intercessions and a request (albeit somewhat unsuccessful) for apostolic intervention. Although Michael's pleas are initially rejected, and the apostles fail to offer any intercession, Christ ultimately yields to the collective supplications of Mary, Michael, and the apostles. And this is exactly the context in which we should expect to find the origins of Marian piety, embedded within the emergent veneration of the saints and angels, of which the early cult of the Virgin is ultimately, as already noted, only a particular variant.

After yielding to the prayers of Michael, the apostles (who don't actually seem to pray), and his mother, Christ closes the pit of Hell and brings Mary and the apostles swiftly back to Paradise. There the apocalypse concludes with a brief tour of Paradise which is not, it should be noted, very well attested in other early witnesses to the ancient Dormition traditions. This final section also is very garbled at times and difficult to understand. Nevertheless, it is clear that, after returning from their vision of Hell, Mary and the apostles are greeted by the souls of many of the Old Testament patriarchs: Abraham, Isaac, Jacob, Noah, David, Enoch, and also Elizabeth. Then they briefly behold God, who is entirely fire and thus cannot really be seen. After some very unclear conversations, the Lord has a throne brought in for Mary to sit on, and he returns the apostles to the earth, telling them to proclaim everything that they have seen, thus bringing their otherworldly journey—and this text—to an end.

Conclusions

Perhaps more than any other text, this early Dormition narrative challenges us to reconsider many traditional notions about Mary's status within the early Christian tradition. Here, instead of the passive, obedient Virgin celebrated by the *Protevangelium* and the early church fathers, we find Jesus' mother revered not for her purity but for her knowledge of the cosmic mysteries and her influence with her son. We also find a Mary who openly confesses that she had once sinned, and a Joseph who sounds a bit like an angry, possibly lecherous drunk. This Mary is not the Mother of God; instead she is the mother of the Great Cherub of Light. The *Book of Mary's Repose* thus depicts her glorious departure from this world and belief in her intercessory powers against a strikingly heterodox backdrop. This quality serves as yet another reminder that this woman who would soon be hailed as the "Scepter of Orthodoxy" was earlier revered by Christian groups that were theologically heterodox—and, indeed, perhaps even more so by them than by the early proto-orthodox. Perhaps, as noted already, this could explain the distance that the early church fathers seem to have kept from Mary—the taint of heresy may have left them a bit hesitant to embrace her completely.

Unfortunately, very little can be said about the early Christian community in which this form of early Marian piety first took hold, other than what can be determined from the text itself. No other similar group is mentioned in the writings of the early heresiologists, and I know of no other comparable text from the first few Christian centuries that could be linked with this one. It seems most likely, however, that these traditions had their origin in Palestine, as indicated particularly by their persistent focus on various locations in Jerusalem associated with the end of Mary's life. Despite the wide range of opinions that have been expressed concerning the early history of the Dormition narratives, there is seemingly a broad consensus that these traditions first took shape in Palestine, where they developed in close association with the sites that would eventually become the focus of pilgrimage and Mary's veneration in the Jerusalem liturgies.[69] Thus this earliest evidence for Marian devotion and intercession seems to arise from the Christian communities of late Roman Palestine, and more specifically, from the Jerusalem area.

CHAPTER FOUR

A Cult Following: The *Six Books Dormition Apocryphon*

IN THE FOURTH CENTURY, evidence of Marian veneration begins to pick up significantly, and perhaps the single most important witness to this phenomenon is the *Six Books Dormition Apocryphon*, a narrative packed with nearly every sort of Marian devotion that nonetheless has been almost completely ignored in regard to the rise of Marian devotion.[1] This text is the oldest exemplar of the second major family of ancient Dormition narratives, the Bethlehem traditions, and true to the name, a significant amount of its action takes place in Bethlehem. Despite its unfortunate neglect, this Dormition narrative is actually every bit as important as the *Protevangelium of James* for understanding the rise of Marian piety in early Christianity, and like its second-century predecessor, there is also significant question as to whether this text should rightly be considered an apocryphon. Like the *Protevangelium*, the *Six Books Dormition Apocryphon* was used liturgically, although in contrast to the *Protevangelium*, the *Six Books Apocryphon* seems to have been used as a liturgical reading from the very start.[2] And while this apocryphon is not nearly as ubiquitous in Greek as the *Protevangelium* (in fact, it does not survive at all in Greek), this is because around the beginning of the sixth

130

century a précis of the *Six Books* was made that replaced it in Greek. This more recent Greek text, known as the *Ps.-John Transitus Mariae*, or the *Ps.-John Dormition of Mary*, abbreviates the much longer *Six Books Apocryphon*, presumably with greater liturgical efficiency in mind.[3] In this abridged form, the traditions of the *Six Books* thus remained very much alive in the medieval Greek (and Slavonic) churches. And for its part the *Ps.-John Dormition* can certainly rival the *Protevangelium*'s popularity: it survives in as many as one hundred Greek manuscripts and over one hundred known Church Slavonic manuscripts, as well as in Georgian, Latin, and Arabic versions.[4] Nevertheless, in Arabic and Ethiopic Christian culture, the *Six Books Apocryphon* was not displaced but retained its currency, and it survives in an as yet still unknown number of Arabic and Ethiopic manuscripts.

Prior to the last decade or so, this text was virtually unknown outside of studies on the early Dormition traditions. Even works on Mary in early Christian tradition would generally afford it no more than a brief mention or footnote, although the text had been published and translated into English already by the middle of the nineteenth century. Its lengthy disregard would appear to owe itself at least in part to the anti-Catholic tendencies that sadly were often on display in earlier scholarship on the history of Christianity. Once it was consigned to the dustbin of "popery" by scholars of this era, the *Six Books Apocryphon* lay largely forgotten for well over a century. For example, Heinrich Ewald, in a rather chauvinistic review of the first edition and translation of this text, ironically highlights the enormous significance of this apocryphon for understanding the rise of Marian piety even as he surely intended to dismiss its value completely. "We can certainly affirm that this book has become from the first the firm foundation for all the unhappy adoration of Mary, and for a hundred superstitious things, which have intruded with less and less resistance into the Churches, since the 5th century, and have contributed so much to the degeneration and to the crippling of all better Christianity. The little book is therefore of the greatest importance for the history of every century in the Middle Ages, and yet today we ought to notice far more seriously than we usually do the great amount of what we have to learn from it. The whole cultus of Mary in the Papal Church rests upon this book; we might search in vain for any other foundation to it."[5] Sadly, this is not even the most colorful remark in Ewald's review, and admittedly his anti-Catholicism was considered exceptional even by the standards of his own peers.[6] But only a few decades later, Agnes Smith Lewis, who published another version of the same text, remarked in her introduction: "It is hardly necessary to say that I endorse the opinion of Dr. Ewald (as quoted by Dr. Wright)," William Wright being the text's initial editor, who also cites Ewald's assessment of the text's content with approval.[7] It is indeed a bit odd to find scholars expressing such disdain for material that they have presumably labored long and hard to bring to light. Yet, despite the obvious prejudice of Ewald's remarks, his assessment of the importance of this ancient Marian apocryphon for understanding the emergence of Marian cult is surprisingly close to the mark.[8]

Somewhat more evenhanded are remarks by Max Bonnet, who shortly thereafter responded to Ewald's review by noting that in fact the opposite of what Ewald has proposed must be true: before ideas such as are found in this text could have been expressed, "Marian veneration and Marian cult must already have been flourishing."[9] Bonnet therefore concludes that Marian devotion must have begun quite early within the Christian tradition, suggesting that the silence of the church fathers from the fourth century and earlier regarding Marian devotion is a sign of its initial emergence somewhere along the margins of "orthodoxy" or in a more "popular" context. Nearly a century later, the publication of the *Book of Mary's Repose* offers possible confirmation of Bonnet's hypothesis, as does also the more "orthodox" *Six Books Apocryphon*, which reveals the emergence of popular devotion to Mary within proto-orthodox circles in advance of its full embrace by the church hierarchs only in the fifth century. In any case, the *Six Books* reveals a Marian piety that had already come into full bloom by the fourth century, within a milieu that appears to conform to the emergent discourse of Christian orthodoxy.

The *Six Books Apocryphon* bears witness to a far more elaborate veneration of the Virgin than we find in the *Book of Mary's Repose*, and this more developed Marian piety would also appear to be consistent with its seemingly more recent origin. The earliest form of the *Six Books Apocryphon* is best known to us through several ancient Syriac manuscripts, even though, like the *Book of Mary's Repose*, it was originally written in Greek. There are at least five different Syriac manuscripts from the fifth and sixth centuries, and accordingly the Greek original(s) lying behind these translations must be even earlier. Only two of these manuscripts are complete, one in the British Library (edited by Wright in 1865) and a still unedited manuscript in Göttingen, both of which are from the sixth century. There are also three different sets of fragments, all of which are palimpsests, that is, manuscripts that have been erased and reused. In such cases one can often, with some difficulty, decipher the earlier script, and in each of these manuscripts the original writing that was erased dates to the later fifth century. The most important of these is an extensive palimpsest codex edited by Smith Lewis and now at the Cambridge University Library, but more limited fragments are also found in the Schøyen Collection (originally from Sinai) and bound together with the Old Syriac Gospel palimpsests from Sinai.[10]

The diversity of the accounts preserved in these early manuscripts already by the end of the fifth century ensures that this apocryphon was composed by the early fifth century at the absolute latest, and a number of internal features locate the *Six Books* almost certainly in the fourth century.[11] Its rather unusual account of the discovery of the True Cross suggests this period, and Richard Bauckham's analysis of the cosmic tour that completes the *Six Books* determines that the apocryphon must date "from the fourth century at the latest, but perhaps considerably earlier."[12] Furthermore, as we will see below, Epiphanius's attack on the so-called "Kollyridians"—a Christian group that made bread offerings in the Virgin's honor and allowed women to serve as liturgical leaders—seems to indicate the circulation of this early Dormition narrative already by the middle of the fourth century. Nevertheless, the interest shown by this narrative in the relic of the True Cross and the Virgin's practice of praying at her son's tomb secure its production sometime after the reign of Constantine, even if many individual traditions from the narrative may possibly be earlier.

The Cult of the Virgin in the *Six Books Dormition Apocryphon*

From the very start the *Six Books Apocryphon* presents a rather different sensibility about the veneration of Mary from the *Book of Mary's Repose*. Whereas in the *Book of Mary's Repose* evidence of Marian piety occurs only in a few instances and involves seeking Mary's intercessions alongside the prayers of other saints, the *Six Books Apocryphon* is suffused with Marian devotion of every kind, making it invaluable for discovering the roots of the fifth century's Marian revolution. The *Six Books Apocryphon* begins with what appears to be a congregational prayer, which, among other things, asks for the Lord's blessings upon "our congregation, which glorifies the commemoration of your mother, my master Mary." Indeed, this initial prayer invokes the context of a commemoration of Mary several times and promises to relate her "coronation."[13] The preface then continues to recount the story of the text's own miraculous discovery. One day some monks at Mount Sinai began to wonder, how did the Virgin Mary depart from this world? They wrote to Cyrus the bishop of Jerusalem, and he searched for an answer. He was unable to locate any written account about this matter, but instead he found a note written by James the bishop of Jerusalem in the year 34/35 CE, in which he describes a work in six books, each written by two of the apostles, that told of Mary's departure from this world. John, Peter, and Paul were all known to have had a copy in their possession. Cyrus replied to the monks of Sinai with this information, and when they received it, they began a search for the lost text. The monks wrote letters to Rome, Egypt, and Alexandria looking for this writing, and they made inquiries of the bishops of various regions, all without any luck. Eventually they came to Ephesus, where they spent the night in the shrine of Saint John. They prayed that John would appear to them, and when they fell asleep, he did. John promised to give them the book that they sought, "so that there will be a commemoration of my master Mary three times in the year, because, if humankind will celebrate her memory, they will be delivered from wrath."[14] In the morning when they awoke, they found the *Six Books Apocryphon*, and they sent copies to both Mount Sinai and Jerusalem.

Obviously this story of the narrative's discovery is not historical, and it seems designed to introduce an unfamiliar text and to apologize for its apparent newness. Presumably the *Six Books Apocryphon* was an older text that originally lacked this introduction, and the preface was supplied to introduce it to a context where it had previously been unknown. A number of more recent manuscripts either lack this etiological introduction or transmit it as a separate text.[15] Likewise, the preface is also absent from the Greek précis mentioned above, the *Ps.-John Dormition*, although admittedly it may be that the preface was omitted in order to shorten what was in fact a very long text. Nevertheless, it seems most likely that this preface was added to the *Six Books Dormition Apocryphon* sometime after its original composition, in order to facilitate its reception. Perhaps this apocryphon was intended as an orthodox antidote to the fairly heterodox traditions of the *Book of Mary's Repose*, and so its adoption required some justification. In any case, this introduction occurs in all of the fifth- and sixth-century manuscripts that preserve the earliest version of this text, and while the text and its traditions are presumably older, it would appear that the account of the narrative's discovery must have been produced sometime after the beginnings of monasticism on Mount Sinai in the fourth century.[16]

In its present state, this preface stands as the first of the six books, and only in the second book does the actual narrative of Mary's Dormition and Assumption begin. As the story opens, we find Mary going to the tomb of Christ to pray, as she did every day. The Jews, however, sought to prohibit anyone from praying at Christ's tomb, and they had stationed guards there to prevent it. When the guards reported Mary's activities to the priests, they went to the Roman governor and asked that he forbid her from praying at the tomb. With the governor's blessing, they admonish her, and suggest that if she cannot abide by their terms, then she should go from Jerusalem to the house that she also has in Bethlehem. So together with the three virgins who lived with her as attendants, she relocates to her Bethlehem house. There the apostles miraculously arrive on clouds for her departure from this world, and the details of their individual travels round out the remainder of this second book.

John is the first to arrive, and when he does, the first thing he does is kiss the Virgin "on her breast and on her knees," both of which are important symbols of her Divine Maternity, the knees being the lap on which the child sat.[17] Likewise, the other apostles, when they arrive, also immediately kiss her breast and her knees.[18] These are the first of many acts of veneration offered to the Virgin in the *Six Books Apocryphon*, and no doubt these representations are intended to encourage similar behaviors in the narrative's audience. Throughout the narrative, those of the most exalted ranks routinely show their obeisance to Mary. The Roman governor, for instance, when he comes to her to request healing for his son, kneels down and venerates the Virgin Mary, speaking praises in honor of her and her son.[19] The patriarchs and prophets, who accompany Christ when he comes to receive his mother's soul, also venerate Mary: Abraham, Isaac, Jacob, and David venerate her, as do the prophets, with censers in their hands.[20] Even the heavenly bodies venerate the Virgin in this apocryphon: while she was in Bethlehem, "the sun and moon … came and worshipped before the upper room" in which she was dwelling.[21] After her resurrection in the Paradise of Eden, Mary enters the heavenly Jerusalem and again the sun and the moon worship her, as do thunder and lightning, fire and flame, the rain and the dew. The angels as well, including Gabriel and Michael, bow down before her, then Mary herself finally worships God the Father in the heavenly city.[22]

Mary's mediation also is a particularly prominent theme of the *Six Books Apocryphon*. In contrast to the infrequent Marian intercessions of the *Book of Mary's Repose*, the *Six Books* is replete with occasions where Mary intercedes successfully with her son on behalf of Christian believers. As in the *Book of Mary's Repose*, Mary embarks on a tour of the heavenly realms after her resurrection in Paradise, although in these two final books of the *Six Books* she travels alone, without Michael and the apostles, led only by her son. When mother and child eventually arrive before the roaring fires of Gehenna, Mary beholds the damned, who await their eternal torment after the final judgment and cry out to Christ for mercy. Mary hears the cries of the wicked, and being saddened, she pleads with her son, "Have mercy on the wicked when you judge them at the day of judgment, for I have heard their voice and am sad."[23] While no specific reprieve is announced on this occasion, as it is in the *Book of Mary's Respose*, the effectiveness of Mary's intercessions is repeatedly acknowledged and demonstrated elsewhere throughout the narrative. The clear message is that one cannot hope for a better mediator with the divine judge than his beloved mother. For instance, in another episode just prior to her death, the apostles ask the Virgin to leave a blessing for the world that she is about to leave. She obliges, praying, "May God, who willed from his own will and sent His Son and He put on a body and dwelled in the palace of my members, have mercy on the people who call upon Him." She continues, praying, "Lord Jesus, receive the prayers of the people who call upon you, and make bad times cease from the earth. And give a crown to old age, and growing up to youth, and help the souls that call upon you."[24] Christ responds by promising his mother, "Everything you have said to me, Mary, will I do to please you; and I will show mercy to everyone who calls upon your name."[25]

Mary's intercessions are especially linked with the numerous miracles that she works in the text, particularly healings. Most of these are gathered together in two large collections, one at the beginning of book 3 and the other at its end. As the third book opens, Mary and the apostles are still at her home in Bethlehem, where its citizens behold "the stammering, the dumb, the blind, the deaf, the sick, the afflicted, those beset by unclean spirits, and everyone who had an illness, going to her and being healed," including "women ... from the cities and regions and from Rome and Athens, the daughters of kings and procurators and prefects."[26] Several accounts of specific miracles follow: two women possessed by demons and another with strangury are healed when Mary prays over them; a woman with leprosy prostrates herself before Mary, and Mary heals her by making the sign of the cross over some water and sprinkling her with it; a woman blind in one eye is healed when Mary signs the cross over it. Then a throng "without number" travels from Jerusalem to Bethlehem to seek Mary's healing, crying out for her to have mercy on them, and when Mary hears their voices, she prays, "Lord Jesus Christ, hear the voice of the souls that are crying out to you." As a result of her prayer, "immediately two thousand six hundred souls were healed, men, women, and children."[27]

At this point in the narrative, Mary's miracles and the crowds that had gathered around her begin to attract the attention of the authorities. The priests again approach the governor and ask that he send soldiers to arrest Mary and the apostles in Bethlehem. Initially he tries to refuse, but the priests threaten to appeal to the emperor if he denies their request. Reluctantly the governor dispatches a captain and thirty soldiers to go and seize them. But as the soldiers are en route to Bethlehem, the Holy Spirit warns the apostles of their approach and promises to deliver them. Then the apostles take up Mary's bed and miraculously fly through the air over the heads of the men coming against them, who fail to see them. Thus, in an instant they are brought from Mary's Bethlehem house to her home in Jerusalem, where she had been living as the story began.

Once Mary returns to Jerusalem with the apostles, the Roman governor organizes a public debate between the Jews and Christians, in which the Christians (unsurprisingly) triumph. Immediately thereafter follows a second anthology of Marian miracles that completes the third book, itself framed by two lengthy miracle stories, beginning with Mary's healing of the Roman governor's son and concluding with the botched Jewish assault on her bier, when Mary dramatically restores the severed arms of her injured attacker. After the Christian victory in the debate, the Roman governor brings his son, who suffers from a stomach disease and strangury, to Mary's house and begs her to heal him. When she prays and stretches out her hands to bless the child, instantly he is healed. Thereupon the governor returns to Rome, where he spreads news of Mary's wonders and miracles among the emperors and the nobility of Rome.[28] Then follows a report sent to the apostles from the disciples of Peter and Paul in Rome, who describe the miracles recounted by the governor there. Remarkably, each of these wonders involves an apparition of the Virgin, and these would seem to be some of the earliest reports regarding this aspect of Marian devotion. When sailors in peril at sea cried out for Mary's mercy, "she rose above them like the sun and delivered these ships, which were ninety-two in number." One day some robbers attacked a group of men and threatened to kill them, and when they called on Mary for mercy, "she rose above them like a flash of lightning and blinded the eyes of the thieves, and they were not seen by them." A widow whose son had fallen down a well cried out to her, "and my master Mary appeared to her, and snatched up the child, and he was not drowned. And she gave him to his mother alive." She also appeared to a man who had been sick for sixteen years: when he brought out a censer and prayed to her, immediately she came to him and healed him. A merchant, who had borrowed a thousand dinars and lost them along the road, prayed to Mary, and she came to him and "took him and brought him to the purse of dinars." Lastly, two women on their way to Egypt were confronted by a giant snake that was about to devour them, and when they called upon Mary, she "appeared to them and struck the snake on its mouth, and it was split in two." Yet perhaps most extraordinary is the fact that while Mary was working these miracles "at Rome and in all places," we are told that she remained simultaneously right beside the apostles in Jerusalem.[29] Finally, book three comes to a close as the apostles process to Mary's tomb at "the head of the valley," with Mary lying on her funeral bier still alive. As they exit the city, a Jew named Yūphanyā (Jephonias in Greek) attacks her, and when his hands touch her bier, "the angel of the Lord struck him with a sword of fire and cut off both of his arms from his shoulders, and they hung like ropes from the bier." Yūphanyā then begs the apostles to heal him, but they advise him to call upon Mary instead. Once he pleads with Mary for mercy, she instructs Peter to give Yūphanyā his arms. Peter then spits on one of them and says, "In the name of my master Mary, the Theotokos, cleave to your place," and his arms are miraculously restored through the prayers of Mary.[30]

Yet petitions to the Virgin alone are not enough, according to this early Marian apocryphon: they must be joined to liturgical commemorations and offerings in Mary's honor. The *Six Books* narrative repeatedly insists on regular observance of ceremonies in Mary's honor, bearing witness to the existence of a formal cult of the Virgin already by this time. As previously noted, the elaborate invocation that opens book 1 introduces a liturgical setting from the very start, asking for the Lord's blessing on "our congregation, which glorifies the commemoration of your mother, my master Mary, O Lord God."[31] Shortly thereafter, when the monks miraculously receive the *Six Books Apocryphon* from Saint John at his shrine in Ephesus, he explains to them that he "has sent you this book so that there will be a commemoration of my master Mary three times in the year, because, if humankind will celebrate her memory, they will be delivered from wrath."[32] Likewise, the women who are healed at Bethlehem in book 3 bring Mary "gifts and offerings" along with their petitions.[33] At the beginning of book 4, when Mary leaves her blessing for the world that she is about to leave, her favors are again closely linked with her commemoration. The apostles ask for her blessing "so that those who make commemorations and offerings to you will be delivered from severe afflictions." She then prays, "Make bad times cease from the earth, when human beings, my Lord, hold a commemoration of my body and spirit, which have gone forth from the world. And make death and captivity, the sword and famine, and every suffering that befalls humankind, pass away from the land in which offerings are offered to me." As Mary continues her blessing, a strong connection emerges between her intercessions and agriculture and fertility. No doubt here the Virgin has already begun to fill a role as protectress of the earth and the harvest that she inherited from the various Mediterranean goddesses. Mary prays for her son to "make pestilence cease from the land in which offerings are offered to me; and bless the garland of the year. And may the lands be kept free from the locust, so that it will not destroy them, and from blight and mildew and hailstones." She stays with this theme, asking, "And the fields that give an offering in my honor, let them be blessed and bring forth the seeds that are buried in the furrows; and the vines from which wine is pressed in my name, let them bear bountiful clusters."[34]

After Mary's son promises to grant her requests, her soul goes forth from her body and is transferred to the Paradise of Eden. The apostles then provide specific instructions for celebrating the annual Marian feasts that the *Six Books* narrative so emphatically enjoins on its audience. In what amounts to a brief liturgical handbook, the *Six Books* directs that three commemorations of the Virgin should be observed at different times in the year, and with each of these, the agricultural connections remain quite strong. The specific dates vary slightly according to the different early manuscripts, but their approximate times and significance remain constant. The first feast ought to be celebrated on the same day as the Nativity, which is 24 December or 6 January according to different manuscripts, but since that date already held a major feast, Mary's memorial should follow two or three days later. The purpose of this commemoration is "that by her pure offerings the seeds that the farmers have borrowed and sown will be blessed," to which the unpublished sixth-century manuscript in

Göttingen adds, "so that by her offerings and prayers, the locusts that hide in the lands will be killed." The second feast is on 15 May in all of the manuscripts, and it is observed "on account of the seeds that were sown, and on account of the flying and creeping locusts, that they might not come forth and destroy the crops, and then there would be a famine and the people would perish," to which some of the early manuscripts add blessings for "the beard of wheat, so that from them there will be an offering to the Lord and the blessed one." Finally, a feast is appointed for 13 August, "on account of the vines bearing clusters and the trees bearing fruit, so that the clouds of hail, which bear stones of wrath, will not come and break the trees and their fruit and the vines with their clusters."[35]

Following this calendar the *Six Books* narrative gives a rather detailed description of the ceremonies to be observed on each of these occasions, which focus on offerings of bread in the Virgin's name and, in a blatant act of self-promotion, the reading of the *Six Books Apocryphon*.

And the apostles also ordered that offerings that have been offered in the name of my master Mary should not remain over the night, but that at midnight of the night immediately preceding her commemoration, it should be kneaded and baked. And in the morning let it go up onto the altar, while the people stand before the altar with psalms of David. And let the New and Old Testaments be read, and the book of the departure of the blessed one [i.e., the *Six Books Apocryphon*]. And let everyone be before the altar in the church, and let the priests make the offering and set up a censer of incense and light the lights, and let the entire service be concerning these offerings. And when the entire service is finished, let everyone take his offerings to his house. And let the priest speak thus: "In the name of the Father, and of the Son, and of the Holy Spirit, we celebrate the commemoration of my master Mary." Thus let the priest speak three times; and with the words of the priest who speaks, the Holy Spirit will come and bless these offerings. And when everyone takes away his offering, and goes to his house, great aid and the blessing of the blessed one will enter his dwelling and sustain it forever.[36]

A nearly identical version of these ritual instructions appears in the sixth-century Göttingen manuscript, but unfortunately the corresponding section is missing from the three fifth-century palimpsests, all of which are fragmentary.[37] Nonetheless, the fifth-century palimpsest codex published by Smith Lewis preserves not only the liturgical calendar but numerous other references to these commemorations as well.[38] Likewise, the palimpsest folios bound together with the Old Syriac Gospels twice mention the observance of these commemorations, and the palimpsest fragments in the Schøyen Collection preserve the liturgical invocation with which all of the early Syriac manuscripts begin, asking for divine blessings on the congregation as they celebrate Mary's memory and departure from the world.[39] It is clear, then, that these ritual practices belong to the earliest layer of these apocryphal traditions, and one would presume that these Marian feasts were observed by communities using the *Six Books* narrative as a liturgical text already by the fourth century. Thus, the *Six Books Apocryphon* appears to bear witness to full-blown Marian cult already by this time, probably somewhere in Palestine, where, like the *Book of Mary's Repose*, this narrative most likely originated. The liturgical instructions come to a close with a prayer for the months of the year, which again underscores the strong connections between Marian veneration and the rhythms of the agricultural seasons. Each of the twelve months is invoked, asking for divine blessings for flowers that may adorn the altar of the Lord, for the grain harvest, for fruits, for the farmers, for the rains and snows, and finally for lambs and sheep. Altogether it is a fairly descriptive account of how these fourth-century Marian feasts were observed in the communities that used the *Six Books Apocryphon*, and the persistent focus on agriculture perhaps suggests a rural rather than urban environment.

Epiphanius, the Kollyridians, and the *Six Books Apocryphon*

Not to be overlooked, however, are the extraordinary similarities between the ritual practices ordained by the *Six Books Apocryphon* and those of the so-called "Kollyridians," a group described by Epiphanius of Salamis during the later fourth century in his *Panarion*, or *Medicine Chest* against heresies.[40] According to Epiphanius, these early Christians allowed women to serve among the clergy and observed annual commemorations of the Virgin at which bread offerings were made in her honor. "On a certain day of the year," he writes, "they put forth bread and offer it in the name of Mary, and they all partake of the bread."[41] Epiphanius's ensuing denunciation of the Kollyridians has led many scholars to the conclusion that these Christians were worshipping Mary either as a part of the Godhead or as some sort of "pagan" goddess cloaked in Christian garb. Yet these interpretations of the Kollyridians' actions owe themselves primarily to Epiphanius's overheated rhetoric and should not be taken as accurately reflecting the liturgical intentions of the early Christians whose practices he describes. Nowhere in his account does he indicate that the Kollyridians actually went so far as to identify Mary with the deity in the way that Trinitarian Christians had come to understand her son as divine, for instance. He does not attack them for advancing a theological belief in Mary's divinity or for reverting to a kind of goddess worship but rather specifically for their practice of offering cult to the Virgin and venerating her in a manner that he considers utterly inappropriate for a human being. Such ritual activities in his view are tantamount to "substituting her for God,"[42] involving worship of a creature in the place of God, regardless of what their intentions may have been.

Nevertheless, it is doubtful that the Kollyridians understood their actions in this way. To the contrary, it appears from Epiphanius's own rhetoric that the Kollyridians were merely offering to Mary a somewhat more elaborate version of the veneration that Christians were increasingly offering to other saints during the late fourth century.[43] Indeed, a careful reading of Epiphanius's invective reveals his opposition to the Kollyridian practices within the context of a broader condemnation of the veneration of saints as a whole, which, as we have proposed, is precisely the context in which the nascent cult of the Virgin should be understood.[44] Reading between the lines of his diatribe suggests that the Kollyridians were no more interested in replacing God with Mary or elevating her to a divine status than were the early devotees of Saint Thecla or Saint John intent on divinizing the subjects of their devotion. According to the terms of his polemic, the Kollyridian "idolatry" was in theory not unique, and any devotees of a particular holy person who dared to cross the threshold of veneration and began to offer some sort of cult to a saint would be equally guilty of the same blasphemy. Epiphanius instead makes clear that the role of the saints in the church should be limited to serving as examples of Christian excellence, and they are not themselves to become objects of devotion.[45] His resistance to this form of "idolatry" is paralleled by his early opposition to the use of images in cultic settings, and in this section of the *Panarion* as well as in the fragments from his now lost iconoclastic writings, Epiphanius joins his censure of venerating the angels and apostles to his condemnation of the use of their images.[46]

146

Yet while Epiphanius may well have regarded the Kollyridians' actions as idolatrous, his attack affords no evidence that these early Christians actually understood themselves to be worshipping Mary as a goddess or a part of the divinity. Indeed, Epiphanius himself even concedes as much toward the conclusion of his attack on the Kollyridians, when he allows for the possibility that their offerings to the Virgin may reflect something quite different from worship of Mary as divine. "And how much is there to say? Whether these worthless women offer Mary the loaf as though in worship of her, or whether they mean to offer this rotten fruit on her behalf, it is altogether silly and heretical, and demon-inspired insolence and imposture."[47] Here Epiphanius is reduced to mere rhetorical bluster: while presumably there would be nothing inherently wrong with presenting such bread offerings on Mary's behalf, instead of *to* her as an act of worship, Epiphanius nonetheless insists that such practices amount to demonic foolishness and thus are best avoided. Although Epiphanius makes his best effort to trump up the charges against the Kollyridians as idolatrous worship of Mary as a goddess, in this passage he himself leaves an important clue that the Kollydridians very likely understood their actions quite differently. Here then, as is so often the case with opposition to the cult of the Virgin (and the saints more generally), critics are quick to impute certain intentions to these practices, such as idolatry, that generally seem to be lacking in the practitioners themselves. For example, Carlos Eire, in his study of the rhetoric of idolatry in Reformation Europe, observes that "one man's devotion was another man's idolatry," and thus the mere accusation from an opponent, such as Epiphanius, does not establish that these Christians were worshipping Mary as a divine goddess, as Epiphanius would apparently have his readers believe.[48] To judge the matter otherwise may ultimately have more to do with the legacy of the Reformation-era debates analyzed by Eire than with the history of ancient Christianity.

In fact, the *Six Books Apocryphon* appears to provide compelling evidence to the contrary. Here we find a very elaborate devotion to the Virgin, complete with regular bread offerings, articulated, and presumably practiced, within a thoroughly monotheist, Trinitarian context. The *Six Books* repeatedly makes reference to veneration or worship (*segdto*) of the Virgin, yet without ever implying that she is divine or equal to her son. More often than not, Mary's miracles are ascribed to intercessions with her son or to the sign of the cross, and the ontological difference between Mary and her divine son never seems to become blurred. One must, of course, admit that there are numerous "pagan" parallels to many aspects of the Marian piety expressed in the *Six Books* and attributed to the Kollyridians, such as the bread offerings or the strong agricultural associations. Yet these alone do not allow the conclusion that in either instance Mary was being worshipped as a divine goddess. As noted already in the introduction, innumerable elements of early Christian faith and piety have obvious precursors in Greco-Roman religious traditions, as seen particularly in certain liturgical practices and the veneration of saints, and while these relationships are historically illuminating and important, the mere existence of such parallels does not control the interpretation of these phenomena or allow us to impute polytheist beliefs to their practitioners, particularly when they themselves profess otherwise.[49]

The *Six Books* thus offers an especially relevant point of comparison to the Kollyridians, inasmuch as some sort of connection between the *Six Books* and Epiphanius's invective against the Kollyridians seems highly likely. While evidence of their relation may not be as direct as some would like, it is perhaps all the more compelling for the manner in which Epiphanius's account seems to obscure the links between the Kollyridians and traditions of Mary's Dormition.[50] The bread offerings in Mary's honor are of course the most significant point of contact: nowhere else in early Christian literature (to my knowledge) do we find bread offerings to the Virgin in the manner that Epiphanius describes, except in the *Six Books Apocryphon*. The remarkable similarities between the ritual practices of this early Dormition narrative and those of Epiphanius's opponents alone invite some sort of connection between the two. Yet there are a number of more subtle indications that Epiphanius's attack on the Kollyridians reacts to the traditions of the *Six Books Apocryphon*, which he may have known about only at second or even third hand. Epiphanius addresses the Kollyridians twice, first in the *Letter to Arabia* (which appears as book 78 of the *Panarion*) and then more extensively in *Panarion* book 79, and both accounts make very clear but unexplained associations between the ritual practices of the Kollyridians and traditions about Mary's Dormition. In the background of Epiphanius's attacks on the Kollyridian bread offerings lurks an unexplained and often veiled concern for traditions about the end of Mary's life that shows an awareness of these specific apocryphal traditions. Since Epiphanius composed his *Letter to Arabia* in 370 while he was still living in his native Palestine, his attacks on the Kollyridians also seem to confirm the circulation of this Dormition narrative in Palestine by the middle of the fourth century.

In his first account, from the *Letter to Arabia*, as Epiphanius excoriates the Kollyridian rituals, he turns suddenly to the question of the end of Mary's life, professing the strict agnosticism on this subject for which he has become so famous in various modern studies on the Dormition and Assumption. Without making any obvious transition to a new topic, he seemingly continues to write about the Kollyridians. He thus explains, "The holy virgin may have died and been buried—her falling asleep was with honor, her death in purity, her crown in virginity. Or she may have been put to death—as the scripture says, 'And a sword shall pierce through her soul'—her fame is among the martyrs and her body, by which light rose in the world, [rests] amid blessings. Or she remained alive, for God is not incapable of doing whatever he wills. No one knows her end."[51] Following this passage, Epiphanius continues his attack on the Kollyridians uninterrupted, offering no explanation for his introduction of this particular topic and thus leaving the unmistakable impression that his discussion of the Dormition has something to do with the Kollyridians. The overall effect is to link his opponents' bread offerings in Mary's honor with the question of how her life ended, a pairing that certainly suggests a connection with the *Six Books Apocryphon*.

A similar association between the Kollyridians' veneration of Mary and the Virgin's Dormition appears in the penultimate section of the *Panarion*, which is dedicated exclusively to refuting this Marian "heresy." After denouncing the Kollyridian practice of allowing female clergy, Epiphanius eventually comes to address their bread offerings to the Virgin, which he attacks by comparing Mary with Elijah, John, and Thecla. In this way he continues his apparent strategy of undermining the veneration of the Virgin through a broader attack against veneration of the saints more generally.[52] The main point here is that just as Elijah, John, and Thecla are not venerated through the use of such blasphemous ritual practices, so too there is no basis for the Kollyridian veneration of Mary. Thecla's appearance in this context is to be expected, since she had long served as an important role model for female virginity, a role that Mary also began to assume increasingly at this time.[53] Yet comparisons with a prophet and an apostle are perhaps somewhat unexpected given the harangue against women's liturgical leadership that precedes his discussion of the bread offerings. Obviously, prophecy and leadership are not the qualities that Epiphanius wants to associate with Mary.

Instead, Epiphanius's comparisons with Elijah and John focus squarely on the miraculous manner in which each ended his life. Mary is like Elijah, he explains, in that he was "a virgin from his mother's womb, he remained so perpetually, and was assumed [*analamba-nomenos*] and has not seen death."[54] Although this passage has been frequently overlooked in various studies of the Virgin's Dormition and Assumption, the last two points deserve particular emphasis. In contrast with the guarded agnosticism of the *Letter to Arabia*, which previous scholarship has overwhelmingly taken as evidence that Epiphanius knew no tradition of the end of Mary's life, here he rather unambiguously proclaims that Mary, like Elijah, "was assumed and has not seen death." Moreover, he makes this assertion in the broader context of rebutting the Kollyridian liturgical practices, again suggesting his awareness of a link between these rituals and a tradition about the end of Mary's life. This connection is reinforced by his comparison between Mary and John, when he invokes John's miraculous dormition, arguing that "John is not to be venerated, even if through his own prayer (or rather, by receiving grace from God) he made of his falling asleep [*koimēsin*] an amazing thing."[55] Here Epiphanius refers to the various traditions of John's "metastasis" and the miraculous removal of his body from this world at death that had begun to circulate already in several versions by this time.[56] Thus, again, without much explanation, Epiphanius returns to the theme of Mary's Dormition in his assault on the Kollyridian ritual practices. His deployment of traditions regarding the miraculous endings of Elijah's and John's lives in the context of attacking the Kollyridian veneration of Mary suggests even more strongly a connection between their bread offerings and a tradition of Mary's Dormition. Indeed, the implied logic of Epiphanius's argument is that his opponents seem to have appealed to a tradition about Mary's Assumption in order to defend their veneration of her, although this is far from certain.

In any case, Epiphanius's own rhetoric reveals in both instances a connection between the Kollyridian bread offerings to Mary and a tradition about her miraculous departure from this world. This configuration can only point to the *Six Books Apocryphon*, whose traditions therefore Epiphanius must have known in either written or oral form. The *Six Books* is the sole source from the ancient church to mandate regular liturgical offerings of bread to the Virgin, which it enjoins within the context of an account of Mary's Dormition, a subject that Epiphanius apparently saw as being closely intertwined with his opponents' bread offerings. Consequently, it would seem that traditions from the *Six Books*, including their liturgical ceremonies in Mary's honor, must have been in circulation already by the middle of the fourth century, when Epiphanius presumably encountered them in Palestine prior to writing the *Letter to Arabia* there. Epiphanius, it is true, says that these women came from Scythia and Thrace to Arabia, which in modern terms correspond roughly to the southern Ukraine, the southeastern Balkans, and Jordan respectively. Yet there is no reason to believe that this information is accurate, and it is quite likely that Epiphanius has invented this information to associate this group with these marginal regions in order to emphasize the exotic nature of their customs and to make them seem peripheral. Instead, for the same reasons that the *Book of Mary's Repose* seems to be connected with Palestine and the Jerusalem area, the *Six Books Apocryphon* also seems most likely to have emerged from the same region.

The "Kollyridians" and the *Six Books Apocryphon* according to *Joseph's Bible Notes*

An additional source has recently come to my attention that strengthens these conclusions considerably, removing all doubt, it would seem, about the connection between the Kollyridians and belief in the Virgin's Assumption that Epiphanius indicates. The source in question is an obscure text, the so-called *Hypomnestikon of Joseph*, or *Joseph's Bible Notes*, as its English translators have decided to name it. Although I suspect that this text is as unfamiliar to many readers as it was to me not long ago, this work has been known since the early eighteenth century, even if it has failed to attract much scholarly attention, and it has been almost entirely overlooked in earlier discussions of the Kollyridians, limited such as they are.[57] No doubt this oversight is in large part a consequence of the peculiar nature of the text itself. It is a sort of a reference manual, concerned primarily with historical questions about biblical traditions. Yet despite its organization in a question-and-answer format, it is markedly different from other similar biblical *Quaestiones* collections insofar as it shows little concern for resolving contradictions in the biblical text. It is instead primarily a collection of facts and names from the Hebrew Bible and early Christian history seemingly aimed at moral instruction.[58] Indeed, one is tempted to think of it as an early Christian manual of Bible trivia. Organized into 167 chapters, its pages address such topics as "Other prophets who did not write", "Idols worshiped by the people", "Johns and Zechariahs", and "Hebrews with gentile names." The chapter titles sound like categories ready-made for a contest of "Bible Jeopardy." Also included is a lengthy chapter on "Heresies," which lists and briefly describes sixty-two different Christian heresies, and among these we find the Kollyridians.[59] Although *Joseph's Bible Notes* names them instead the "Marianites," there is no question that this is in fact the same group that Epiphanius rebukes both in his *Letter to Arabia* and again in the penultimate chapter of his *Panarion*.

The description of the Marianites in *Joseph's Bible Notes* is, like the other "heresies" it catalogues, extremely brief. The Marianites, it informs us, "raise up Mary to a divine substance (*tēn Marian eis theian ousian anagousi*), and they say that she was assumed into heaven (*eis ouranon aneilēphthai*), commemorating her with an offering of bread (*mnēnēn autēs en artou prothesei poioumenoi*)."[60] The account is terse, particularly in comparison with Epiphanius, but these "Marianites" are clearly the same group that Epiphanius names the Kollyridians. And this is no coincidence: it has long been recognized that the inventory of heresies in *Joseph's Bible Notes* somehow relates to Epiphanius's *Panarion*, although the precise nature of this relationship has been a matter of some discussion. Nevertheless, in this particular case the account of the Marianites from *Joseph's Bible Notes* shows relative independence from Epiphanius, not only in its name for the group but also in its distinctive phrasing. More importantly, *Joseph's Bible Notes* is quite unambiguous where Epiphanius remains cagey, relating directly that these early Christians believed in Mary's Assumption into heaven, an event that they commemorated with bread offerings in her honor.[61]

Although it is not entirely out of the question that *Joseph's Bible Notes* has somehow made use of a common source that it shares with Epiphanius, some sort of dependence on the traditions of Epiphanius's *Panarion* seems to be the most likely explanation. There is a more substantial debate as to whether *Joseph's Bible Notes* depends directly on the *Panarion* itself or has instead made use of the *Epitome (Anakephalaiosis)* of the *Panarion* that had begun to circulate widely not long after Epiphanius's death.[62] As far as the date of *Joseph's Bible Notes* is concerned, there would appear to be a fairly broad consensus favoring the first decades of the fifth century. A handful of scholars, most notably Stephen Goranson and Simon Mimouni, have opted for an earlier date, largely in hopes of identifying its author with Joseph of Tiberias, a Jewish convert to Christianity whom Epiphanius had met in Palestine sometime around the middle of the fourth century.[63] Despite their arguments for an earlier date, composition of *Joseph's Bible Notes* before 393 seems unlikely, and this chronological limit is difficult to reconcile with Joseph of Tiberias's relatively advanced age already by the mid-fourth century.[64] As for the latest possible date, a prediction of the world's end in the year 500 seems to ensure its composition before the sixth century. A number of other features can narrow the range further. The absence of Nestorius from *Joseph's Bible Notes* suggests its composition before the controversies surrounding the Council of Ephesus, and a variety of other elements seem to indicate that the reign of Emperor Julian was not long past. All of this points to the late fourth or the early fifth century as the time when this peculiar assemblage of trivia was compiled.[65] Thus, despite the abiding mystery of its authorship, *Joseph's Bible Notes* has been rather persuasively dated to sometime around the turn of the fifth century: the only dissenters would favor an even earlier composition. The location of its production remains unknown, although its most recent editors have tentatively proposed Alexandria as a strong possibility, with some good reason.[66]

Joseph's Bible Notes is then a text composed some twenty to fifty years after Epiphanius's *Panarion* that also addresses the beliefs and practices of the Kollyridians, or the Marianites, as this writing names them. Its apparent dependence on Epiphanius's earlier heresiology, of course, limits somewhat its usefulness as an independent witness. Yet there are elements of this brief report that make it invaluable as both a supplement and a confirmation of Epiphanius's account of the Kollyridians. Its initial accusation that these early Christians elevated Mary to the status of a divine being is, for reasons already explained above, almost certainly inaccurate. Here *Joseph's Bible Notes* simply repeats, it would seem, Epiphanius's calumnies against the nascent Marian piety of these early Christians. The second point regarding the Kollyridians is perhaps the most interesting: in unequivocal terms *Joseph's Bible Notes* relates that they believed that Mary had been "assumed into heaven." This text thus makes explicit the connection between these early Christians and belief in the Virgin Mary's Assumption that Epiphanius seems almost reluctant to reveal. *Joseph's Bible Notes* unambiguously confirms the link that Epiphanius strongly implies, leaving little doubt that belief in Mary's Assumption was a distinctive characteristic of this early Christian group.[67] No less important is the third and final point that these Christians "commemorate her with an offering of bread," which solidifies the identity of these "Marianites" with the Kollyridians and also the *Six Books Dormition Apocryphon*.

The *Six Books Apocryphon* once again is the only other early Christian source where we find regular bread offerings in Mary's honor combined with belief in her Assumption. Accordingly, a connection between this ancient Dormition narrative and these references to the so-called Kollyridians/Marianites seems almost impossible to deny. Although Epiphanius himself strongly implies such a link between the Kollyridians and a belief in Mary's Assumption, he fails to make this explicit. Yet what Epiphanius will only cryptically allude to, *Joseph's Bible Notes* plainly relates: these early devotees of the Virgin Mary regularly offered bread in her honor *and* believed in her Assumption. *Joseph's Bible Notes* thus confirms that Epiphanius indeed knows more about a connection between the Kollyridians and belief in the Virgin's Assumption than he is willing to relate directly, for whatever reason. Much more importantly, however, the correspondence between these key elements of this early Dormition narrative and the accounts from Epiphanius and *Joseph's Bible Notes* allow us to conclude with a high measure of confidence that the traditions of the *Six Books Apocryphon*, and almost certainly the apocryphon itself, date to the middle of the fourth century and can be associated with the early Christian group that Epiphanius names the Kollyridians. The similarities are simply too great to be a mere coincidence, or to be ignored. Nevertheless, before we turn to the final topic of this chapter, it is perhaps worth noting that there is no mention whatsoever in the account from *Joseph's Bible*

Notes of women serving as priestesses or in any other liturgical capacity. What this difference means is not entirely clear, but it certainly raises some question as to just how central these practices may or may not have been within this particular early Christian group.

Women's Liturgical Leadership in the *Six Books* and the "Kollyridian" Priestesses

In a previous publication on these same topics, I concluded that while there are clear connections between the *Six Books Apocryphon* and the Kollyridians with respect to the bread offerings and their association with Mary's Dormition and Assumption, there is in the *Six Books* no evidence of women's' liturgical leadership, although at the same time there is nothing in the text that would contradict such a practice.[68] Recently, however, Ally Kateusz has published an article in which she purports to have identified significant evidence of women's' liturgical leadership in the *Six Books Apocryphon*, and more specifically in the particular version preserved by the late fifth-century palimpsest manuscript that was published by Smith Lewis.[69] While I find a number of problems with this article and particularly its assumptions about how the early Dormition traditions developed in relation to one another, there is, I think, possibly some important insight here regarding this question that I did not previously consider. If it is highly improbable that this Dormition narrative witnesses to traditions of Mary as a liturgical leader that go back to the second century, as Kateusz contends,[70] there certainly is something to be said for Mary's representation as liturgically active in this text in ways that I previously overlooked. Kateusz takes as her touchstone Tertullian's rebuke of heretical Christians who allow women "to teach, to dispute, to enact exorcisms, to undertake cures—it may be even to baptize."[71]

Certainly Mary is recalled in the *Six Books Apocryphon* as having engaged in some of these activities, which admittedly does point toward certain kinds of liturgical leadership. As we have already seen, Mary is said to have cured the sick, healing thousands of people in the lead-up to her death. On one occasion she even heals a boy by "sealing" him: exactly what this term means is not entirely clear, but it certainly seems sacramental, and may be an anointing of the sick.[72] Mary also exorcizes demons from the afflicted on more than one occasion. There is even evidence of Mary preaching the gospel, at least in one of the early witnesses to this apocryphon.

One of the strengths but also one of the weaknesses of Kateusz's approach is her focus especially on the particular version of the *Six Books Apocryphon* preserved in Smith Lewis's late fifth-century palimpsest codex. This is a strength insofar as it leads her to highlight some important traditions found in this version but not preserved in the sixth-century manuscripts. It becomes a problem, however, when she simply assumes that the version from the late fifth-century manuscript is earlier than those of the sixth-century manuscripts and furthermore presumes that the versions in these later manuscripts are direct redactions of the longer version extant in the late fifth-century palimpsest. Neither of these assumptions is warranted in the current state of our evidence, and in fact they both seem rather dubious. Moreover, these rather doubtful assumptions undermine many of the arguments that Kateusz advances regarding the development of the early Dormition traditions. Nevertheless, one particularly important tradition in this earliest manuscript is a scene in which Mary evangelizes the Roman governor, an episode that is, for whatever reason, lacking in the sixth-century manuscripts.[73] This clearly seems to suggest a type of women's liturgical leadership. The same is true of another passage that describes Mary as teaching the gospel to other women who seek her instruction, and she entrusts them with some "writings" and charges them to use these to convert their families.[74] Again, this portrayal clearly would seem to put Mary on an equal footing with the male apostles and their role as liturgical and doctrinal leaders of the community.

Much less persuasive, however, in my opinion, is Kateusz's claim that Mary is portrayed as baptizing individuals in this text. In one instance Mary is said to heal some women by sprinkling water on them and "sealing" them in the name of the Trinity. According to Kateusz this should be understood as Mary's baptism of these women.[75] While this interpretation certainly is not impossible, I find it extremely improbable, and her actions more likely reflect some sort of anointing of the sick, as noted of the sealing above, particularly since their effect is the healing of the women's afflictions. In another passage Mary leads the male apostles in prayer, and when she finishes, they bow down and pray. Kateusz concludes that Mary here leads the apostles in prayer while they are bowed down before her, but this is not what the text says.[76] Still, Mary clearly appears here once again in a liturgical role. Most problematic, however, is Kateusz's claim that this version of the *Six Books* depicts Mary behaving like a priest. It is true that Mary performs many of the tasks that a priest might perform, such as teaching and evangelizing, leading prayer, healing the sick, and exorcising demons, both for men and for women, and some of these actions might have been regarded as sacramental in some sense. But the act of leading prayer alone does not mean that Mary is portrayed here "like a priest as well as like a bishop." As Kateusz herself notes, there is no evidence of Eucharistic priesthood by Mary or any other women in this text. Kateusz proposes instead to read Mary's Eucharistic priesthood back into the *Six Books* on the basis of Epiphanius's report about the Kollyridians and their women priests, but this seems dubious in the extreme: not only does it rely too much on the accuracy of Epiphanius's polemics but in many

159

respects it simply begs the question. Furthermore, the *Protevangelium* does not offer any evidence of Mary in this sort of priestly role, nor can Mary's other appearances in apocrypha of the second and third centuries establish her priesthood in this text, as Kateusz tries to argue.[77] In the end, one simply must concede that neither Mary nor any other woman is portrayed as a Eucharistic priest in the *Six Books Apocryphon*.

Nevertheless, that does not mean that there is no evidence of women's liturgical leadership in the *Six Books*, as I once incorrectly proposed. Accordingly, there also may be some truth behind Epiphanius's accusation that these "Kollyridians," with their bread offerings to Mary and their apparent belief in her Assumption, may also have involved women in the worship of their community in ways that Epiphanius could misconstrue—or deliberately misrepresent for polemical purposes—as women priests. If Mary's representation in these narratives bears any relation to the roles that women played in the communities that produced and used this text, then clearly women must have served as liturgical leaders in some capacities. Mary's depiction establishes a precedent for women to teach and evangelize, to disseminate scripture and supervise other preachers, to lead prayer in the congregation, and to perform exorcisms and healings using the rite of "sealing." Certainly, these are things that a male "priest" would have done in Epiphanius's community, which then would allow him or even encourage him to excoriate this Christian group for having women serve as priests based on their performance of such activities. It certainly is no stretch to imagine that Epiphanius of all people might have exaggerated the status of these women within the community in order to achieve a polemical point. Epiphanius is almost notorious in modern scholarship on early Christianity for his very fertile imagination when it comes to defaming the precisely eighty heresies that he set out to denounce in his *Panarion*. Accordingly, it is no wonder to find that he seemingly may have played a bit loose with the facts here as well in order to cast his opponents in the worst possible light, at least as he conceived of it.

As noted above, Epiphanius misrepresents his knowledge of the early Dormition traditions and seems to disguise their connection to the Kollyridians. Likewise, he exaggerates their devotion to the Virgin, whom they venerate merely as one of the saints rather than worshipping her as a goddess, a point that even he ultimately concedes at one point. As for their bread offerings, he deliberately misrepresents this ritual as a Eucharistic offering, when both his own description of the ceremony and the instructions given by the *Six Books Apocryphon* show it to be something quite different from the Eucharist.[78] Moreover, the *Six Books Apocryphon* specifies that the context for presenting these offerings in Mary's honor is either Matins (according to one manuscript) or Vespers (according to the other), at which there would be no Eucharistic rite.[79] Instead, the bread offerings of the Kollyridians and the *Six Books Apocryphon* resemble nothing so much as the Eastern Orthodox service of Artoklasia, "the breaking of bread," which is often observed after Great Vespers (and sometimes also after Matins or the Liturgy).[80] In this ceremony several loaves of wheat bread and sometimes a bowl of wheat are placed before the icons at the altar and censed and blessed by the priest, and at the end of the service, the bread is distributed to the congregants. This ritual seems very much like what the Kollyridians are said to have done and also quite similar to the commemorations of the Virgin ordained by the *Six Books Apocryphon*. And there can be no question that this service is completely different from the Eucharistic service.

So if Epiphanius has distorted the Kollyridians' veneration of Mary as goddess worship and misrepresented their bread offerings in Mary's honor as a Eucharist, one can readily imagine that he has also escalated women's involvement in teaching, communal prayer, healing, and exorcism to their status as priests within the community. Again, in all fairness, these are the sorts of things that male priests would presumably be found doing in the communities that Epiphanius recognized as orthodox. Moreover, if women were somehow involved in the bread offerings, it would be even more logical for Epiphanius to draw the conclusion that the women were serving as priests, since he misconstrues this ceremony as the Eucharist. The *Six Books*, it is true, only mentions priests in its description of this ritual, although there does seem to be a high level of lay involvement. Yet at the same time we certainly should not exclude the possibility that women may have served as priests in the communities that used the *Six Books Apocryphon*: there is nothing in the text that would preclude this practice, even if there is no direct evidence for it.

Therefore, Epiphanius's report that the Kollyridians allowed women to serve as priests is consistent both with the evidence afforded by the *Six Books Apocryphon* and with the pattern of exaggeration and misrepresentation that characterizes Epiphanius's account of this group, not to mention so many of his other victims. What this means, then, is that in actuality the "Kollyridians," whose name is quite likely Epiphanius's invention,[81] were a group of Christians who had begun to venerate the Virgin in the way that many other Christians had similarly begun to venerate other saints. Their veneration of Mary involved regular offerings of loaves of bread in Mary's honor, a practice that links them strongly with the *Six Books Apocryphon*, as does Epiphanius's persistent interest in traditions of Mary's Dormition and Assumption in his discussion of these Christians. His report that women served as liturgical leaders is also seemingly confirmed by Mary's depiction in the *Six Books Apocryphon* as performing a number of different liturgical activities, even if she does not serve as a Eucharistic priest. Presumably Mary's portrayal in the *Six Books* reflects similar involvement by women in the communities that used this text, and this is the basis for Epiphanius's invective against their allowance of women priests. Whether women actually served as Eucharistic priests in these communities is not especially important, since Epiphanius's hyperbolic polemic against this practice could just as easily have arisen from other kinds of liturgical leadership by women.

Admittedly, this is all perhaps a little less exciting than it would be to take Epiphanius's report at face value, as much previous scholarship has done. After all, it is hard for many modern readers to resist the enticing idea that there were, in the middle of the fourth century, Christians who had women priests and worshipped Mary as a goddess. Sadly, however, so much of this seems to be the product of Epiphanius's particularly active and malicious imagination. Yet at the same time, it is all the more satisfying to find that behind Epiphanius's harangue there seems to be an actual group of relatively "orthodox" Christians who allowed women to participate in some forms of liturgical leadership and were pioneers in the veneration—not worship—of the Virgin Mary, a portrait that emerges particularly through comparison with the *Six Books Dormition Apocryphon*. This long overlooked early Christian text allows us to peer behind Epiphanius's distorting rhetoric to discover this group of early Christians who venerated the Virgin Mary with bread offerings and no doubt called themselves something other than "Kollyridians" or "Marianites"—perhaps instead "Christians."

Conclusions

Along with the *Book of Mary's Repose*, which we considered in the previous chapter, the *Six Books Dormition Apocryphon* shows significant evidence of the growth of Marian piety during the "tunnel period" between the second-century *Protevangelium* and the

Nestorian controversy of the early fifth century. The *Book of Mary's Repose*, as we noted, is especially significant for its remarkable portrayal of Mary as one learned in the cosmic mysteries and for its early witness to the practice of Marian intercession. Nevertheless, the Marian veneration of this earliest Dormition narrative is rather basic, as perhaps one might expect from such an early text: one finds only scattered references to the efficacy of Mary's intercessions with her son, which are framed within a setting that also includes intercessory prayers from the apostles and angels. The *Six Books Apocryphon*, however, shows that a much more developed cult of the Virgin had come into existence already by the middle of the fourth century, in which the focus on Mary's intercessions has intensified considerably and has been joined to belief in Mary's power to work wonders and her apparitions. In addition, the *Six Books* narrative affords what is most likely the earliest witness to liturgical commemorations of the Virgin, in the form of three annual liturgical feasts celebrated in her honor with bread offerings on her behalf.

Perhaps Epiphanius stumbled across these traditions while searching for knowledge about the end of Mary's life. Clearly, however, he did not care very much either for the Dormition traditions themselves or for the Christians who followed them, inasmuch as he published two separate invectives against both. Although in one instance he feigns ignorance of any Dormition traditions in rather dramatic fashion, undoubtedly he had in fact encountered the traditions of *Six Books*. Accordingly, his insistence that he could not find any traditions at all about the end of Mary's life should be taken with a grain of salt: it would appear that he had found some traditions but just none that he could approve of. Moreover, the explicit connection between the ritual practices of the Kollyridians and belief in Mary's Assumption in *Joseph's Bible Notes* affirms that these two traditions almost certainly were already linked when

Epiphanius encountered them, leading us straight to the *Six Books Apocryphon.*

It is also worth noting that in this instance, once again, early veneration of the Virgin is associated with heterodox Christianity, at least as judged by Epiphanius. In actual fact, there is nothing at all in the *Six Books* or even in Epiphanius's account of his opponents' reverence for Mary that would suggest even the slightest hint of heterodoxy. Epiphanius objects to the fact that these Christians are offering veneration to Mary in the context of a broader argument that reveals his opposition to the veneration of any figure other than God. Such ritual actions, whether directed to Mary, Thecla, Elijah, or John, are tantamount to idolatry and must be condemned as such. Yet in this respect Epiphanius seems to have actually been in the minority among orthodox Christians, and even by the standards of his own time, Epiphanius was something of a conservative watchdog in general. Epiphanius was on the wrong side of history here, and within several decades of his death the sort of Marian piety reflected in the Kollyridians' veneration of the Virgin and in the *Six Books Apocryphon* would be officially embraced as the very epitome of Christian orthodoxy. It is nonetheless noteworthy that in his time the veneration of Mary could still be regarded as a heresy, at least by some, and this offers another possible clue, I suspect, as to why many of the church fathers may have kept their distance from this phenomenon in its earliest stages. Yet as we will see in the next chapter, during the second half of the fourth century the ice begins to break quickly, and suddenly we start to find evidence of the cult of the Virgin emerging from a number of different sources.

CHAPTER FIVE

The Memory of Mary: The Fourth and Early Fifth Centuries

Marian Devotion and Cult in the Fourth-Century Church Fathers

IN THE FOURTH CENTURY, and especially the second half of that century, the cult of the Virgin starts to come more fully into view, and we find evidence of emergent Marian veneration from a variety of different sources, including, at long last, the church fathers. Many of the most important orthodox Christian writers of this age begin to take a significant interest in the Virgin Mary, although they are mostly concerned with her doctrinal role and often express little interest or even knowledge of her veneration. The fourth century of course witnessed convulsive debates about the question of Christ's divinity, as theologians fought fiercely over the Son of God's relation to God the Father. Not surprisingly, this era also saw a corresponding interest in Mary's Divine Maternity, and from the very beginning of the century she was increasingly called by the title Theotokos.[1] Both Peter of Alexandria (bp. ca. 300–311) and Alexander of Alexandria (bp. ca. 312–328) called Mary the Theotokos in their writings from the beginning of the fourth century.[2] Athanasius (ca. 296–373) was the first Church Father to use this term with regularity, and in doing so it seems that he sought to channel the force of popular devotion to his cause: as others have noted, the title Theotokos first came into widespread use in the context of devotion and worship rather than theological speculation and dispute.[3] The Cappadocian fathers, Basil the Great (ca. 330–379), Gregory of Nazianzus (ca. 329–390), and Gregory of Nyssa (ca. 335–395), who emerged as the great defenders of the Son's divinity and the doctrine of the Trinity in the next generation, would continue to place strong emphasis on Mary's Divine Maternity and her role as Theotokos.[4] Their contemporary Julian the Apostate (361–363), who sought to reverse the Christianization of the Roman Empire, complained that the Christians of his age simply would not cease from calling Mary the Theotokos.[5]

Perhaps no one embraces Mary's Divine Maternity with as much fervor and eloquence as Ephrem the Syrian (ca. 306–373), whose frequent meditations on this theme are saturated with the language of devotion.[6] For Ephrem, since Christ's flesh came from Mary's flesh, she shares directly in the process of redemption through the Incarnation. Ephrem also develops the idea of Mary as the New Eve much further than his predecessors, so that Mary becomes the mother of the new life, in contrast to Eve who was the mother of the old life.[7] Yet despite Mary's doctrinal elevation to new heights, and the rich, poetic nature of Ephrem's hymns, his writings somewhat surprisingly give no indication of any veneration or cult of the Virgin. While Mary's veneration often seems almost implicit in his songs in praise of the Virgin, nowhere in his authentic works do we find evidence of intercessory prayer to Mary, a feast in her honor, or any other sign of cult. Of course, there is much more that could be said about the Mariologies of the Cappadocians and Ephrem, and of the other fathers of the fourth century for that matter, than we will offer here. But these topics are by now relatively well-covered territory, and one can readily consult any number of studies dealing with Marian doctrine in this era.[8] Accordingly, in the interest of maintaining a focus on Marian devotion, we will necessarily cut this thread short.

At the other end of the spectrum, however, stands John Chrysostom (ca. 347–407) who, perhaps as a harbinger of the Antiochian tradition that Nestorius would soon make infamous, does not think so highly of the Virgin as many of his contemporaries. John did not hesitate to identify flaws in Mary's character, using them as moral examples for his congregations. For instance, John interprets the Synoptic tradition of tension between Jesus and his relatives, including his mother, as indicating their disbelief, which Jesus aims to correct. Mary did not understand who her son was, and as his mother she mistakenly thought that she should have authority over him and was superior to him. It was outrageous for her, according to Chrysostom, to demand that he should come out to see her. Likewise, at the wedding of Cana, John explains that Mary's motive was to impress the guests and draw more attention to herself, which accordingly explains Jesus' curt response. As for the Annunciation, John maintains that this took place lest Mary should be confused by what was happening to her and might have stabbed or drowned herself to avoid disgrace.[9] In holding these opinions, Chrysostom is definitely an outlier when it comes to reverence for the Virgin Mary and her special sanctity in this age, and there is no other comparable voice that so openly identifies imperfections and failings in her character. But at the same time there is no evidence that such remarks sparked any sort of outrage among his congregation or his peers, such as would befall his fellow Antiochian Nestorius only a few decades later.[10] Instead, in Chrysostom's time, controversy swirled around the question of whether or not Mary remained a Virgin, and on this topic at least, Chrysostom was solidly in line with his orthodox colleagues.

Mary as Ascetic Model

The doctrine of Mary's virginity became a subject of some significant debate during the later fourth century. All of those writers whom the later orthodox tradition remembers as church fathers were on board with affirming not only Mary's virginal conception, but now also the preservation of her virginity while giving birth (*virginitas in partu*) and her persistence in virginity until the end of her life (*virginitas post partum*), that is, her Perpetual Virginity. Both of the two latter doctrines came sharply into question during the later fourth century, particularly in the Latin West, and the fierce debates over Mary's virginity that ensued were interwoven with broader conversations about the status of asceticism, which was on the rise in the later fourth century. The controversy arose in no small part because Mary and her virginity had both been enlisted for the ascetic cause as the paradigm of the virginal life, especially for women. Alexander of Alexandria, Athanasius's predecessor, seems to have been the first to recommend that Christian ascetics should have Mary as their model. After him Athanasius would himself advance belief in Mary's Perpetual Virginity, and in his *First Letter to the Virgins* he recommends to virgins that they should examine the life of Mary and imitate her. He describes Mary's conduct in some detail, suggesting that it should serve as a mirror for those who would follow in her footsteps: in essence, Mary was hardworking, charitable, and docile, and she remained at home, avoiding any contact with men. It was in part a strategy, as David Brakke explains, to undermine the support that his "Arian" opponents received from many virgins and to prevent others from being lured away.[11] Athanasius's view of the perpetually virgin Mary as the exemplar for other virgins would also influence Ambrose of Milan (ca. 340–397), whose writings offer one of the most developed Mariologies of the early church. Drawing directly on Athanasius's early work, he developed this idea further, and in a treatise on virginity addressed to his sister, he similarly describes Mary the model virgin, whose humility, industry, modesty, and reserve other virgins must strive to emulate.[12]

By contrast, a certain Helvidius published a treatise sometime around 380 CE that challenged the doctrine of Mary's Perpetual Virginity, arguing against it especially on the basis of New Testament passages that suggest Mary and Joseph had sexual relations after the birth of Jesus as well as those mentioning Jesus' brothers. It would appear that Helvidius was writing in response to a now lost pamphlet that had been published previously by someone named Carterius, which had argued for the superiority of the ascetic life over marriage on the basis of Mary's Perpetual Virginity. Helvidius answers by defending the strict equality of both the married and the celibate life, and so Mary must be a model not only for virgins but for the married as well. Therefore, Helvidius argued that Mary's virginal conception served as an example for Christian virgins, while her life as Joseph's spouse offered a model for the married. To this he adds a list of married patriarchs from the Old Testament, asking if Christian virgins would dare to think themselves better than these biblical heroes. Broader issues also were at stake for Helvidius regarding the inherent goodness of the material realm and sexuality, and he saw in the exaltation of virginity over marriage a potentially dangerous denigration of God's creation. Jerome (ca. 347–420) somewhat reluctantly penned a response, refuting Helvidius's arguments, which were beginning to persuade many, and in the process he authored the first treatise defending Mary's Perpetual Virginity. Jerome eventually won the debate, and as a result Helvidius's views are known only through their rebuttal.[13]

Nevertheless, we get some sense of what Mary might have looked like as a model for married asceticism from an anonymous Spanish letter written toward the end of the fourth century.[14] The author, whom the text's editor argues is a woman, writes to a married woman and advises her to look to Mary as a model for her own ascetic practice. Rather surprisingly, however, the letter identifies Mary's pain and anguish in giving birth as the main quality that she should imitate: by this time, one should note, it is rather rare to encounter the belief that Mary suffered in labor. Yet according to the letter, as Mary brought forth the hope of her salvation with toil and travail, so other women likewise will only bear spiritual fruits through struggle and suffering. The letter also anticipates objections from its married recipient: "But perhaps you will say, '... Only virgins may serve Christ.'"[15] The author then answers her own question, insisting that since a virgin has not experienced sexual intercourse or the pains of giving birth, she is in no way superior to married women, and furthermore that God's grace is not limited to any single class of people. Mary is thus an ascetic model even—if not especially—for married women. They are to imitate her by periodically refraining from sexual relations, and so the letter specifically recommends that its addressee should spend some time away from her home in a monastery. She should also expect some resistance from her husband, but the author notes that Joseph was absent when Mary endured her pains of labor, and so it must be in her case as well. Others too may object that such a practice is unprecedented, but the newness of all things in Christ warrants the transformation of old ways and customs. And object they did, it would seem, if the response to Helvidius offers any indication. But this anonymous letter gives us some idea of how he—and other like-minded Christians—might have envisioned the Virgin Mary as a model for ascetic practice among married Christians, who were every bit the equal of the continent.

Not long after Helvidius published his treatise, a Roman monk named Jovinian began similarly teaching against the superiority of the ascetic life, refusing, like Helvidius before him, to allow that Christians who pursued such rigors were any better than those who chose instead to marry and have a family. And here again, issues regarding the goodness of creation and sexuality come to the fore, so that Jovinian accused the champions of the ascetic cause, like Ambrose and Jerome, of having embraced Manicheanism in their disregard and denigration of the material world and sexual inter-course, both points for which the Manicheans were widely known and condemned by orthodox Christians. But the question of Mary's virginity also emerges in this controversy as well, even though Jerome in his response to Jovinian oddly fails to mention this point. We know only from Ambrose that Jovinian rejected the preservation of Mary's virginity in the process of giving birth. Why Jerome does not respond to this point is admittedly something of a mystery. But for Jovinian, it seems, the doctrine of Mary's virginity after giving birth smacked of Docetism, an early Christian heresy that denied the reality of Christ's physical body, so that he only appeared to be flesh and blood. For him, Mary's failure to lose her virginity in giving birth implied that Christ was some sort of immaterial being who passed through her womb without opening it. And so Jovinian was able to enlist this Marian doctrine in support of his accusation that these architects of asceticism were in fact embracing the errors of Manicheanism by privileging celibacy over marriage. In order to clear their names of this heinous charge both Jerome and Ambrose had to respond, and in doing so they were largely successful in persuading their peers of the superiority of the ascetic life over Christian marriage. Through their efforts Mary would ultimately emerge as the paragon of female virginity, whom all other virgins should strive to imitate.[16]

Perhaps, then, we should add Mary's role as an ascetic model to the mounting evidence that we find for devotion to the Virgin in early

Christianity. For instance, Stephen Davis in his book on *The Cult of St Thecla* identifies "acts of asceticism" among the various forms of devotion that early Christians would offer to the saints.[17] Would not then a Christian virgin's attempt to emulate Mary's perfect model of virginity also indicate a kind of devotion to the mother of Jesus? It is true that in earlier centuries Thecla was frequently held forth as the model of female virginity, and even as Mary became ascendant in this role during late antiquity, Thecla still continued to appear often as an example of virginity. For instance, Athanasius also commends Thecla as the consummate model of virginity in another writing, *On Virginity*, a treatise that Davis notes would have been directed toward the same female monastic communities in Alexandria as his *First Letter to the Virgins*, mentioned above. On the basis of Athanasius's recommendation of Thecla as their ascetic exemplar, Davis concludes that "What we have here, then, is evidence suggesting that Thecla devotion was practiced by fourth-century monastic women in Alexandria." Moreover, he also maintains that Athanasius used Thecla to align these Alexandrian virgins with his political and theological campaign against the Arians, much as Brakke before him had argued was the case with Mary.[18] Accordingly, if Athanasius's promotion of Thecla as a model for these ascetic women can serve as evidence that they were practicing Thecla devotion, then the same must also be true of the Virgin Mary, and we may conclude that devotion to the Virgin Mary was an important component of female monastic life in fourth-century Alexandria. Likewise, the same would presumably hold true for female monastics in northern Italy, Jerusalem, and elsewhere on the basis of Ambrose and Jerome's endorsement of Mary as the ideal model for female virginity. Accordingly, following Davis's reasoning, we can attach Marian devotion in the fourth century to communities of female ascetics in various locations throughout the empire. And, moreover, based on the Spanish letter considered above, it would appear that, at least in Spain, Marian devotion had also taken hold within the Roman household as well by the end of the fourth century.

Patristic Evidence for Marian Intercession and Apparitions

Some of the earliest patristic evidence for Marian cult comes from the two great Cappadocian Gregorys mentioned above, Gregory of Nyssa and Gregory of Nazianzus. The latter, Gregory of Nazianzus, offers what is perhaps the earliest patristic witness to the practice of Marian intercession in his *Oration 24*. In this rather peculiar work, a panegyric on "Cyprian," Gregory freely mixes traditions about Cyprian of Carthage with those of Cyprian of Antioch (in Pisidia), whose feast the oration was presumably intended to commemorate.[19] Cyprian of Antioch was, according to legend, originally a magician who sought with his spells to seduce a beautiful Christian virgin named Justina. Justina, however, successfully defended herself by calling on her "husband," Christ, as well as by praying to the Virgin Mary for her aid, since she too was a virgin who had once faced danger. When Cyprian recognized his defeat, he made the sign of the cross over himself, thereby freeing himself from Satan's influence and allowing him to become a Christian.[20] Whether or not a virgin named Justina actually sought the Virgin's assistance and protection through prayer in the early fourth century, as the legend suggests, is perhaps beside the point: the primary significance of this story lies in its witness to the practice of intercessory prayer to the Virgin among the Nicene Christians of Constantinople by 379, when Gregory delivered this oration.[21] From Gregory's representation of Justina, we may assume that such Marian prayers were a fairly common practice in the community that he led, which included, we should note, a number of aristocratic women who were devoted to the cult of the saints and their relics.[22]

At approximately the same time, Gregory of Nyssa records the earliest known account of a Marian apparition, in his panegyric on yet another Gregory, the third-century Gregory the Wonderworker. This biography, written in the fall of 380, describes Gregory the Wonderworker's waking vision of the Virgin. One night Gregory found himself unable to sleep because of worries about the heresies that were threatening the church. Two figures then appeared to him to explain the true doctrines of the Christian faith, and in the process of their conversation, Gregory realized that they were John the Evangelist and the Virgin Mary. Mary, he says, appeared as a woman "whose noble aspect far surpassed normal human beauty," even though she was so extraordinary that he could not bear to look upon her.[23] While this story offers no guarantee that Gregory the Wonderworker actually had such a vision, it does seem an odd thing for Gregory of Nyssa to have invented from whole cloth. And in any case, its inclusion in this biography shows that appearances of the Virgin Mary were something familiar to the Cappadocian Christians in Gregory of Nyssa's flock.[24] That both Gregorys would describe these phenomena so matter-of-factly suggests that prayers to the Virgin and her apparition were a regular part of the Christian faith in their communities.[25] As Nicholas Constas rightly observes, even though these are the first reports of such phenomena, "these accounts do not have the air of novelty or innovation," and presumably they reflect already well-established traditions of Marian piety.[26] Yet, for whatever reason, those scholars who would maintain a post-Ephesian origin for Marian veneration generally have looked past these early witnesses.

Another early account of Marian apparitions also comes to us second hand. According to the fifth-century church historian Sozomen, similar experiences were common at Gregory Nazianzen's church in Constantinople. Sozomen reports these occurrences as follows:

Gregory of Nazianzus presided over those who maintain the "consubstantiality" of the Holy Trinity, and assembled them together in a little dwelling, which had been altered into the form of a house of prayer, by those who held the same opinions and had a like form of worship. It subsequently became one of the most conspicuous in the city, and is so now, not only for the beauty and number of its structures, but also for the advantages accruing to it from the visible manifestations of God. For the power of God was there manifested, and was helpful both in waking visions and in dreams, often for the relief of many diseases and for those afflicted by some sudden transmutation in their affairs. The power was accredited to Mary, the Mother of God, the holy virgin, for she does manifest herself in this way. The name of Anastasia was given to this church.[27]

One cannot know for certain if these apparitions were experienced during Gregory's time as the leader of this church, as reported, but again it seems unlikely that Sozomen has invented this account. The fact that Gregory's close friend Gregory of Nyssa relates a Marian apparition at around the same time certainly suggests that this phenomenon was not uncommon within their intellectual circle. Accordingly, it seems quite plausible that in Gregory Nazianzen's time the Virgin Mary was believed to appear regularly in the midst of his congregation in Constantinople.

Another important and often overlooked witness to early Marian veneration is Severian of Gabala, a contemporary of John Chrysostom who was in large part responsible for Chrysostom's dismissal as patriarch of Constantinople. Like Chrysostom, Severian was also from Syria, but unlike his compatriot he took a much more positive view of the Virgin Mary, a point that should remind us that not all of those in the Antiochian tradition shared the same opinions about her as Nestorius and Chrysostom. In the last of his six *Homilies on Creation*, which he delivered in February of 401,[28] Severian develops the Eve/Mary typology that we have noted before, and in the process he reminds his audience: "Of course she hears our prayers, the mother of salvation and the source of light, because she is in the glorious place and the land of the living."[29] Here, as Brian Reynolds notes, Mary's intercessions seem to be linked with the belief in her Assumption, since she is especially able to intercede for others because she has already gone ahead to the heavenly rewards.[30] Although the Assumption admittedly is not mentioned directly, it nonetheless seems implicit in the notion of Mary's presence already in Paradise.

Likewise in his homily *On the Lawgiver*, delivered the previous summer in 400, Severian also addresses the theme of Mary's intercessions, once again seeming to link her intervention with her Dormition.[31] Following a discussion of Deborah and Jael, two women who showed great prowess in battle in the book of Judges (4–5), Severian says the following about the Virgin Mary. "And we also have Saint Mary the Virgin and Theotokos who intercedes for us. For if an ordinary woman can be victorious, how much more will the mother of Christ humiliate the enemies of truth. The enemy, armed to the teeth, thought that the woman was worthy of derision, but he found her to be a valiant general. He did not think that he [or she?] would be placed in the tomb, but he found the grave. He thought that she was dead, but he was put to death by her. We have our master Saint Mary the Theotokos."[32] Two themes are particularly intriguing in this passage. Firstly, we find here, seemingly for the first time, the image of Mary as a valiant general, a portrait of the Virgin that would proliferate in the centuries to come as she was increasingly imagined as the protectress of the imperial capital, Constantinople. After the Avar siege of the early seventh century, for instance, there were stories that Mary had been seen on the city walls wearing battle armor, slaying many of the enemy by her own hand.[33] It was a tradition that would continue into the Byzantine period and still finds expression today in the Eastern Orthodox hymn to the Virgin, "O Champion General," sung as a part of the Akathist hymn and on other occasions as well. Secondly, much like the passage from the previous homily, Severian again appears to refer, albeit elliptically, to the Virgin's Dormition and Assumption. Presumably this is the meaning of the cryptic sentence, "He thought that she was dead, but he was put to death by her." Admittedly, the meaning is not entirely clear, but this reference to Mary's death and her triumph over the enemy (Satan) is perhaps best explained by the tradition of her death and resurrection, which Severian seems to know. What is unmistakable, however, is the belief in the power of Mary's intercessions that he professes in both of these homilies.

Liturgical Evidence for the Cult of the Virgin: Feast Days and Shrines

The earliest patristic references to a liturgical feast in honor of the Virgin Mary seem to come from Athanasius of Alexandria, who in two letters written in the final years of his life refers to a "commemoration of Mary."[34] On both occasions he uses the Greek word *mnēmē*, which in the most general sense means "memory," but in Christian Greek the word also is used in a more technical sense for the liturgical commemoration of a saint or martyr. Such in fact was the title of the earliest Marian feast in Jerusalem at the beginning of the fifth century: the Memory of Mary (*hē mnēmē tēs Marias*). The first of these two letters, the *Letter to Epictetus*, was written in 370 to address a new form of Docetism that had recently emerged in Egypt. Here Athanasius argues against this renewed heresy that its beliefs about the nature of Christ "render superfluous the commemoration and office of Mary [*perittē tēs Marias hē mnēmē kai hē chreia*]."[35] One imagines that this feast, which presumably celebrated Mary's Divine Maternity, is here invoked as a refutation of any claim that Christ was not born and did not have a real human body: in previous centuries Mary's birthing of Christ was upheld as evidence against Docetist views. Likewise, in his *Letter to Maximus*, written not long thereafter, Athanasius rebuts a different Christological error regarding Jesus' humanity in similar fashion, maintaining that "if this were so, the commemoration of Mary would be superfluous [*perittē tēs Marias hē mnēmē*]."[36] Once again, faith in Mary's Divine Maternity as commemorated at her feast ensures the reality of his humanity.

Nevertheless, what Athanasius has in mind here by the "commemoration" of Mary is admittedly not entirely clear. It is possible, of course, that he simply means to call to mind the memory of Mary's role in the Incarnation as a point capable of refuting the two heresies in question. Nevertheless, it makes for a bit of an odd expression to read the passage, "if this were so, calling to mind a remembrance of Mary is superfluous." Something more specific than just recalling her memory seems to be in view here, and understanding his mention of "the memory of Mary" as reference to a liturgical commemoration makes a great deal more sense. In fact, I would suspect that any doubts about such a liturgical interpretation have arisen primarily from traditional scholarly assumptions about the late onset of Marian veneration. Yet the *Six Books Apocryphon* shows that such commemorations had already begun elsewhere by the middle of the fourth century. Moreover, within just a few decades we find annual feasts of the Virgin in both Jerusalem and Constantinople. Accordingly, the existence of a similar feast of Mary in Egypt during the later fourth century, as Athanasius appears to indicate, would not be in the least bit peculiar and perhaps is even to be expected. This is all the more so given that many scholars have proposed Egypt as the place where Marian veneration first developed.[37] The popularity in Egypt of the title Theotokos, which seems to derive from devotional practice, also strengthens the possibility that Athanasius refers to an actual liturgical feast of Mary. Taken on the whole, then, the evidence for a feast of Mary in Egypt during the later fourth century seems quite credible, even if a degree of uncertainty necessarily remains.[38]

In the imperial capital, the feast of the Memory of Mary is first attested in the famous *First Homily on the Theotokos* by Proclus of Constantinople, the future bishop of Constantinople and one of Nestorius's most ardent opponents, who will be discussed in more detail in the following chapter.[39] Proclus delivered this homily in 430 at the height of the Nestorian controversy in the presence of Nestorius himself, responding directly to what he perceived to be Nestorius's attacks on Marian piety. In the process, Constas observes, Proclus "established the veneration of the Theotokos upon theological and exegetical principles which defined the rhetoric and rationale for the cult of the Virgin Mary throughout the Byzantine period."[40] Yet most important for the present purpose, however, is the occasion for this homily. Proclus delivered his homily, he informs us, for "the Virgin's festival," a recently established feast in Mary's honor commemorating her Divine Maternity and virginity. The feast was most likely observed on 26 December, a date that corresponds not only with the feast of Mary following the Nativity in the *Six Books Apocryphon* but still today is observed as the Feast of the Theotokos in the Eastern Orthodox churches. As Constas concludes in his exhaustive study of Proclus, this new feast of the Virgin had almost certainly been established by one of Nestorius's immediate predecessors as bishop of Constantinople, and for a variety of reasons Atticus of Constantinople, bishop from 406 to 425, stands out as the most likely suspect.[41] Without any doubt, then, there was in Constantinople already a liturgical feast honoring the Virgin as Theotokos even in advance of Nestorius's arrival.

Yet the most plentiful and pronounced evidence for an early Marian feast comes from Jerusalem. The Christians of late ancient Jerusalem took full advantage of their uniquely consecrated terrain, fusing feast with place through ritual commemoration, and with processions between the city's major shrines and beyond to more remote stations in Bethany and Bethlehem, they visibly wove the Christian faith into the fabric of Jerusalem's urban landscape. These stational movements and memorials comprise one of the most distinctive qualities of the early Jerusalem liturgy, and although there is limited evidence for similar practices elsewhere, in Rome and in Constantinople,[42] nowhere else is the public worship of a late ancient city on such rich display. By the early fifth century, Jerusalem's calendar included an annual commemoration of the Memory of Mary on 15 August (perhaps corresponding to the 13 August feast in the *Six Books Apocryphon*?).[43] A number of early fifth-century witnesses attest to the observance of this commemoration, including liturgical materials and homilies for the feast as well as the archaeological remains of an early fifth-century church where the feast was celebrated.[44]

The most direct evidence for this annual Marian feast comes from the *Jerusalem Armenian Lectionary*, a manual outlining the yearly liturgical celebrations of the Holy City that was compiled sometime between 417 and 439. Among its many commemorations is a feast of the Memory of Mary, celebrated on 15 August at the third mile from Bethlehem, midway between Jerusalem and Bethlehem.[45] The prescribed lectionary readings for the feast all relate to Christ's birth from Mary, signaling a commemoration of Mary's Divine Maternity similar to the feast of the Virgin in Constantinople witnessed by Proclus. Such a focus is not at all surprising, since the site of this commemoration was itself strongly connected with the events of the Nativity: as we saw in the first chapter, according to the second-century *Protevangelium of James*, Jesus was not born in the city of Bethlehem but halfway between Jerusalem and Bethlehem in a cave just off of the main road, the precise location of this early Marian feast.[46] There are even some indications that both this location and its feast were originally connected with the events of the Nativity itself, but by the early fifth century the festival had become an annual commemoration of the Virgin Mary.[47]

At the beginning of the fifth century, this site boasted an important church, the church of the Kathisma, or "Seat," of the Theotokos, which according to tradition stood on the spot where the Virgin sat to rest briefly before giving birth in a nearby cave.[48] The main focus of this holy place was a large rock, upon which the Virgin was believed to have sat, at least according to later tradition (the *Protevangelium* does not mention any rock). Over the past several decades, two fifth-century churches have been unearthed at this location, and their relations to each other and to the traditions of the Kathisma and the Memory of Mary remain somewhat uncertain. One church is a much smaller basilica that was constructed in the late fourth or early fifth century as part of a monastery overlooking the field where the holy rock is found, some 300 meters to the southwest.[49] The second, much larger church is an octagonal structure that was built in the middle of the fifth century, right around the very rock itself. At first glance it might seem perfectly clear that this larger church should be identified as the Kathisma, since it obviously serves to commemorate this sacred stone where Mary once rested, and there is no doubt that, at some level, this is correct. Yet the literary evidence for the history of this site seems to require a slightly more complex interpretation, and it would appear that both of these churches may in some way be connected with the tradition of Mary's resting.

The earliest sources of information about this church—other than the *Armenian Lectionary*—are two sixth-century lives of a fifth-century Palestinian monk named Theodosius. According to one of these accounts, Theodosius was sent at the beginning of his monastic career to live at the church and monastery known as the Old Kathisma, a designation which, as others have noted, seems to imply the existence of a New Kathisma from which it was distinguished. Moreover, the same text informs us that a woman named Ikelia financed the construction of a church at this site sometime around 455.[50] Theodosius's other biography also mentions Ikelia's benefaction and further notes that Theodosius was living there at the time when Ikelia's church was being built. This second report similarly seems to indicate both an old church, attached to the monastery in which Theodosius was living, and a new one that was in the process of being built during the mid-fifth century.[51] When we add to this the fact that we know from the *Armenian Lectionary* that an annual feast took place at this church prior to 439, and in fact before 428 according to evidence noted immediately below, it seems hard to avoid the conclusion that there must have been a church of the Kathisma that predated Ikelia's foundation. Moreover, the *Jerusalem Georgian Calendar* from the tenth century reports two different dedication dates for the church of the Kathisma, which also suggests the existence of two churches, each with its own consecration date.[52] It is admittedly not entirely clear how this information should be related to the two churches at this site, but I have proposed that the smaller church and its monastery were likely constructed in the late fourth or early fifth century to serve as the earliest site of this Marian feast. The larger church, then, which was built around the rock but does not appear to have any monastic cells connected to it, presumably was built with Ikelia's support during the middle of the fifth century to accommodate increasing pilgrimage traffic.[53] In any case, whatever the solution to this liturgical and archaeological puzzle may be, it is quite certain that at least one of these two churches stood in this location by the beginning of the fifth century, housing an altar for the annual observance of Mary's feast.

In addition to these material remains from the early cult of the Virgin, a pair of homilies for the feast of the Memory of Mary also survive from the Jerusalem church in this era, two homilies in honor of Mary by Hesychius, a priest of Jerusalem during the early fifth century. Hesychius delivered his *Homily V* to commemorate the Memory of Mary sometime between 431 and 433, and his *Homily VI* was most likely delivered for the same occasion sometime prior to 428.[54] Presumably, both homilies were pronounced in the church of the Kathisma, and even if by some chance the shrine was not yet so named, it is safe to assume that Hesychius spoke in a church standing at the site identified by the *Armenian Lectionary*. In any case, Hesychius's homilies confirm the observance of this Marian feast in Jerusalem by the early fifth century and before the Council of Ephesus, adding precision to the witness of the *Armenian Lectionary* by establishing the commemoration of the Memory of Mary before 428.

One important omission, however, is the absence of this feast from the famous pilgrimage account of Egeria, a wealthy woman from late ancient Spain who traveled to the Holy Land and elsewhere in the eastern Mediterranean. Egeria stayed in Jerusalem for several years, from 381 to 384 it would seem, and so her account of the Holy City's ceremonies at this time is especially well-informed and detailed.[55] Egeria makes no mention of the Memory of Mary in her description of Jerusalem's annual liturgical practices, recorded while she was in the Holy City in 383.[56] Yet Egeria's silence offers no assurance that the establishment of this Marian feast postdates her visit, inasmuch as her account does not offer a complete liturgical calendar but focuses only on certain major feasts. Although Egeria describes rather extensively the observances surrounding Epiphany, Lent, Holy Week, Easter, and Pentecost, outside of this cycle and in the period of "ordinary time" she notes only the dedication feast of the Holy Sepulcher in mid-September. Her account is both selective and incomplete, a problem compounded by the fact that the sole manuscript preserving this remarkable account is missing a number of pages, so that her description of Jerusalem's liturgical cycle breaks off suddenly in midsentence: perhaps the missing pages may have continued with some information regarding the Memory of Mary.

Moreover, as Walter Ray observes, Egeria's account as it presently stands "describes only dominical feasts and ... does not mention any commemorations of saints,"[57] which severely limits its usefulness for understanding liturgical practices outside of the Epiphany to Pentecost cycle. Likewise, John Baldovin cautions, "The liturgical data provided by Egeria must be considered carefully in contrast with the A[rmenian] L[ectionary]. Since she does not pretend to give a complete liturgical calendar for Jerusalem but only describes major feasts, one cannot tell how many individual saints were honored by the Christian community in Jerusalem in the late fourth century. On this level, that of a more complete sanctoral calendar, we must overlook differences with the A[rmenian] L[ectionary]."[58] Consequently, Egeria's failure to mention the Memory of Mary cannot be taken to indicate the absence of this feast from Jerusalem's liturgical calendar in the later fourth century. As Ray, Baldovin, and others have observed, it seems likely that many of the commemorations of the saints described by the *Armenian Lectionary* extend back into the fourth century, and it is certainly possible that the feast of Mary was among these. Nevertheless, only the observance of this feast prior to 428 is certain, as evidenced by the homilies of Hesychius of Jerusalem.

Finally, the church of Mary's (empty) tomb in Jerusalem, which is next to the Garden of Gethsemane, also seems to have been built during the fifth century; nevertheless, its absence from the *Armenian Lectionary* seems to limit the possibility of its construction prior to the Council of Ephesus. While the lectionary may potentially have been compiled a decade or so before the Council of Ephesus, its failure to mention this church is likely telling. The archaeology of the site itself indicates its construction during the fifth century, and the church is said to have been a center of resistance to the Council of Chalcedon, so that when the patriarch of Jerusalem Juvenal returned from the council in 451, he had to use imperial troops to take control of the church. The various early accounts of pilgrimage to Jerusalem are also consistent with a fifth-century date for this church. And the earliest Dormition traditions for their part describe Mary's burial in a tomb just outside of Jerusalem, but these third- and fourth-century narratives fail to provide a more specific location. Thus, in the current state of our evidence it is not possible to identify a church commemorating the Virgin's tomb in Jerusalem before the Council of Ephesus with any certainty, although it would appear that this church existed and was highly revered by the time of the Council of Chalcedon, just twenty years later.[59]

Liturgical Evidence for the Cult of the Virgin:
Early Hymnography

The *Armenian Lectionary* and also the somewhat later *Jerusalem Georgian Lectionary* open up the world of Jerusalem's early liturgies in a spectacular way that is truly unique within late ancient Christianity. They specify not only the appointed readings for dozens of annual liturgical feasts, but they also provide the specific locations for their celebration in Jerusalem and its immediate environs. Yet, while these two documents are unequaled for what they reveal about the evolving feasts of the Palestinian church in late antiquity, their terse accounts

of these annual commemorations offer little sense of how these celebrations came to life in the context of early Christian worship.[60]
Thankfully, however, there is now another important early liturgical
source that can provide such a perspective, the ancient *Chantbook* of
the Jerusalem church, a work that survives only in Old Georgian
where it bears the title *Iadgari* (*Tropologion* in Greek).[61] This remarkable collection of texts reveals for the first time the hymns that were
sung in the churches of Jerusalem during the sixth, the fifth, and even
the fourth century. Not surprisingly, the Virgin Mary figures prominently in these early Christian hymns, and not only on the occasion
of feasts in her honor, but also in the context of regular Sunday
worship as observed throughout the course of the year. From this
collection of hymns we can see that already by the later fourth century
devotion to Mary and her unique powers of intercession had become
an important feature of regular Christian worship, at least in Jerusalem.

Although these hymns have been well known to Georgian scholars
for some time now, they are still largely unknown to specialists on
late ancient Christianity in Western Europe and the Americas, with
the exception of scholars of early Christian liturgy, who have been
quick to recognize the unique value of this collection. We know from
Egeria that the singing of hymns was a central element of Christian
worship in late ancient Jerusalem, since she refers to the singing of
hymns and antiphons over one hundred times in her fourth-century
pilgrimage account. It is true that the *Armenian Lectionary* gives
some idea of Jerusalem's early psalmody, and the *Georgian Lectionary*
provides incipits for the hymns appointed for its various feasts.[62] But
the *Jerusalem Georgian Chantbook* reveals for the first time the words
of the songs that once filled Jerusalem's churches, offering an unri-
valed perspective on early Christian music and worship. The various
layers of this early liturgical collection reveal a rich corpus of sophis-
ticated theological poetry steeped in biblical allusions, such that, as

Peter Jeffery observes, "the importance of this material for the history of Christian hymnody and theology . . . cannot be overstated."[63]

In its present format this ancient hymnal dates to sometime around the turn of the seventh century, at which time its various elements were gathered together into a liturgical manual that could be used for numerous occasions throughout the church year.[64] Nevertheless, this early version of the *Chantbook* contains within it three distinct collections of hymns, and each of these appears to have been individually assembled earlier still. The first and largest collection consists of hymns appointed for the evening office, the morning office, and the Eucharist for each of the year's major liturgical feasts, according to the order of the liturgical calendar.[65] Jeffery persuasively dates this collection to the middle of the sixth century, on the basis of the calendar that organizes this section of the *Chantbook*, and so he concludes that its hymns thus must date even earlier.[66] A short collection of festal hymns then follows this larger cycle, and it too is organized according to the same liturgical calendar. The purpose of these hymns is not entirely clear, but Jeffery suggests that these are "supplementary troparia" for the major feasts.[67] The *Chantbook*'s third and final section presents the "Hymns of the Resurrection," which are hymns for the weekly Sunday services.[68] Thanks to the seemingly tireless industry of Charles (Athanase) Renoux, these particular hymns have now been made accessible to a larger scholarly audience in French translation.[69] Moreover, Renoux has persuasively dated most of these hymns to the late fourth or early fifth century, meaning that we now have a sizable corpus of hymns that were regularly used by early Christians for their Sunday worship. Renoux identifies one of the *Chantbook*'s manuscripts as a particularly faithful witness to the actual liturgical practices of late ancient Jerusalem's churches, and accordingly this manuscript, Sinai Georgian 18, forms the basis for the study of liturgical chant and poetry during this period.[70]

One of the most remarkable features of these Sunday hymns is their organization according to an eightfold tonal structure, known more commonly in the Eastern Orthodox tradition as the "Oktoechos." According to this liturgical system, which is used primarily during the period from Pentecost to the beginning of Lent, the music for each week rotates in sequence through each of eight distinct "modes" or melodic themes. Given the importance of this liturgical practice for much of Christian history, liturgists have understandably focused their attention largely on this aspect of the Sunday hymns, since they provide the earliest evidence for this practice and seem to link its origins with late ancient Jerusalem.[71] Nevertheless, we shall turn our attention instead to another quality of these hymns that has gone largely unnoticed so far, that is, their evidence of significant devotion to the Virgin Mary during the Sunday liturgies already before the Council of Ephesus in 431. The *Jerusalem Georgian Chantbook*'s hymns offer particularly early evidence of veneration of Mary and prayers for her intercessions, and accordingly these hymns would appear to afford one of the richest and also one of most overlooked sources for exploring the beginnings of Marian piety.

There is some significant diversity among the various manuscripts of the early *Jerusalem Chantbook*, and one of the most notable differences in fact is the inclusion by several manuscripts of a collection of "Praises of the Holy Theotokos" as a part of the hymns for Sunday worship. These Marian hymns constitute a remarkable corpus in their own right, and it would appear that they represent the earliest surviving collection of hymns devoted specifically to the praise and veneration of the Virgin Mary.[72] In the *Chantbook* these hymns appear individually at the end of the matins service for each of the eight tones, and their length varies from 30 to 150 lines, averaging about 50 lines. Sinai Georgian 41, the manuscript that best preserves these hymns, has a total of 54 strophes in its hymns to the

Virgin, and the other manuscripts also preserve some variant strophes. According to Renoux, these hymns most likely were not intended specifically for use in the matins service, but instead he proposes that their position at the end of matins and before the liturgy provided a convenient location for gathering Marian hymns for each of the tones so that they could be easily found.[73]

Altogether these "Praises of the Holy Theotokos" amount to a rather sizable collection of Marian hymnography, which again seems to have been a part of regular Sunday worship in late ancient Jerusalem. The only problem, however, is that these hymns are absent from two of the most important manuscripts. There is certainly no question that these hymns were in use by the sixth century at the absolute latest, since the *Chantbook* itself dates to the beginning of the seventh century. Yet Renoux argues persuasively on the basis of their content that they must be even earlier: their theology and imagery of the Virgin Mary correspond very closely with other witnesses from the fifth century and find their closest parallels in Hesychius of Jerusalem (whom we have just met) and other writers of the same period.[74] One of the strophes is even cited by Proclus of Constantinople in his famous *First Homily on the Theotokos* (also mentioned above), which he delivered in 430 for the Feast of the Virgin. The hymn, as it was sung at Jerusalem in the early fifth century, is as follows:

> You, the fleece of the holy rain from heaven,
> By whom the shepherd of the sheep was clothed,
> Handmaid and mother and virgin, heaven of the heavens,
> The only bridge for God's coming to humankind,
> Awesome loom of our economy,
> On which the garment of the Lord was ineffably woven,
> Pray for us, O holy Queen,
> Do not cease to intercede for the salvation of our souls.[75]

This hymn, at least, was clearly in use before the Council of Ephesus ever met, and on the whole it would appear that these Marian hymns as a group belong to the early fifth century. In the case of this particular hymn, Proclus presumably recites a hymn already familiar to his audience, and the fact that it was included in both the Constantinople and Jerusalem liturgies by this time indicates that it must have come into use even earlier, presumably during the fourth century.

There is a single strophe in this collection, however, that seems to reflect the influence of the Council of Chalcedon, making brief reference to the unity of Christ's two natures without confusion.[76] On the basis of this lone passage, Renoux suggests the possibility that these hymns may belong to the latter half of the fifth century, at least in part.[77] Nevertheless, the bulk of his arguments seem to favor much more strongly a dating to the first half of the fifth century, which seems to be the preferred era for these hymns. The use of *asynchytos/ asynchytōs* ("without confusion") to describe the union of natures in Christ was not the Fourth Council's invention, and there is significant precedent for such usage in writers of the fourth and early fifth centuries.[78] Likewise, it is equally possible that this isolated passage may in fact be a later intrusion into this corpus of early hymns to the Virgin. In any case, there can be little question that many of these hymns date to the pre-Ephesian period (as, for instance, Proclus demonstrates), and the absence of the issues that gave rise to the Fourth Council, with only this one exception, seems to indicate their composition before the events of this divisive council. Accordingly, we have in the Marian hymns of the early *Jerusalem Chantbook* a substantial collection of hymns to the Virgin that is at least as old as the Akathist hymn and is quite possibly even earlier.

Yet the *Jerusalem Chantbook* has still more to offer scholars of early Marian piety than this important collection of hymns to the Virgin. Indeed, evidence of Mary's veneration is littered across its hymns for the Sunday services. In addition to these special "Praises of the Theotokos," the regular Sunday hymns of the *Chantbook* routinely feature acclamations of the Virgin and invocations of her intercessory powers.[79] This is true for all of the manuscripts, including those believed to reflect the very earliest recensions of the *Chantbook*. Praises of the Theotokos and pleas for her intercession are so diffuse and interwoven with the rest of the hymnography that they clearly form an integral part of this ancient collection of hymns rather than a more recent addition. For example, in the first hymn of the first mode for matins the congregation sings:

> She who gave birth to God, by word and without seed,
> Let us sing to her, the Virgin Mary,
> Who intercedes for the salvation of our souls.[80]

Similar pleas for Mary's intercessions abound throughout these Sunday hymns, which Renoux persuasively dates as a whole to the late fourth and early fifth centuries. The absence of any influence from the debates of the Fourth Council appears to confirm their composition before the middle of the fifth century, as does the appearance of many of the same hymns in early Armenian hymnography, which drew heavily from the Jerusalemite tradition as practised at the beginning of the fifth century.[81]

Thus, the hymns of the *Jerusalem Georgian Chantbook* reveal a remarkably advanced level of devotion to the Virgin already at the heart of the Sunday liturgy much earlier than most scholars would have thought to expect. The hymns focus especially on praising Mary's purity and holiness and her Divine Maternity, themes that one might anticipate from such an early source. Nevertheless, alongside of these acclamations are also frequent pleas for Mary's intercessions with her son, an indication that the cult of the Virgin had already begun to take root within the Jerusalem church.[82] There is, moreover, as Renoux observes, nothing in the *Chantbook*'s hymns that betrays any influence from the early traditions of Mary's Dormition and Assumption, which first began to circulate within the discursive arenas dominated by the bishops and church fathers only toward the end of the fifth century. The titles given to the Virgin in these hymns are also, according to Renoux, "sober and classical," a quality that he contrasts with the "luxuriance of appellations and images" for Mary in the special collection of "Praises of the Holy Theotokos."[83] Since these early fifth-century "Praises of the Holy Theotokos" seem to be slightly later than the rest of the Sunday hymns, one is tempted to conclude that the comparative restraint of the Sunday hymns is a sign of relative antiquity. Yet even these earlier hymns envision Mary's pleas as having an unequaled ability to influence her son, a sign that already by this time veneration of the Virgin was beginning to assume the unique position within Christian devotion to the saints that it would soon attain.

The Sunday hymns of the early *Jerusalem Chantbook* thus offer impressive evidence that the cult of the Virgin had established itself at the heart of Jerusalem's Sunday liturgies in advance of the Council of Ephesus. For many scholars this finding may come as a bit of a surprise, no less so because the earliest and most compelling evidence for public veneration of the Virgin Mary comes from Jerusalem, and not from Constantinople or Egypt, as some scholars have occasionally suggested. Yet the emergence of congregational devotion to Mary in late fourth and early fifth-century Jerusalem is actually not so unexpected. Undoubtedly, the Marian veneration embedded in the *Chantbook*'s hymns is closely related to Jerusalem's early commemoration of the Virgin in the 15 August feast of the Memory of Mary. So, while scholarship on early Marian piety has often tended to look elsewhere for the first shoots of devotion to Mary, it seems that late ancient Jerusalem stood at the forefront of the emerging cult of the Virgin, as witnessed especially by its early liturgies and shrines. And among the most important witnesses to this incipient veneration of Mary now stands the ancient *Jerusalem Georgian Chantbook*. Moreover, these hymns also add significant weight to the possibility that the *lex orandi* of ancient Christianity, that is, its practice of prayer and devotion, was possibly a bit ahead of its *lex credendi*, that is, its doctrinal formulations, at least with respect to honoring and venerating the Virgin.[84] Of course, Marian piety is but one of many topics that remain to be explored across the vast richness of the *Chantbook*'s hymns, and here we have merely scratched the surface even of this particular theme. Nevertheless, the Jerusalem *Chantbook* provides crucial evidence for organized Marian devotion at a time when sources for such practice are scarce, and these hymnic invocations of the Virgin and her intercessory powers unquestionably invite further exploration in order to determine the full value of their witness to early Marian veneration.

Material Culture and the Early Cult of the Virgin

Not surprisingly, evidence from material culture for early devotion to the Virgin is difficult to come by during the period that concerns us. This is in part because distinctively Christian art and architecture is almost non-existent prior to the third century, and the practices of pilgrimage and the cult of the saints did not become widespread until the fourth century. Only after the Constantinian revolution do we begin to find Christian artifacts relevant to the veneration of saints in any meaningful quantities.[85] Nevertheless, one of the great virtues of Stephen Davis's book on *The Cult of St. Thecla* is its frequent attention to evidence from material culture for devotion to this early Christian apostle. Since some scholars have identified the cult of Thecla as a kind of milestone against which to measure the allegedly late emergence of cult of the Virgin, we will want to consider the comparable evidence from early Christian art and archaeology indicating Mary's veneration, beyond what has already been covered with regard to Mary's early shrines in Jerusalem. Although such evidence is rather scant, as we will see, once again Mary can seemingly hold her own against Thecla.

When one thinks of early Christian art, and more specifically of the earliest representations of the Virgin, there is a good chance that thoughts turn immediately to the Roman catacombs. These ancient burial places beneath the city of Rome and its environs are one of the richest repositories of Christian art from the first few centuries. Among the various images that adorn many of these crypts are several that have been identified as representations of the Virgin dating to the second or third century.[86] Unfortunately, however, as is often the case with such depictions, the figures and scenes portrayed are frequently open to a wide range of interpretations. Moreover, in the case of the alleged representations of the Virgin Mary, there is also the issue that most of these identifications were first established by Roman Catholic priests during previous centuries, and the catacombs remain under the control of the papacy to this day. Still, there is perhaps some basis for finding in these ancient frescoes evidence of early Marian devotion.

The most famous of these images is found in the catacombs of Priscilla, where a fresco dated to the third century portrays a woman with a child on her lap. Although the image itself is not labeled, traditionally this portrait has been interpreted as the earliest representation of the Virgin with child. A similar image is found in the catacombs of Agnes, where again a woman and her child have been identified with Mary and Christ. There are also other images believed to portray Mary at the Annunciation and the Adoration of the Magi. Yet, in each case, the identifications of these scenes with specific episodes from the New Testament and with Mary are uncertain, and other interpretations are possible. It was not uncommon, for instance, to find representations of a mother and child in Roman funerary contexts, and so it could be that these images from the catacombs were originally intended to represent those individuals who had been buried there.[87] Nevertheless, one should also note the very persuasive arguments that Michael Peppard has recently raised for identifying the woman at the well from the third-century Dura-Europos house church with Mary at the Annunciation.[88] To be sure, some uncertainty remains regarding this woman's identity as well, but even if these ancient images were not originally intended to represent the Virgin Mary, many early Christian viewers likely would have understood them as such. As Maxwell Johnson observes in this regard, "whatever hermeneutical key might have been available to interpret such iconographic depictions of a 'Christian woman with her child' would have long been displaced by the interpretive lens or key provided by the Virgin and Child. And, given the overall context that appears to have been developing with regard to Marian symbols and theology, it would be surprising if, at least, the possibly third-century St. Priscilla image did not come quickly to be interpreted as the prophet Balaam or Isaiah pointing to the star of Jacob and the woman with her child as the Virgin and Christ Child."[89] However these images may have originally been intended, one can readily imagine how the early Christians might soon have invested them with very different meanings related to Mary and her son.

Also from the Roman catacombs are several representations of the Virgin Mary on gold glass dating to the later fourth century, and in this case there can be little question who is portrayed: Mary is specifically named on the objects themselves. These five small glass tokens depict Mary in the *orans* position, that is, with arms raised in prayer, either alone or in the company of Saint Agnes or Peter and Paul. Hermann Vopel dates them on the basis of their style to before the completion of the mosaics portraying Mary in the church of Santa Maria Maggiore at Rome, which was almost complete when the Council of Ephesus convened in 431.[90] The exact purpose of these objects unfortunately is not entirely known, but clearly they seem connected with the rising belief in Mary's powers of intercession. As Davis observes of other similar images, "the *orans* comes to symbolize the prayer and intercession of the deceased (or more specifically, the martyr) on behalf of the faithful viewer."[91] Therefore these small medallions afford yet another sort of evidence for the cult of the Virgin and belief in the power of her intercessions during this period, presumably coming from within a more private devotional context.

A tombstone from Gaul dated to sometime between the fourth and sixth centuries also seems to show Mary as an *orans*. It depicts a woman in the *orans* position with the inscription MARIA VIRGO MINESTER DE TEMPULO GEROSALE, that is, "the virgin Mary, servant of the Jerusalem Temple." Some interpreters have suggested that this portrays the Virgin Mary, and that the reference to the Jerusalem Temple reflects the tradition of her childhood in the Temple as related by the *Protevangelium of James*. N. P. Kondakov suggests instead that Mary is the woman buried in the tomb, who must have served as a deaconess or in some other ministerial function. This interpretation follows Kondakov's hypothesis that these early *orans* figures should be associated with the orders of widows and virgins in the third and fourth centuries.[92] Nevertheless, it seems difficult to date this tomb so early, and moreover, the connection to the Jerusalem Temple seems a bit strange if we understand this woman as a deaconess from Gaul. On the whole, it seems most likely that the tombstone portrays the Virgin Mary, but its date is too uncertain at present to make it of much use for our purposes. Another possibly early portrait of Mary is found in south-central Egypt, where she appears again as an *orans* at the early Christian cemetery at el-Bagawat near the Kharga oasis. In the Chapel of Peace at this site, one finds a fresco that Gerard Wellen dated, along with the building itself, to the fourth or fifth century. More recent scholarship, however, tends to favor a date in the fifth or sixth century for this structure, which places this image most likely outside the scope of our analysis.[93]

At the same time, recent publications have added to our inventory of early Marian representations. For instance, Arne Effenberger identifies several new objects in his study of Mary's depiction as a mediator and intercessor in late ancient art, including: 1) scenes from the life of Mary on a fourth-century sarcophagus from Rome; 2) Mary with child – perhaps nursing – on a sarcophagus from around 400 found in Constantinople; 3) a crater from around 380–390, also from Constantinople, that depicts the Virgin nursing her son; 4) a silk tunic from around the year 400 with a cycle of scenes from the life of the Virgin Mary in the Abegg Stiftung; and 5) a fifth-century (without greater precision) fresco from the necropolis of Antinoë, where the deceased, a certain Theodosia, stands in the orans position between the Virgin Mary and St. Kollouthos.[94] To this we should also add Ally Kateusz's recent analysis of the early depictions of the "Ascension," in which she persuasively argues that these images originally portrayed the Assumption (*analēpsis*) of Mary but only later came to be identified as representations of the Ascension (*analēpsis*) of Christ.[95] For our purposes the most significant part of this study – and also one of the most persuasive – is its clarification of two panels from the carved wooden doors of Santa Sabina in Rome, which were carved sometime between 422 and 440 and thus roughly contemporary with the Council of Ephesus. One panel clearly depicts the Ascension of Christ into the clouds, with no depiction of the Virgin. Yet on the same door is a panel in which Mary stands *orante* while seeming to receive a crown with Christ in the heavens above her – a scene very much like the traditional iconography of the Ascension of Christ. Yet art historians have long agreed that this cannot be the Ascension of Christ, since it is clearly represented in a very different fashion elsewhere on the door. Instead, the Princeton Index of Christian Art only vaguely identifies this image as "*Madonna advocata*," that is Mary the intercessor, which, if correct, would be interesting in its own right. Nevertheless, Kateusz is no doubt correct that instead we find here a very early representation of the Virgin's Assumption, again, roughly contemporary with the Third Council.[96]

Turning to a different kind of material evidence, two interesting papyri from the third or fourth century, in addition to the *Sub tuum praesidium* papyrus, seem to indicate early devotion to the Virgin Mary. One of these is an amulet text that invokes a blessing in Mary's name: "[in the most blessed name] of the holy Theotokos and ever-virgin Mary and the holy Longinus, the centurion." Although this fragmentary prayer does not explicitly seek Mary's intercessions in its present state, it seems clear that it envisions a mediatory role for the Virgin Mary.[97] The second papyrus is a Latin hymn to the Virgin, also probably from Egypt, which draws heavily on the *Protevangelium* as well as the canonical gospels. Its focus, however, is squarely on Mary's Divine Maternity, and there is no indication of any belief in her intercessory powers. Even so, this extensive hymn from the third or fourth century shows evidence of a sustained interest in Mary as a figure in her own right, continuing the second-century traditions of the *Protevangelium*.[98]

In the fifth century, material evidence of devotion to the Virgin becomes slightly more plentiful but still is relatively limited. There are, for instance, a number of Egyptian amulets from the fifth century that seek the Virgin's intercessions. There is also the recently published *Gospel of the Lots of Mary, the Mother of the Lord Jesus Christ*, a handbook for divination preserved by a Coptic manuscript from the fifth or sixth century, as well as several papyrus fragments. The text itself derives from an earlier Greek original, which perhaps was composed prior to the Council of Ephesus[99] Likewise, we know of a fifth-century church at Oxyrhynchus dedicated to the Virgin, adding to the churches in Jerusalem and Rome that we have already mentioned, as well as the church of the Virgin at Ephesus in which the Ecumenical Council itself met in 431.[100] The relic of the Virgin's robe at the Church of St. Mary at Blachernae in Constantinople dates to the later fifth century, and the church itself was probably built under the empress Pulcheria's patronage during the middle of the fifth century.[101] The earliest evidence for Marian devotion in pilgrimage art comes only in the sixth century, at which time we find a number of ampullae (small flasks), pilgrimage tokens, and lamps from Palestine that invoke the Virgin's blessings. One of these tokens, however, appears to date to the fifth century, and it asks for "a blessing of the Theotokos of the rock," seemingly a reference to the church of the Kathisma, one would imagine.[102] But on the whole, this later material evidence does not add much to our effort to understand the emergence of Marian devotion prior to Ephesus.

By comparison, material evidence for devotion to Thecla in the fourth and early fifth century is not particularly better. In his study of her early cult, Davis identifies from this period a Coptic curtain fragment from the fourth or fifth century; a fourth-century comb bearing her image, also from Egypt; a wall painting from the fourth century at el-Bagawat; a fourth or fifth-century limestone relief from Oxyrhynchus; and fourth or fifth-century fragments of the *Acts of Paul and Thecla* from the Fayyum oasis.[103] Nevertheless, we also have extensive papyrus fragments of the *Protevangelium* from fourth-century

Egypt in the Bodmer papyrus, one should note. On the whole, then, the early material evidence for Thecla devotion—a comb and wall painting from the fourth century, and a tapestry and relief from the fourth or fifth—does not surpass the comparable evidence for devotion to Mary. If one were to include the disputed representations of the catacombs, then Thecla would not come close. Yet even without these portraits, the fourth-century gold glass from Rome, the *Sub tuum praesidium* papyrus (and the Bodmer Papyrus), the amulet and hymn from the third or fourth century, and now the series of early objects identified by Effenberg—not to mention the fifth-century pilgrimage token and Mary's possible depiction on a tombstone—show evidence of Marian devotion in the material record that can easily match that for Thecla.

In the fifth and sixth centuries, Davis is able to identify more abundant evidence of Thecla devotion, including a number of pilgrimage flasks from Egypt, another fifth or sixth-century wall painting from el-Bagawat, a few Egyptian churches dedicated to Thecla, and an oil lamp.[104] But at this point material evidence for devotion to the Virgin also becomes much more plentiful and easily is comparable if not in fact superior to that for devotion to Thecla. Davis also looks for namesakes of Thecla found in documentary papyri and inscriptions from Egypt as evidence of devotion to Thecla. In all, he finds four such namesakes from the fourth century and seven from the fifth, although he was admittedly looking only in certain regions.[105] By comparison, however, a quick search of the main online database of published papyri yields fifteen examples of individuals named Mary from between 300 and 450, ten of which date to before 400.[106] In most cases these individuals appear to be Christian, and Roger Bagnall, in his study of Egypt's Christianization based on naming practices, identifies Mary as a specifically Christian name in the Egyptian countryside at this time.[107]

Accordingly, with respect to material culture as in the other relevant areas, the early cult of the Virgin fares very well in comparison with the early cult of St. Thecla, and thus it no longer seems possible to imagine that Mary's cult was somehow lagging significantly behind Thecla's. We have seen evidence of belief in the power of Mary's intercessions already in the third century, and accounts of her many miracles in a fourth-century Dormition narrative. This same fourth-century Dormition narrative also enjoins on its audience three annual feasts in Mary's honor, which are commemorated with offerings of bread. To my knowledge no other saint, Thecla included, could boast of such an annual liturgical program in this era. By the later fourth and early fifth centuries Christians in Jerusalem had begun to seek Mary's intercessions during their regular Sunday worship, something which, to my knowledge, is entirely unknown for Thecla (or any other saint, for that matter). And by the late fourth and early fifth centuries we have annual liturgical feasts in Mary's honor in Alexandria, Jerusalem, and Constantinople. Antioch's absence from this list perhaps has something to do with the disputes about Mary that would soon come to a head in the Third Council. It is true that the first indisputable evidence of a Marian shrine comes several decades after Egeria's visit to Thecla's Seleucia shrine. Nevertheless, despite the absence of any mention of a feast or shrine of Mary in Egeria's account, there is good reason to suspect that both are probably closer in date to Egeria's travels than the current state of our sources would suggest. Indeed, Athanasius's likely witness to such a feast in Egypt would be nearly contemporary with Egeria's visit. Now also, in regard to material culture, we see that the early evidence for devotion to Thecla is only marginally better at best, and the comparable evidence for early Marian devotion is in no way meaningfully deficient. Indeed, the attestations of Marian cult in this arena once again seem to confirm that her veneration was developing at a pace at least comparable to that of other non-martyr saints in this era, including St. Thecla.

Conclusions

While the first three Christian centuries are certainly not devoid of interest in the mother of Jesus, both devotional and otherwise, clearly it is in the fourth century that she begins to come into her own. While the *Protevangelium*'s reverence for Mary's sacred purity is certainly a sign of intense interest in her person and a harbinger of things to come, such sentiments remain seemingly isolated and exceptional in their time. Otherwise, in the second and third centuries Mary seems to have been held in esteem especially among Christian groups that prized esoteric knowledge as the way to salvation, and saw in Mary a revered and learned teacher of these mysteries. Also in the third century we see the first evidence of belief in the power of Mary's intercessions, some of it coming from within such an esoteric Christian milieu. But in the fourth century we find the proto-orthodox church fathers taking a significant interest in Mary for the first time. Drawing on the language of devotion, they embraced her status as Theotokos with a newfound enthusiasm. Such devotion to Mary's Divine Maternity would prove to be useful as Athanasius and his allies sought to combat the influence of other Christians who saw Christ as something less than "true God of true God." Likewise, with the rise of the ascetic movement, Mary was quickly identified as the exemplar of the virginal life, offering an ideologically conservative role model for female virginity. And also, the fathers begin to show familiarity with different aspects of Marian cult in this era, including the power of the Virgin's intercessions especially.

With the *Six Books Dormition Apocryphon* we encounter for the first time the full range of Marian cult. This mid-fourth-century text indicates the observance of three annual feasts in Mary's honor, belief in the power of Mary's intercessions, miracles ascribed to her power, and even Marian apparitions. Not long thereafter, Athanasius seems to refer on two occasions to a feast of the Memory of Mary that was observed in Alexandria in the later fourth century, and by the early fifth we know of a similar feast in Constantinople and Jerusalem and have even discovered the remains of the church where the latter was first observed. The later fourth century also saw Mary and her intercessions enter into the public worship of Jerusalem, in the hymns that were sung every Sunday during ordinary time. One wonders if this practice may in fact have been more widespread at this time, given the near invisibility of early Christian worship otherwise during the fourth century. If only we had comparable sources from Alexandria, Constantinople, or Rome, perhaps we would find similar invocations of Mary in liturgy. Also at this time we begin to find evidence of Marian cult in the material record, perhaps in the paintings of the Roman catacombs, but certainly in the gold glass taken from these catacombs as well as a few other bits and pieces. All in all, it is a pretty impressive record, one that compares well with devotion to Thecla or most other non-martyr saints. By the second half of the fourth century, then, the cult of the Virgin had begun, and we do not have to wait until the Council of Ephesus, let alone the sixth or seventh century, in order to find evidence of Mary's veneration, her intercessions, her miracles, feasts in her honor, and prayer to her in the Sunday liturgies. All of this is on display in the fourth century if we simply know where to look. Thus, Mary's cult does not develop significantly later than Thecla's, but to the contrary, the evidence for Mary's veneration in the fourth century is at least as good as that for Thecla and in fact is seemingly much better.

CHAPTER SIX

The Scepter of Orthodoxy: The Cult of the Virgin and the Council of Ephesus

THE COUNCIL OF EPHESUS in 431 was unquestionably a major turning point in the history of Marian piety. Things were not the same afterward as they had been before. While it is certainly a mistake to imagine that the events of this council somehow were generative of the cult of the Virgin, there can be no denying that they transformed Marian piety in significant ways. What is perhaps less obvious, however, is the extent to which the cult of the Virgin seems to have played a pivotal role in the controversies leading up to the council itself as well as its outcome. Toward the end of the twentieth century, a number of important studies drew new attention to the impact that an already vibrant Marian piety seems to have had in galvanizing the resistance to Nestorius in Constantinople and elsewhere. These studies also frequently identify the Empress Pulcheria, sister of Emperor Theodosius II, as an instrumental figure who was particularly responsible for deploying popular devotion to Mary as a means to accomplish Nestorius's downfall, in part for personal reasons.[1] More recently, however, Pulcheria's direct involvement in all of this has come into serious question, and it would seem that there are in fact some significant problems with aspects of this narrative of Pulcheria's conflict with Nestorius, which derives partly from later and possibly tendentious sources.[2] Nevertheless, there is some concern that in these efforts to remove Pulcheria from the scene we may also be in jeopardy of losing sight of the significant impact that both she and Marian piety appear to have had in fomenting opposition to Nestorius and even on the outcome of the Council of Ephesus itself. Therefore, in this last chapter we will present the controversies of the Third Council in terms that underscore the role that the cult of the Virgin and also Pulcheria played in bringing about Nestorius's demise.[3]

As noted in the previous chapter, the cult of the Virgin had become established in many of the major urban centers of the eastern Roman Empire already in advance of the controversy over Nestorius and the Third Council. Constantinople in particular had begun to observe an annual Feast of the Virgin on 26 December sometime before 425, and so the reaction to Nestorius's refusal to call Mary the Theotokos both in the imperial capital and elsewhere must be interpreted against the backdrop of existing Marian veneration.[4] Of course, if one reconstructs this debate primarily by reading the theological writings of those church fathers who stood at its center, as has often been done, it is possible to miss the role that popular devotion to the Virgin Mary seems to have played in the controversy. As a result, there is no shortage of accounts that describe the events of the Council of Ephesus in terms that are strictly theological and Christological.[5] Mary does not come into the picture much at all from such a perspective, except insofar as the theological principle of her Divine Maternity impacted the different understandings of the relation between the divine and human in her son. Mary and her veneration were otherwise not part of the equation, and any interest in Mary beyond this theological concern should be viewed as a by-product of the council and its debates rather than a catalyst. In such a reading it appears almost as if the church fathers inadvertently stumbled into a whole set of issues regarding Mary's significance for Christian faith and practice that they had not previously recognized. The result was a sudden explosion of Marian devotion, as the Christians of the mid-fifth century suddenly discovered this amazing thing that they had previously been missing. Mary, who had long stood at the margins of early Christian discourse, suddenly became all the rage among the Christians of the eastern Mediterranean.

Our perspective on the Third Council changes dramatically once we recognize that Marian piety had already begun to flourish in Constantinople and elsewhere before Nestorius refused to allow Mary the honor of being called Theotokos. Perhaps it is true that Nestorius merely wished to make an important Christological point in denying Mary this title. Yet, once he diminished the holy mother of Christ in this way by lowering her status, one can readily imagine how this would inflame Christians who were devoted to the Virgin and had come to believe that the power of her petitions with her son could release them from punishment for their sins and secure their salvation. If Mary was not in fact God's own mother, then this would undermine the effectiveness of her intercessions. If she had merely given birth and been a mother to the human part of Christ, then what gave her the capacity to stand before God and ask God to yield and relinquish the right to punish the wicked for their sins? It was primarily because she had given birth to God the Word, the Son of God, that she could boldly entreat God to show mercy in a way that no other being could. Therefore, if Mary was not the Theotokos, the one who gave birth to God, but instead only gave birth to Jesus' humanity, then the logic of Mary's uniquely powerful intercessions would be significantly undermined. Accordingly, one can understand how those who had faith in Mary as their most trusted advocate before the Lord would view Nestorius's rejection of the title

Theotokos as a grave theological error that denied Mary the very quality that made her petitions so effective, thus shattering their hopes in her ability to deliver them from divine judgment.

The Controversy over Nestorius

Nestorius came to Constantinople and was consecrated as its new bishop in April 428. With the death of his predecessor Sisinnius in 427, the factions in Constantinople were deadlocked between two rival candidates, Proclus and Philip of Side, and so the emperor called in Nestorius from Antioch, where he was admired as a gifted orator and austere ascetic. When Nestorius arrived he was already unwelcome in the eyes of many who had backed the two local candidates, and, of course, in the eyes of the two candidates themselves. It would not take long before Nestorius found himself in open conflict with Proclus, particularly over the question of whether it was correct to call Mary the Theotokos. The controversy began when a close associate of Nestorius, one Anastasius, a priest who had come with him from Syria, preached a sermon late in 428 in which he said, "Let no one call Mary Theotokos. For Mary was human and it is impossible that God should be born of a human." His words sparked immediate outrage among many of the clergy and all of the laity (*laikous pantas*).[6] In response, Nestorius himself delivered several public discourses in which he similarly rejected the use of the title Theotokos for the Virgin Mary. But if he hoped that this might perhaps diffuse the uproar that Anastasius had created, his actions only served to escalate the controversy, as the clergy in Constantinople soon divided into factions and the dispute quickly spread throughout the eastern Mediterranean. Indeed, within several months the bishop of Alexandria, Cyril, had entered the conflict and soon emerged as Nestorius's main theological opponent.

In Constantinople, however, it was Proclus who responded for the other side, delivering his famous *First Homily on the Theotokos*. The occasion was the Feast of the Virgin in 430, and none other than Nestorius himself was in the audience. Proclus directly attacked the position of Nestorius and those like him who would deny Mary the honor of being named Theotokos, and he answered them with an extensive and eloquent discourse offering what he calls "a clear proof" that Mary is Theotokos.[7] The message was apparently well received, so that the crowd rose up with enthusiastic applause. Nestorius, however, took no time in giving his rebuttal, and he spontaneously delivered a sermon of his own to the congregation. While he initially praised the audience for showing such respect for the Virgin Mary in their response, he quickly warned them not to honor Mary too much, since excessive veneration of the Virgin comes at the expense of giving proper worship to God. It makes for an interesting beginning, since Nestorius himself seems to highlight the issue of Marian piety as being particularly relevant to those in the assembly. The bulk of this homily, however, consists of a direct response to Proclus's teaching, followed by a concluding defense of his own theological position.[8] We do not know how Nestorius's homily was received, but one would imagine that it may not have gone over as well as Proclus's initial oration. In any case, the battle lines had been clearly drawn, and the confrontation would continue to escalate until the Council of Ephesus eventually decided against Nestorius and in favor of the Theotokos.

The fact that Nestorius began his response to Proclus's homily by addressing the issue of Marian veneration is surely telling. His approach seems to indicate that devotion to Mary, and not just Christology, was from the very start already a vital part of the debates about Mary's status as Theotokos. For many in the audience—especially those who were not particularly attuned to the nuances of Christological debate—the issue of Marian devotion was likely paramount. Yet there is also further evidence to suggest that Marian piety was indeed a central element of this larger debate, particularly for those who opposed Nestorius. As W. H. C. Frend was seemingly the first to notice, popular devotion to Mary as the Theotokos appears to have been instrumental in turning the tide of popular opinion against Nestorius and his supporters.[9] To be sure, if one were to focus only on the theological exchanges of the church fathers who were involved in these disputes (including in this instance Nestorius), one might overlook this important aspect of the controversy, as much previous scholarship has done. It certainly is no surprise to find that the fathers were by and large themselves engaged with a particular set of abstruse theological questions. They were trying to persuade one another according to the terms that their classical education had taught them to value the most: philosophy, logic, and rhetoric. But at the same time there was a rather different contest taking place on a different playing field regarding devotion to the Virgin, and it would seem that this conversation was no less important in determining the outcome of this dispute.

Pulcheria vs. Nestorius

Despite the missteps of some previous scholarship on this topic, one simply cannot deny that there is a significant body of evidence indicating the empress Pulcheria's direct involvement in the opposition to Nestorius.[10] While it may be problematic to attribute his downfall especially to her actions, there can be little question that she was allied against Nestorius with her spiritual mentor Proclus. Moreover, in the portrait of Pulcheria that emerges from these sources, her objections to Nestorius appear to center not on his Christology but rather on matters related to Marian piety and may have been driven by personal conflicts as well. It is true that some of the sources presenting Pulcheria in this role are relatively late and not always completely reliable, as others have now noted. Nevertheless, some of the relevant witnesses are of particularly high quality, and after sifting through them all carefully, it is possible to reconstruct a credible approximation of Pulcheria's position in these controversies as an opponent of Nestorius.

One of the most problematic documents relevant to this question is the *Letter to Cosmas*, a letter supposedly written sometime shortly after Nestorius's downfall by several of his closest supporters. Both Ken Holum and Vasiliki Limberis place this letter squarely at the center of their studies of Pulcheria, focusing their attention on its well-known story of a confrontation between Pulcheria and Nestorius when she attempted to enter the sanctuary to receive the Eucharist.

At the great feast of Easter the Emperor used to receive communion in the Holy of Holies. Pulcheria wanted to do the same: she won over Sisinnius [of Constantinople, d. 427], and began to receive communion in the Holy of Holies together with the Emperor. Nestorius did not allow this. On one occasion when she was making her way as usual to the Holy of Holies, he saw her and asked what this meant. Peter the archdeacon explained the matter to him. Nestorius ran, met her at the entrance to the Holy of Holies, stopped her, and would not let her enter. The Empress took offence and said to him, "Let me enter according to my custom." But he said, "This place is reserved for priests." She said to him, "Why? Have I not given birth to God?" He replied, "You have given birth to Satan!" and chased her from the entrance to the Holy of Holies. She left in a rage, and went and reported the incident to the Emperor, her brother Theodosius II. "On your life, my sister," he replied, "and by the crown that is on your head,

211

I will not rest until I have taken vengeance on him." From that day forth Nestorius enjoyed no credit with the Emperor.[11]

This certainly makes for a dramatic and exciting story, but unfortunately its veracity is somewhat questionable. In the first place, the letter itself is known only from a single nineteenth-century manuscript, and while this in and of itself does not necessarily mean that its report is unreliable, it does invite a certain measure of suspicion. Richard Price is seemingly a bit too quick to dismiss the entire *Letter* completely, particularly when other specialists on this topic are convinced that much of the text likely dates from sometime around 436. But these same specialists have also expressed some skepticism regarding specific parts of the letter, including particularly the initial section in which this story of Pulcheria and Nestorius appears.[12] Price is certainly correct that parts of this account simply cannot be true: for instance, if the emperor had actually turned against Nestorius at this point, then presumably there would have been no future controversy regarding the Theotokos.[13] It is a fairly sketchy tale from a rather recent manuscript, and, accordingly, it makes for a poor foundation on which to reconstruct Pulcheria's opposition to Nestorius. A more persuasive account of her role in the controversy needs a more solid basis.

This first section of the *Letter to Cosmas* also relates that Nestorius discontinued Sisinnius's practice of inviting Pulcheria and her retinue to dinner at the episcopal palace after the Sunday service—a minor snub that she surely would have soon gotten over, particularly if she was not especially fond of Nestorius. More serious are its reports that Nestorius defaced a portrait of Pulcheria that had been placed above the altar of the Great Church, Hagia Sophia, and he removed her robe from the altar, where it had previously been in use as the altar cloth during the Eucharist.[14] The first point also is hardly to be believed, since as Price observes, defacing a portrait of the empress would have amounted to treason and would have been punishable accordingly.[15] Nevertheless, the story of both her portrait and her robe are also reported in a more reliable and earlier source, albeit in slightly different fashion. A late sixth-century East Syrian (i.e., "Nestorian") author named Barhadbeshabba 'Arbaya writes in his *Ecclesiastical History* that Pulcheria sought to have Nestorius hang her portrait in the altar and also asked that he use her garment as an altar cloth, but he refused: a much more believable story. According to Barhadbeshabba, he instead had her image painted elsewhere, only later on to have it blackened when he learned that she had been married seven times. Yet once again, it seems unlikely that he actually would have been able to get away with such an outrageous act.[16]

Nevertheless, the decisive passage in this matter comes from Nestorius himself, who writes the following of Pulcheria in his *Bazaar of Heracleides*, a text written after he had gone into exile:

You have further with you against me a contentious woman, a princess, a young maiden, a virgin, who fought against me because I was not willing to be persuaded by her demand that I should compare a woman corrupted of men to the bride of Christ. This I have done because I had pity on her soul and that I might not be the chief celebrant of the sacrifice among those whom she had unrighteously chosen. Of her I have spoken only to mention [her], for she was my friend; and therefore I keep silence about and hide everything else about her own little self, seeing that [she was but] a young maiden; and for that reason she fought against me. And here she has prevailed over my might but not before the tribunal of Christ where all [will be] laid bare and revealed before the eyes of him in whose presence our judgement and theirs will come in the days that have been appointed by him.[17]

There is little question who this contentious princess is, and scholars agree that Nestorius is writing here about Pulcheria. According to Nestorius himself, then, Pulcheria "fought against" him and likewise "prevailed over" him. This would seem to settle the matter decisively: Nestorius tells us that Pulcheria schemed against him and played a decisive role in his downfall. This does not mean that the scene at the altar actually took place, or even that Pulcheria once asked to have her portrait and garment placed within the sanctuary, to be sure. Yet before we discard the story of the Easter altercation altogether, it is worth noting that Nestorius refers here to his disagreement with Pulcheria in the context of a Eucharistic liturgy ("the chief celebrant of the sacrifice") where she presented herself as "the bride of Christ" ("Have I not given birth to God?"). In any case, so long as the *Bazaar of Heracleides* is considered an authentic work of Nestorius, it seems impossible to avoid the conclusion that Pulcheria actively opposed him and was instrumental in his defeat. This evidence, one should note, also gives other reports of her antagonism toward him more credibility. Nestorius also confirms that Pulcheria had styled herself as a consecrated virgin, even if, according to him, in truth she was not. It is admittedly odd, however, that Nestorius describes Pulcheria here as having been his "friend": I am not at all sure what to make of this, given what else he has to say about her. Perhaps they had once briefly been friends before he openly preached against calling Mary Theotokos.

In view of the words then from Nestorius's own pen, I think that Richard Price pushes too far in the other direction in his critique of Holum and Limberis and their portraits of Pulcheria. While in some respects his correction is needed, at the same time it is a bit of an overcorrection. Indeed, even Price must ultimately yield in some fashion to Nestorius's own testimony of Pulcheria's hostility and contribution to his demise. In order to explain this account he invents a pretext for Nestorius's words. This statement, he maintains, "must surely be read as the elderly Nestorius a decade or more later playing his part in the development of the Pulcheria legend," since he could not "forgive Pulcheria for stabbing him in the back after the Council of Ephesus."[18] It is frankly hard to accept the notion that Nestorius is here just "playing his part" almost passively in the creation of a legend of Pulcheria's opposition to him, which, although supposedly false, seemingly was well in place soon after the events of Ephesus.[19] Indeed, such an interpretation is a bit too convenient to be very persuasive. Nonetheless, Price further maintains "that weight of the evidence continues to be that [Pulcheria] had supported [Nestorius] up to that date [i.e., the Council of Ephesus]." Yet the evidence for this assessment is insufficient, at least as Price presents it, and does not warrant such a conclusion.

Price cites two main sources, the first of which is a homily preached by Nestorius in December of 430, in which he "expressed his continuing confidence because 'the emperor is pious and the empresses love God.'"[20] Now Nestorius does not actually say here that he has Pulcheria's support, only that he is certain that he will prevail because he knows that the empresses are godly women. One suspects instead that this line, taken from a homily, is rhetorical in nature and not an accurate report of how Nestorius was faring at the time in his efforts to shore up support within the imperial family. And we know, in fact, from his own words that he did not actually believe Pulcheria to be a godly woman. Instead, we find here presumably an oratorical expression of confidence, aimed to encourage his supporters and perhaps to send a message to a certain empress that she should soften her opposition toward him. Indeed, one would certainly expect the bishop of Constantinople to proclaim publicly that he was confident in the support of the godly emperor and empresses, at least if he still had any hope of keeping his job. One thinks particularly here of a politician who, down in the polls, nonetheless assures his constituents that he is certain that the good people will come out on election day and do the right thing—that is, vote for him. Accordingly, I fail to see this rhetorical phrase as providing any evidence that Pulcheria was actually supporting Nestorius at this time. It does seem that the emperor supported him until the bitter end, but not so for his sister, and in any case, this brief remark can hardly provide evidence that she was in his camp.

Price also notes a letter that was sent by agents of Cyril of Alexandria to the bishop of Constantinople after the Council of Ephesus in 432 or 433 in order to shore up the opposition to Nestorius in the imperial capital. The letter mentions a number of substantial bribes that Cyril had delivered in order to win support for his cause and it mentions Pulcheria by name. We know from other sources that Pulcheria, like many others, received bribes from Cyril in order to secure her backing, so that is not in question. But Price maintains that this letter also complains of "Pulcheria's lack of zeal for the anti-Nestorian cause," despite the bribes she has accepted.[21] Yet that is not exactly what the letter says. Rather, the author, Cyril's archdeacon, laments that Pulcheria is not doing *enough* to support Cyril, which is quite a different matter.[22] In the aftermath of the Council of Ephesus, Cyril certainly could not count on imperial support as a matter of course, particularly since he had defied the will of the emperor in opposing Nestorius. The emperor continued to favor Nestorius after the council until he eventually realized that it was no longer in his best interest to do so. And when he finally did side against Nestorius, it was not because of any affection for Cyril or his views or his role in bringing about the downfall of his chosen bishop.

Cyril was in fact in something of a precarious position with the emperor following the council. The emperor was so angered with

Cyril that he actually had him arrested, although soon thereafter he was able to escape and flee to exile in Alexandria.[23] Accordingly, Cyril sent significant bribes to Pulcheria at this time in order to encourage her to pave the way for his rapprochement with the emperor and thus secure his victory over Nestorius in the aftermath of what had been a very irregular and disputed council. Undoubtedly, these are the circumstances that the letter addresses: despite the bribes, Cyril and his allies did not think Pulcheria was doing enough to smooth things over with the emperor after the council and his own arrest.[24] The fact that the author hopes that she will "*once again* devote herself to the cause of the Lord" certainly implies that she had previously been allied with Cyril's cause against Nestorius.[25] I simply don't see any angle from which this brief passage can be interpreted as indicating her support for—or even lack of opposition to—Nestorius, his ideas, and his supporters.

It seems, then, that we should not write Pulcheria out of the picture, even if we are left with a somewhat less colorful portrait of her involvement in the Nestorian controversy than we once thought. To be sure, the dramatic tale of her confrontation with Nestorius from the *Letter to Cosmas* probably should not be taken as an historical event. And comparison with Barhadbeshabba's *Ecclesiastical History* gives us good reason to suppose that the opening section of the *Letter* has embellished matters quite a bit. Nevertheless, there is solid evidence indicating that Pulcheria did indeed actively oppose Nestorius and worked to have him removed. Nestorius himself tells us as much, and other related evidence suggests that she was at odds with her brother the emperor over Nestorius and had close ties to Cyril of Alexandria. For instance, Cyril had previously written to Pulcheria at the height of the controversy, urging her support against Nestorius. When the emperor became aware of their correspondence, he rebuked Cyril for trying to foment the theological disagreements between him and his sister. Leo of Rome directly credits Pulcheria with bringing down Nestorius in a letter written to her, as does John Rufus in his early sixth-century *Plerophories*.[26] No less importantly, the evidence that has been alleged to show her support for Nestorius prior to the Council of Ephesus is not at all convincing. Therefore we should continue to count Pulcheria among the key opponents of Nestorius, and no doubt she must have played an important role in undermining his support in Constantinople.

I suspect that some readers will continue to maintain that Pulcheria's opposition is a complete fiction, invented by Nestorius and his supporters in order to portray him as the innocent victim of a scheming, wicked woman, much like the traditions about John Chrysostom and Eudoxia. Nevertheless, such hyper-skepticism does not sufficiently acknowledge the sum of the evidence in favor of her active opposition to Nestorius, in my opinion. While it would be a mistake to lay his downfall primarily at her feet, the evidence considered above converges to reveal a high probability that she was opposed to Nestorius and aligned with his theological opponents. Nestorius himself tells us as much, writing not long after the council of Ephesus, and his report is confirmed by Leo the Great's letter to Pulcheria as well as the letter from Cyril's archdeacon written shortly after the council that expresses hope that she will once again support Cyril's cause. When we add to this her close relationship with Proclus and her apparent personal devotion to the Virgin, it seems extremely unlikely that the reports of her opposition to Nestorius were invented soon after the council only as part of some sort of conspiracy to exonerate him by shifting blame to her.[27] There can be little question then, it would seem, that Pulcheria must have allied herself with Nestorius's opponents and not, as Price maintains, with Nestorius himself.

Pulcheria, Proclus, and the Cult of the Virgin

Pulcheria had been closely allied with the bishops of Constantinople from her childhood. While she was still a young girl, bishop Atticus served as her spiritual director and confessor, and he even composed a work *On Faith and Virginity* for Pulcheria and her sisters.[28] Unfortunately, this treatise has not survived, and we know of it only through Gennadius of Marseilles, who writes in the middle of the fifth century: "Atticus the bishop of Constantinople wrote a very fine book *On Faith and Virginity*, addressing it to the princesses, the daughters of Arcadius. In it Atticus attacked in advance the teaching of Nestorius."[29] The last sentence here is particularly interesting: presumably Atticus did not address the niceties of Nestorius's two-person Christology in this treatise for the young princesses, and so his anticipation of Nestorius must refer instead to the promotion of Marian piety. Moreover, in the lone homily by Atticus that survives, a homily on the Nativity, he specifically identifies Mary as a figure that virgins should strive to emulate.[30] One would imagine, then, that he must have similarly done so in the treatise that he wrote for Pulcheria and her sisters, particularly since, as we have already seen, by this time it had become relatively common to present Mary as the ideal exemplar for female virginity.[31]

There is a good chance, however, that many of Atticus's homilies were actually written by his protégé and personal secretary, Proclus, who also enjoyed a very close relationship with the imperial family and Pulcheria in particular.[32] After Atticus, he seems to have taken over as Pulcheria's spiritual advisor, and Sozomen reports that together they recovered the relics of the Forty Martyrs of Sebaste.[33] Numerous sources connect them in various other ways, but perhaps none as dramatically as Proclus's *Homily on the Resurrection*, where he takes the occasion to praise Pulcheria for her piety and virginity.

"When we see the trophies, there can be no doubt that the victory has been won. We wonder at the great soul of the empress, a brimming source of spiritual blessings for all. As long ago the Jews flung stones at Stephen, wishing to cast down the matchless preacher and first athlete of the Crucified One—so she devoted her virginity to Christ, exhausting her wealth in pious works and making her body dead to its passions, bringing the Crucified One into her bride-chamber, beautifying the heaven which we can see on earth."[34] Moreover, we know that Proclus delivered his *Homily 3: On the Incarnation* for the feast of the Virgin in 429 (the year before his more famous *Homily 1*) in the "Pulcherian quarter," a section of the city where Pulcheria had built a number of chapels and churches. In this instance it seems that Pulcheria offered her spiritual confidant refuge in one of the quarter's churches at the height of his confrontation with the city's patriarch, Nestorius.[35] Pulcheria was thus a close associate, indeed one might even say a disciple, of the man who was the main architect of Mary's cult in the imperial capital, Proclus. Therefore it is difficult to imagine that she would not have shared his devotion to Mary and enthusiasm for her veneration; to the contrary, she must have been immersed in the culture of Marian piety from a young age, particularly as a consecrated virgin herself.

There is also the matter of several Marian churches in Constantinople that Pulcheria is said to have founded. While Holum, Constas, Limberis, and other scholars take these reports more or less at face value, in recent years they have come under some increased scrutiny and skepticism. The churches in question are the three main Marian shrines of late ancient Constantinople: the churches of Blachernai, Chalkoprateia, and Hodegoi. While doubts have recently been raised, particularly by Cyril Mango, regarding Pulcheria's establishment of the first two churches, Blachernai and Chalkoprateia, in both cases the literary evidence nonetheless strongly favors their foundation by Pulcheria. This is most clear for the church of Blachernai, which Mango alleges was instead built by Verina, who followed Pulcheria as empress in 457. Yet the source that Mango cites as evidence of this does not in fact say what he claims: to the contrary, it actually describes the church of Blachernai in terms indicating that it was already in existence before Verina came to the throne! Thus this report actually appears to *support* the tradition that Pulcheria was Blachernai's foundress, as most of the relevant sources indicate and most scholars have accordingly concluded.[36] The same is also true of the church of Chalkoprateia, whose foundation is assigned to both Pulcheria and Verina by different sources. Although Mango again favors Verina (not for any particularly compelling reason), most scholars attribute this church also to Pulcheria, supposing that Pulcheria had initially founded it but that it was only completed later under Verina's patronage.[37] So we may add to Pulcheria's Marian dossier the likelihood that she was responsible for establishing the three most important Marian churches in Constantinople, an accomplishment that certainly would seem to indicate her active involvement in promoting the cult of the Virgin there.

While we might perhaps wish for more direct evidence of Pulcheria's participation in the cult of the Virgin and her personal devotion to Mary, the evidence that we have seems sufficient to establish these things. Her early instruction by Atticus suggests that in all likelihood she would have understood her consecration to virginity as an imitation of the Virgin Mary and an act of devotion to her. Likewise, Pulcheria's foundation of the three most important Marian shrines in Constantinople shows her to have been active in promoting Mary's veneration in that city. Her close association with both Atticus and Proclus since childhood indicates that she must have been steeped in Marian piety from her youth. These two devotees of the Virgin surely would have instilled in her a deep reverence and affection for the mother of Jesus. Thus we can say with a fair degree of confidence that Pulcheria was herself devoted to the Virgin Mary and actively involved in Constantinople's emergent Marian piety even before Nestorius's arrival. No doubt Nestorius's refusal to allow Mary to be called by the long-established devotional title Theotokos would have offended her reverence for Christ's mother, and this snub must have fueled her opposition to Nestorius.

Marian Devotion and Nestorius's Defeat

We are left then with the question of just how much popular devotion to Mary in Constantinople and elsewhere may have actually contributed to Nestorius's ultimate downfall. This is not a matter, however, of trying to determine whether the Nestorian controversy was *really* about either Mariology or Christology. The prevailing opinion, as already noted, has long been that these debates were truly about Christology, plain and simple, and popular devotion to the Virgin was a consequence, rather than a cause, of the controversy. Yet scholars such as Holum, Limberis, and Kate Cooper have more recently argued that Marian piety was instead an engine driving the controversy, and that its eventual outcome was largely determined by Nestorius's perceived attacks against the Virgin.[38] Surely, however, it is a mistake to insist too strongly on one or the other of these issues as *the* basis for the controversy: both played a significant role. For the educated bishops and Christian intellectuals who were involved, it seems that their primary concerns in the controversy were in fact the Christological implications of the word Theotokos rather than anything having to do with the Virgin Mary herself. And since our knowledge of these events owes itself primarily to what these church fathers have to say about them, it is rather easy to come to the conclusion that Christology, which was their main interest, fueled the controversy. Yet now that we have become aware of Marian cult's introduction to Constantinople prior to the controversy's outbreak and also of the devotional commitments of several key players, these events suddenly appear in a new light. While the controversy may have been primarily about Christology for the theologians and bishops involved, clearly Marian piety also played a decisive role in the outcome, and one would imagine that this was especially so for those less learned members of the Christian community.

Already we have seen that Atticus promoted the Virgin Mary as an ascetic model for women and also for the young empresses specifically, it would seem. Likewise, during his tenure an annual feast commemorating the Virgin Mary was added to Constantinople's liturgical calendar. But there are other signs that Marian piety was an important part of religious life in Constantinople and elsewhere at this time, and, moreover, that popular devotion to the Virgin made a significant contribution to Nestorius's downfall. Proclus's homilies, for instance, show further evidence of the inroads that Marian cult had made in Constantinople before Nestorius's arrival. Proclus's *Homily 5: On the Theotokos* also was delivered for Constantinople's feast of the Virgin, seemingly much earlier than his other two homilies for this occasion, since it aims to promote the observance of this newly established feast in Mary's honor. Proclus justifies the feast of the Virgin through an appeal to the veneration of the saints more broadly: "But even though all the commemorations of the saints are marvelous, none of them can compare with the glory of the present festival." Then, after mentioning several of the biblical patriarchs and their respective greatness, he exclaims, "But there is nothing as exalted as Mary the Theotokos. . . . Traverse all creation in reflection, O man, and try to see if there is anything equal to the Holy Virgin Theotokos. . . . Marvel at the victory of the Virgin, for him whom all creation praises in fear and trembling she alone admitted into the bridal chamber of her womb."[39] Here, then, we find early Marian veneration located within the broader context of the cult of the saints, while at the same time Proclus exalts Mary beyond all other saints and even beyond all of creation.

It is especially noteworthy that the Council of Ephesus was itself convened in a church dedicated to the Virgin Mary. While scholars have occasionally sought to link this church either with the popularity of the goddess Artemis in Ephesus or with traditions about Mary's life coming to an end there, neither of these connections seems particularly warranted.[40] This is especially so in regard to Mary's death in Ephesus, since there is no evidence for such a tradition prior to the ninth century.[41] Admittedly, Cyril does on one occasion oddly refer to Ephesus as "the place where John the Theologian and the Virgin Theotokos St. Mary are," but it is not at all clear what he means by this.[42] Perhaps there was in Ephesus already a local tradition that Mary had accompanied John to Ephesus in light of Jesus' words from the cross, but this would be the only evidence for it in this era. But this Marian church certainly shows that devotion to the Virgin and perhaps even her veneration had taken hold in Ephesus also prior to the council's commencement. It is true that some question has now been raised as to whether or not the archaeological remains that have traditionally been identified with this church can be dated to the era of the council. Nevertheless, such findings in no way raise any question about the existence of a church of Mary the Theotokos in Ephesus where the Third Council met, but only as to whether or not we have yet discovered its remains. The existence of the church itself is clearly indicated by the acts of the council, even if its ruins have still not been identified.[43] The choice of a church dedicated to the Virgin Mary as the venue for this convocation surely is telling. The setting gave Cyril and his allies a kind of home-field advantage, and as Holum writes, Pulcheria seems to have had a hand in its selection, presumably in hopes that "if the bishops gathered in Mary's church ... surely with Mary's help and guidance they would punish Nestorius."[44]

The council convened on 22 June 431, and after a one-day session, those who were present (Nestorius refused to attend and many of his supporters had not yet arrived) voted in favor of Nestorius's condemnation. When the session had concluded, Cyril and many of his allies gave a series of sermons. Cyril spoke last, and he delivered a homily that went well beyond mere Christological concerns in its exalted praises of Mary, addressing her in language of intense devotion: "Hail Mary the Theotokos, the revered treasure of the whole world, the inextinguishable lamp, the crown of virginity, the scepter of orthodoxy, the indissoluble temple, the container of the uncontainable, mother and virgin."[45] A crowd of people had gathered outside of the church, anxiously awaiting news of the bishops' decision. When they came out of the church, the crowd spontaneously erupted with joy that Nestorius had been condemned. According to Cyril's own testimony, "when [the crowd] heard that the blasphemer had been deposed, all with one voice began to praise the holy council and glorify God, because the enemy of the faith had fallen. While we were coming forth from the church, they went before us with lamps even unto our lodgings—for it was evening. And there arose much joy and illumination in the city, so that even the women went before us carrying censers."[46]

There was then popular acclaim and enthusiasm for the council's decision from the people of Ephesus. Scholars seemingly agree that the reason for this was their devotion to Mary: in the people's eyes, the council had vindicated Mary's honor and denounced her despised detractor, Nestorius.[47] Admittedly, Cyril does not explicitly mention the Virgin Mary in this report, but Marian piety seems to be the most likely explanation for the crowd's outburst and demonstration of support. Surely the citizens of Ephesus were not so overcome with joy because the council had condemned Nestorius's overly precise separation of Christ's divinity from his humanity according to two distinct personalities. One would imagine that most of the people understood very poorly the abstract and complex Christological issues at stake. But they would easily have recognized in Nestorius's refusal to call Mary the Theotokos an affront to the mother of the Lord, whom they revered as uniquely holy and prayed to for intercession. Surely it was the council's condemnation of this vile blasphemer of the Virgin Mary, rather than its vindication of Christ's unity of personality, that so elated the populace. Cyril's account of the Ephesian crowd's response offers some of the clearest evidence that popular devotion to Mary seems to have played an important role in Nestorius's downfall. One would imagine that many of the council's members were well aware that popular opinion was swelling against Nestorius, and this factor may have swayed their decision as much as any of the theological arguments that were made before the assembly.

There was apparently a similar reaction in Constantinople just two weeks later. Since the emperor had not yet accepted the council's decision, its outcome was still not decided. Theodosius II, after all, had supported Nestorius prior to the council, and the council itself had been held before many of Nestorius's strongest allies had been able to arrive. It was by no means certain that the emperor would back its determinations, particularly since its proceedings had been so irregular. So the people of Constantinople took to the streets to demonstrate in favor of the council's decision, and they gathered in the Great Church to voice their denunciations of Nestorius. Among other things they are alleged to have shouted acclamations to "the holy Virgin Mary, who overthrew Nestorius." Likewise, they cried out, "Many years to Pulcheria! Many years to the empress! Many years to Pulcheria! She is the one who strengthened the faith!"[48] Of course, there is little chance that we have here a verbatim transcript of what the mob was actually saying. Yet the crowd's praise of Mary for her defeat of Nestorius likely reflects how the controversy was understood in popular opinion. And their acclaim for Pulcheria as the "orthodox empress" who defended the faith confirms her role in bringing about Nestorius's downfall. Altogether the report provides a fascinating snapshot of the issues and players in this controversy that, while perhaps a bit embellished, pulls together many of the threads examined in this chapter.

In Ephesus and Constantinople, then, as well as in Egypt and elsewhere one would imagine, Nestorius was reviled in the popular mind not so much for the deficiencies of his Christology as for his disrespect for the Virgin Mary. Alongside the recondite debates among the church fathers over the proper understanding of unity and division in Christ, popular devotion to Mary appears to have also played a decisive role in the outcome of this controversy.[49] This is certainly no great surprise when we recall that the title Theotokos itself seems to have originally belonged to the language of devotion rather than dogmatics. Only in the Nestorian controversy did the theological implications of this title first emerge, even though it had been in common usage for well over a century. So while Marian piety certainly received a substantial boost from the council's decisions, there can be little question that the cult of the Virgin was already in place prior to the Council of Ephesus in many of the Roman Empire's major urban centers. Moreover, both Proclus and Pulcheria in particular appear to have held a deep personal devotion to the Virgin Mary, and their dedication to her veneration no doubt fueled their fierce opposition to Nestorius. And whatever one may ultimately wish to conclude about the different memories of the empress Pulcheria preserved in various sources, her active opposition to Nestorius seems fairly certain. Accordingly, we must abandon the older perspective that saw the Council of Ephesus as the primary cause and inspiration for the cult of the Virgin. The cult of the Virgin was instead already well established before the council ever met, and personal and popular commitments to Mary's veneration seem to have played a decisive role in the controversies over Nestorius's teaching and the outcome of the Council of Ephesus itself. It was then Marian piety in the form of the devotional title Theotokos that gave rise to the Third Council, rather than vice-versa.

Conclusions

Despite the Marian minimalism encountered in much previous scholarship on early Christianity, the mother of Jesus was in fact rather quick to emerge as the most significant female figure of the Christian tradition. It is true that Mary is not very prominent in the writings of the New Testament, but already in the gospels according to Luke and John she comes more into view, and these two texts in particular sowed many of the seeds that would eventually grow into the cult of the Virgin during late antiquity. By the end of the first century Mary's virginal conception had come to be widely accepted among proto-orthodox writers. Otherwise Mary remains largely out of the picture in the writings that have survived from the first century of Christianity. Only in the second half of the second century does she begin to emerge as a figure of doctrinal significance, as Justin and Irenaeus develop the idea of Mary as the New Eve, whose obedience and virginity have undone the transgressions of Eve. The earliest evidence of Marian devotion also appears during this period, in the *Protevangelium of James*. Although this text offers no evidence of Marian cult or veneration, its interest in Mary as a figure in her own right and its reverence for her sacred purity mark the beginnings of

Marian piety within early Christianity. Yet at the same time the *Protevangelium* is something of an anomaly, indeed even a mystery. There is nothing comparable to it in the early Christian literature of the century before or after. The *Protevangelium* stands alone in its era, making it all the more remarkable for its witness to Marian piety at a time when we have little else to go on: without it we would have almost no idea that Christians had begun to develop devotion to the Virgin Mary as early as the later second century.

One of the abiding riddles of the *Protevangelium* is how this seemingly isolated biography of the Virgin relates to later developments in Marian devotion, during the fourth and later centuries. The best answer would appear to lie in early Christian apocryphal literature, where Mary often figures much more prominently than she does in the writings of the church fathers from the second and third centuries. Nevertheless, while these extra-canonical writings show a sustained interest in Mary and her significance for the Christian faith, their portrayals do not always match well with the *Protevangelium*. While this unfortunately means that we cannot draw a straight line from the *Protevangelium* to the fourth-century cult of the Virgin, more positively it allows us to consider how various early Christian communities revered Mary in some surprisingly different ways. In the second and third centuries, one of the most popular alternatives to proto-orthodox Christianity came from a variety of Christian groups who believed that salvation was attained not through Christ's Incarnation, Crucifixion, and Resurrection, but instead through esoteric knowledge that he had brought into the world. Possession of this knowledge enabled the soul to escape from its imprisonment in the material world at death and return to the realm of light and spirit whence it originally came. In a number of apocryphal texts connected with this early Christian esotericism, Mary is revered especially for her expert understanding of this saving knowledge. Often she is portrayed as one of the most learned of Christ's followers, and his other disciples either seek her instruction or resent her authority and special relationship with the Savior. It is a remarkably different image from the *Protevangelium*, to be sure: this Mary is esteemed for her knowledge and teaching rather than her purity and passivity. In these communities, the mother of Jesus was honored, often in conflation and conjunction with Mary of Magadala, not so much for her virginity but instead as a founder and guardian of the true Christian faith.

Like the *Protevangelium*, however, most of these late second and third-century apocrypha offer no indication of Marian cult or veneration. Nevertheless, in the third century we find some of the first clear evidence for belief in the power of Mary's intercessions. Toward the end of this century the *Sub tuum praesidium* papyrus was copied somewhere in Egypt, preserving a small fragment of a prayer seeking Mary's intercessions. The "anaphora of Egyptian Basil," from the early fourth century, provides a similar witness to Marian intercession at around this same time. Also from this third century, it would appear, is the earliest narrative of the Virgin's Dormition and Assumption, the *Book of Mary's Repose*. This apocryphon shares the Christian esotericism of the many other early apocrypha mentioning Mary, knowing many of the same traditions as well as some rather peculiar traditions of its own. Mary's son, we learn from this text, was a manifestation of the Great Cherub of Light, and he brings to her a prayer that is required for souls to escape from the world at death. Likewise the *Book of Mary's Repose* holds Mary in high esteem for her knowledge of the saving cosmic mysteries, which she transmits to the apostles. Yet this text also reveres Mary for the power of her intercessions with her son, as we see particularly in the heavenly journey that completes this story of Mary's ascension into heaven. Clearly in some Christian esoteric circles belief in Mary's privileged understanding of the sacred mysteries had become joined with belief in the effectiveness of her intercessory prayers with her son. This combination invites a strong possibility that Marian piety and veneration may have first emerged and flourished within heterodox Christian communities, and only gradually did these practices become more accepted among the proto-orthodox Christians during the course of the fourth century. Such a hypothesis certainly could go a long way toward explaining the relative silence of the church fathers during the first few centuries. Marian piety's association with "deviant" forms of Christianity may have encouraged them to disregard such practices and focus instead on the theological importance of Mary's Divine Maternity, which was central to proto-orthodox belief in salvation through God's Incarnation in Jesus of Nazareth.

In the fourth century, evidence of Marian devotion and veneration picks up considerably, and the single most important source that we have from this period is the *Six Books Dormition Apocryphon*, which also is one of the most important Marian texts of ancient Christianity. In the *Six Books Apocryphon* the full range of the cult of the Virgin is on display: not only do we find appeals for Mary's intercessions, but also Marian apparitions, miracles ascribed to the Virgin, and even three annual liturgical feasts in her honor. Each of these feasts involves offerings of bread in Mary's honor, a ceremony that links this text unmistakably with the fourth-century Christian group that Epiphanius names the Kollyridians, who observed an identical practice and believed in the Virgin Mary's Dormition and Assumption. According to Epiphanius, the Kollyridians also allowed women to serve as liturgical leaders, and Mary's representation in the text as performing certain liturgical acts may reflect similar roles played by women in this early Christian community. In terms of doctrine, the *Six Books Apocryphon*, in contrast to the *Book of Mary's Repose*, is thoroughly compatible with the emergent orthodoxies of fourth-century Christianity. It is true that Epiphanius considers these

Christians heretical, but his objections are primarily to their practices: they venerate the Virgin by offering bread in her honor and allow women to serve as liturgical leaders. The latter practice was increasingly condemned in the fourth century, but in offering veneration to the Virgin, the *Six Books* and the Kollyridians are in fact more "orthodox" than Epiphanius himself. It is perhaps significant that in this instance as well, Marian veneration and cult are connected with an early Christian group that at least one church father considered deviant. While the *Six Books* and the Kollyridians are in no way divergent from fourth-century orthodoxy, with the possible exception of women's liturgical leadership, they witness to an early Christian group that seemingly stood somewhere along the margins of the proto-orthodox "mainstream" in the fourth century.

The fourth century also sees the church fathers suddenly begin to take more interest in the Virgin Mary. For some she is the ideal virgin whom other virgins should strive to emulate; other fathers show faith in the power of her intercessions and her apparitions to the faithful. Toward the end of the fourth century and into the beginning of the fifth we become increasingly aware of commemorations and shrines in Mary's honor. In Alexandria, Constantinople, and Jerusalem there were annual feasts in Mary's honor, and in Jerusalem we have discovered the early fifth-century church(es?) where this feast was celebrated. The evidence for late ancient Jerusalem's liturgies is especially helpful for tracking the development of the Virgin's cult, and the relatively recent publication of the *Jerusalem Georgian Chantbook* is particularly important. In this collection we discover that most likely by the late fourth century or by the early fifth century at the latest the cult of the Virgin had already become integrated into the Holy City's Sunday worship. Likewise, in the fourth century we find significant traces of Marian devotion in material culture, and while this evidence is not abundant, it is not notably deficient in comparison with paucity of early Christian material culture more generally. And if Mary is depicted in the Roman catacombs, then that changes things considerably.

Finally, the events of the Council of Ephesus reveal a vibrant cult of the Virgin standing behind the controversies over Nestorius. We know that a feast of the Virgin had already become a part of Constantinople's annual liturgical cycle in advance of Nestorius's arrival, and likewise that the discourse of Mary as the model of virginity had become established there. In the years leading up to the council, Proclus had been active in promoting the cult of the Virgin in the imperial capital, and not surprisingly he emerged as Nestorius's main theological opponent in the imperial capital. Moreover, the empress Pulcheria was closely allied with Proclus and his circle and seemingly had been from her childhood: by all indications, Proclus was her spiritual mentor. We know from Nestorius himself, as well as other sources, that Pulcheria had actively opposed Nestorius and was instrumental in his downfall. Given that she herself was a consecrated virgin (or at least presented herself as such) and was strongly influenced by Proclus, it stands to reason that her opposition to Nestorius was largely determined by his perceived criticism of Marian devotion and the Virgin herself. Recent efforts to marginalize Pulcheria from this controversy or even to argue that she actually supported Nestorius in the controversy are not persuasive in light of the accumulation of evidence indicating otherwise.

Moreover, the role played by Pulcheria's own personal Marian piety, significant though it must have been, was apparently not singular, and devotion to the Virgin in general seems to have been a much more powerful force in this controversy than traditional, narrowly Christological accounts of the Third Council have recognized. Popular response to the council both in Ephesus and in Constantinople demonstrates that devotion to the Virgin was an important factor in its outcome. The fact that the controversy erupted largely over the use of the term Theotokos is itself quite telling. This title, taken from the language of devotion, only secondarily became the catalyst for raging Christological debate. Indeed, on the whole it is rather difficult to disregard the evidence that Marian piety was looming large in the backdrop of the recondite Christological issues contested in the church of Mary the Theotokos at the Council of Ephesus in 431.

The evidence for Marian devotion and veneration in early Christianity is thus not nearly as deficient as much scholarship on this topic has previously maintained. No doubt the lingering influence of Protestantism over the disciplines of religious studies and early Christian studies in particular has had something to do with the persistence of this perspective. Likewise one imagines that Mary's enormous significance in the centuries to come has perhaps also heightened expectations of just how prominent she must have been during these early centuries. Yet when we measure early Christian devotion to Mary against the veneration of the saints more generally in ancient Christianity, it would seem that she comes out possibly even a little ahead. Devotion to non-martyr saints, the category into which Mary falls, did not really begin until the second half of the fourth century, at which time we find ample evidence that the cult of the Virgin had already begun.

Evidence of early devotion to St. Thecla in particular, as we have often noted, has frequently been identified as a kind of barometer against which to measure the relatively late emergence of Mary's cult. Nevertheless, as we have demonstrated, Mary can equal if not best Thecla in just about every category where one might search for indications of devotion. The *Protevangelium of James* and the early Dormition narratives certainly compare well with Thecla's literary corpus. Thecla's shrine is admittedly attested a few decades before the earliest Marian shrines are known with certainty, but this may very well be merely a matter of serendipity. A number of fourth-century church fathers advocate Thecla as a model for female virginity, but the same is also true of Mary. In terms of material evidence, Thecla again has no advantage, and Mary's representation is seemingly comparable, at least. Nevertheless, once we turn to liturgical evidence, suddenly the cult of the Virgin gains a significant advantage: Mary's commemoration in the liturgies of Jerusalem, Constantinople, and seemingly also Alexandria, is documented during the late fourth and early fifth century. Thecla cannot, so far as I am aware, claim as much. Thus if we take devotion to Thecla as our standard for comparison, and for numerous reasons this is a fitting point of reference, devotion to the Virgin Mary actually fares quite well. Marian veneration thus was not largely absent from early Christianity, as many scholars have supposed, but to the contrary we find it precisely where we ought to expect it: emerging right along with the cult of the saints.

Nevertheless, the relative silence of the early church fathers regarding Marian devotion admittedly remains a bit of a puzzle, especially since they often show considerable interest in her doctrinal significance. It is not entirely clear how to account for their collective reticence, but it certainly should not be taken as a sign, as scholars once concluded, that there was no devotion to the mother of Jesus until the fifth century or even later. Some other reason must be found for this disconnect between the fathers and early Marian piety. In the course of this book we have occasionally pointed toward two different hypotheses that may perhaps explain, at least in part, this Marian void in the writings of the early Christian literati: the potentially heterodox associations of early Marian piety, and the possibility that early Christian devotion may have developed more quickly than related dogmatic formulations. It is true that the two explanations are not especially complementary, but at the same time neither are they contradictory. Indeed it is possible that both may offer some clue as to why the fathers were seemingly slower to embrace Marian devotion than, apparently, some other early Christians.

Much of the earliest evidence for devotion to Mary comes from texts whose understanding of Christianity differs significantly from the emergent proto-orthodoxy that was the early church fathers' calling card. Although the *Protevangelium of James* is itself perfectly "orthodox," most other witnesses from the late second and third centuries show strong affinities with various kinds of esoteric Christianity. In these texts Mary is revered not as a virgin mother but instead for her mastery of the secret knowledge that brings salvation. The *Book of Mary's Repose* mixes this portrait of Mary as one learned in the cosmic mysteries with some of the earliest evidence for her veneration. Could it be then that before the fourth century devotion to the mother of Jesus and prayer for her intercessions were more common in esoteric Christian communities than among the proto-orthodox? One can only speculate, but the available evidence certainly could be interpreted as pointing in this direction. And if Marian devotion was largely associated with early Christian groups that the church fathers considered heretical, then one can perhaps understand their lack of interest in the topic. In the fourth century, Christian esotericism entered into significant decline, as the Roman Empire steadily embraced proto-orthodox Christianity and empowered its leaders to eliminate differing points of view. Not coincidentally, this is precisely the moment when the church fathers began to take an interest in Marian devotion and veneration. Perhaps with the taint of heresy removed, it was now possible for them to embrace Marian piety and claim it for orthodoxy.

Another possibility is that devotion to the Virgin Mary does not register in the works of the early church fathers because they were more concerned with doctrine and morality than with practices of personal piety and prayer. Mary thus appears in their writings only to the extent that she impacts their expositions of orthodox theology and conduct. Whatever devotion to the Virgin may have begun to take hold during the early centuries presumably held little interest for them, unless it had some sort of doctrinal significance. Indeed, the early fathers have comparatively little to say about Christian worship and prayer in general (with some important exceptions, of course), and yet such practices must have been developing apace alongside of their doctrinal conversations, even though they are now largely invisible to us. Accordingly, Marian piety may have escaped the fathers' acknowledgment simply because it was of little significance for the topics that occupied their attention. Only when devotion to the Virgin became directly relevant to questions of dogma did they engage with it, and this, it seems, is exactly what happened in the early fifth century, when the devotional title Theotokos suddenly became acutely significant for discussions of the precise relationship between divine and human in the Incarnation.

There is in fact much to favor this interpretation of Marian devotion's invisibility during the early centuries. A look at the broader history of Marian veneration confirms that lay piety frequently stood well in advance of dogmatic developments and ecclesiastical recognition during the medieval and modern periods. Time and again popular devotion to the Virgin outpaced Mariological doctrine, and only gradually would theologians and bishops yield to the will of Mary's faithful devotees, adjusting their doctrinal formulations and liturgies to account for her new attributes and accolades. In an article surveying Mary's portrayal in more "popular" genres during the Middle Ages, Jane Baun wonderfully draws our attention to "the people-led nature of Marian belief."[1] Baun identifies the Marian apocrypha of early and medieval Christianity as "the conceptual and devotional vanguard" of Marian piety. These texts form an anonymous and popular corpus not authored by clergy or theologians but which nonetheless "exerted steady pressure on official religion."[2] At times popular developments in Marian devotion were rejected for their excesses, but often they were "prophetic," propelling existing faith and practice into new directions.

For a more recent example, one need only consider the Roman Catholic Church's definition of the dogma of Mary's Assumption in 1950. The papal decision to declare this doctrine as a fundamental principle of the faith came only after a century of constant letters and petitions sent to the Vatican between 1849 and 1950. By one count the total number of petitioners in this era amounted to 18 patriarchs, 113 cardinals, 2,505 archbishops and bishops, 32,000 priests and male religious, 50,000 female religious, and 8 million lay people.[3] Then only after decades of careful study and consultation did the papacy eventually conclude that Mary's Assumption, which had been a focus of popular devotion at least since the third century, should be recognized as an essential tenet of the Christian faith. In more recent years, and indeed still at this very moment, there is a popular movement within the Roman Catholic Church to have Mary officially proclaimed as Co-Redemptrix and Mediatrix of All Graces by papal definition. According to the website associated with this movement, so far 550 cardinals and bishops and over seven million lay people have signed on over the past twenty years, and petitioners are still actively being sought.[4] Pope John Paul II is said to have personally favored such a proclamation but failed to do so because he recognized that there was still too much controversy over these Marian titles within the broader church.[5] His successors have shown less interest in this topic, and for the moment it seems unlikely that we will see such a new Marian dogma proclaimed anytime soon. But with this we see that even up until the present, Marian devotion and doctrine continue to be driven largely by popular piety, to which the hierarchs and theologians largely respond. Given the persistence of this pattern across the ages, one can readily imagine that something similar was at work in the early Christian centuries, thereby explaining the silence of our patristic sources on the matter of Marian piety.

Of course, these are again two rather different explanations for the failure of Marian piety to register in the writings of the church fathers, and I suspect that ultimately personal preference will largely dictate which of the two possibilities individual readers might favor. Many Roman Catholic and Eastern Orthodox readers, I imagine, will likely prefer the reading that understands Marian devotion as something that took hold early on among the pious faithful but was embraced by the bishops and theologians only later when its practice intruded upon their pursuit of doctrinal order. Others, and especially those interested in the diversity of early Christianity, will perhaps be more attuned to the idea that devotion to Mary first emerged within heterodox Christian communities and was embraced and amended by "orthodox" church authorities only later on. For my part, I see no need to settle for one interpretation over the other, and I think that the evidence is open to both understandings. Perhaps some combination of these two proposals can offer an even better explanation. After all, alongside of the heterodox evidence from the Coptic apocrypha and the *Book of Mary's Response* stand the *Protevangelium of James* and the *Six Books Dormition Apocryphon*, both of which are thoroughly orthodox. No doubt there are other possible explanations as well, and I suspect that many Protestants will still wish to remain firmly entrenched in the older narrative of Marian devotion's late appearance. Nevertheless, it is no longer possible to maintain that there is no evidence for Marian devotion in ancient Christianity: as we have seen, the evidence is both significant and varied and should accordingly inform our understanding of early Christian history going forward.

Notes

Introduction

1. As noted over twenty-five years ago in Cameron, "Theotokos in Sixth-Century Constantinople," 79, and more recently, for instance, by Peltomaa, "Towards the Origins"; and Cameron, "Introduction (2011)," 3–4. One should also note that, despite its title as well as some fine essays, Maunder, ed., *Origins of the Cult*, does not deliver such a study.
2. Brown, *Cult of the Saints*, 1.
3. Again see, e.g., Cameron, "Theotokos in Sixth-Century Constantinople," 79; Cameron, "Introduction (2005)," xxvii–xxviii; and Peltomaa, "Towards the Origins," esp. 76–7.
4. See, for instance, the following examples, which reflect a variety of eras and approaches: von Campenhausen, *Virgin Birth*, esp. 7–9; Carroll, *Cult of the Virgin Mary*, xiii; Belting, *Likeness and Presence*, 34; Cameron, "Early Cult of the Virgin," 5; Johnson, *Truly Our Sister*, 117–18; Avner, "Initial Tradition," 20. For a more popular example, see Warner, *Alone of All Her Sex*, 65–6.
5. E.g., Pentcheva, *Icons and Power*, 16; and Benko, *Virgin Goddess*, 152–3.
6. Daley, *On the Dormition of Mary*, 6.
7. Cameron, "Introduction (2011)," 3–4.
8. See also Limberis, *Divine Heiress*, 145–6, which also notes the value of early apocrypha for understanding early Marian devotion.
9. See, e.g., Bradshaw, *Search for the Origins of Christian Worship*, 98–117.
10. Gaventa, *Mary*. See also Peltomaa, "Towards the Origins," esp. 76–7. From a slightly different perspective, George Tavard similarly notes this divide, observing that while Protestants and Catholics have eagerly discussed issues such as papal primacy, infallibility, and justification in ecumenical dialogues, Mary is very often, it would seem, a "third rail" that both parties are reluctant to discuss. See Tavard, *Thousand Faces*, vii–viii.
11. For example, see Gambero, "Patristic Intuitions"; likewise, without passing judgment on any of the individual essays, one can note a similar sort of optimism regarding the early evidence in the various studies published in the following six-volume collection: Marianus, *De primordiis cultus Mariani*.
12. For instance, the work of Martin Jugie is often characterized by such an approach, particularly in Jugie, *La mort et l'assomption*, and even more so Jugie, *L'Immaculée Conception*.

13. See, e.g., the sort of reasoning expressed in Fehlner, "Immaculata Mediatrix," 314–15.

14. Clark, *Founding the Fathers*, esp. 264–9. For specific examples of Protestant Mariology, see Delius, *Geschichte*; and von Campenhausen, *Virgin Birth*. Examples of recent interest in Mary's biblical representation (which also frequently extend to include the *Protevangelium of James*) include Gaventa, *Mary* (and see pp. 2, 12 on Protestant neglect); Foskett, *A Virgin Conceived*; and Gaventa and Rigby, eds., *Blessed One*.

15. E.g., Benko, *Virgin Goddess*; Carroll, *Cult of the Virgin Mary*. The latter is particularly crass for its definition of Marian devotion as a "cult" in the modern sense of the word (that is, what are also called "new religious movements") and its explicit (and completely bizarre!) equation of Roman Catholic Marian piety with such modern movements as the Church of Scientology, the Hare Krishnas, and the Unification Church: ibid., xi–xii. Examples of anti-Catholic rhetoric linked with the historical analysis of early Marian devotion abound in earlier Protestant writings (e.g., Clark, *Founding the Fathers*, esp. 264–9), but for a more recent example in a Protestant study on early Marian devotion, see von Campenhausen, *Virgin Birth*, 7–8 and esp. p. 8 n. 1.

16. See, e.g., Gaventa and Rigby, eds., *Blessed One*; Braaten and Jenson, eds., *Mary, Mother of God*; Brown, *Mary in the New Testament*; and Blancy, Jourjon, and Dombes, *Mary in the Plan of God*. The half century since the Second Vatican Council has seen something of a decline in Marian scholarship, as observed by both Reynolds, *Gateway to Heaven*, 3, and Cunningham, *Mother of God*, 95. As an example of how far Roman Catholic scholarship has come in terms of accepting historical criticism, see for instance Meier, *Marginal Jew*, vol. 1, which rejects the Virgin Birth on historical grounds and yet was published with the official church sanction of a *nihil obstat* and an *imprimatur*.

17. To date the works of Hippolyte Delehaye remain the best discussion of what constitutes the cult of a saint or martyr. According to Delehaye, we may speak of a cult when we begin to find evidence of the following elements: appeals for intercession; a feast day; a shrine or churches named for the saint; relics; images of the saint; an account of the saint's life and miracles; and taking the saint's name at baptism. See Delehaye, *Sanctus*, esp. 123–5.

18. And here again one can only lament Carroll's unfortunate and misguided mistake.

19. To be sure, the precise distinction between *proskynesis* and *latreia* is formulated most clearly later on in the eighth century in the context of the first Iconoclast controversy. Nevertheless, in the later fourth and early fifth centuries, that is, when the cult of the saints was first developing and starting to expand, we witness the emergence of a new pattern of vocabulary in which *proskynesis* becomes an increasingly accepted term for describing the veneration of saints: see esp. Maraval, *Lieux saints*, 145–7. Likewise Augustine, for instance, had begun by the later fourth century to focus on the Greek *latreia* as the proper term designating the worship reserved for God alone, arguing that Latin lacked an equivalent word. Augustine's earliest discussion of this topic comes in response to Faustus the Manichean, *Against Faustus the Manichaean* 20.21 (Zycha, ed., *De utilitate credendi*, 561–65); see also *Questions on the Heptateuch* 2.94 (Zycha, ed., *Quaestionum in Heptateuchum libri VII*, 156) and *City of God* 10.1 (Dombart, Kalb, and Divjak, eds., *De civitate Dei*, 1:400–404).

20. For examples of these differing approaches, roughly in order, see Benko, *Virgin Goddess*; Barker, *Mother of the Lord*, vol. 1; Carroll, *Cult of the Virgin Mary*; Kearns, *Virgin Mary*; and Warner, *Alone of All Her Sex*.

21. Peltomaa, "Towards the Origins," 79.

22. See the excellent discussion in McGuckin, "Early Cult of Mary," 7–18. With regard to the cult of the saints more generally, see esp. Brown, *Cult of the Saints*, which emphasizes the importance of the saints' status as fellow human beings in the Christian tradition, thus rebutting the false notion that they are somehow merely Greco-Roman deities in Christian guise.

23. McGuckin, "Early Cult of Mary," 7–16, is particularly compelling on this point.

24. See Brown, *Cult of the Saints*, 1–22; Bradshaw, *Search for the Origins of Christian Worship*, 21–3, 213–21, 229–30. On a more general level, see the classic study by Jaeger, *Early Christianity and Greek Paideia*; Geffcken, *Last Days*, esp. 295.
25. See, e.g., Cameron, *Christianity and the Rhetoric of Empire*, esp. 17–21.
26. Smith, *Drudgery Divine*; Brown, *Cult of the Saints*, 4–22. Lawrence Cunningham also notes that the comparison of Marian devotion with pagan goddess worship has long been a "commonplace of anti-Catholic polemics": Cunningham, *Mother of God*, 94. Nevertheless, in all fairness, it should also be noted that Marian devotion in particular was often emphasized as a point of Catholic self-definition against Protestantism in the Catholic Reformation, and against modernity in the nineteenth and early twentieth century: see Rubin, *Mother of God*, 400–14; and MacCulloch, *A History of Christianity*, 417–27.
27. For a fairly recent example, see Delius, *Geschichte*, 33–4.
28. Jaroslav Pelikan rightly rejects such interpretations of the rise of Marian piety as "facile": Pelikan, *Mary through the Centuries*, 57–8. In this regard, see also, e.g., Peltomaa, *Image of the Virgin Mary*, 122–3; and Reynolds, *Gateway to Heaven*, 14.
29. Cameron, "Cult of the Virgin," 13.
30. E.g., Fulton, *From Judgment to Passion*; and Rubin, *Mother of God*.
31. Cameron, for instance, rightly calls attention to "how much of our understanding has been shaped by later ideas, wishes, and religious agendas": Cameron, "Cult of the Virgin," 1. As examples, one could note Carroll, *Cult of the Virgin Mary*, which largely explains the origins of Marian veneration through the analysis of later Catholic piety, or Kearns, *Virgin Mary*, where the medieval idea of Mary's compassion at the Cross is introduced (along with other ideas) to interpret Mary's representation in earliest Christian literature.
32. Cameron, "Early Cult of the Virgin," 5. See also Cameron, *Mediterranean World*, 149. In a more recent article, however, Cameron identifies the late fourth and fifth centuries as the formative period of Marian piety, while still pointing to the determinative influence of Ephesus: Cameron, "Cult of the Virgin," esp. 1–10.
33. Perhaps most recently, see, e.g., Talbot and Johnson, *Miracle Tales*, ix, referring to the more extensive discussion in Johnson, *Life and Miracles*, 221–6.
34. Cameron, "Virginity as Metaphor," 193.
35. Davis, *Cult of Saint Thecla*, 4.
36. Cameron, "Cult of the Virgin," 3–5, 17, which presents her most thorough discussion of the topic, but see also Cameron, "Early Cult of the Virgin," 5.
37. Belting, *Likeness and Presence*, 34. Karwiese, "The Church of Mary."
38. At least according to the evidence cited by Cameron: Maraval, *Lieux saints*.
39. The dates are taken from ibid., which Cameron cites as her source for the early development of these cults. See also Crisafulli, Nesbitt, and Haldon, *Miracles of St. Artemios*.
40. See, e.g., Kelly, *Early Christian Doctrines*, 490–1; Cunningham, *Brief History of Saints*, 8–27; and Price, "Martyrdom." The classic historical studies of the early history of the veneration of martyrs and saints remain Delehaye, *Les origines du culte des martyrs*; and Delehaye, *Sanctus*.
41. E.g., Brown, *Cult of the Saints*.
42. E.g., Cameron, "Cult of the Virgin," 3–5, 17; Pentcheva, *Icons and Power*, 16; Tsironis, "From Poetry to Liturgy."
43. E.g., Fulton, *From Judgment to Passion*, 3–4, 216–18. See also Shoemaker, "Mary at the Cross."
44. Shoemaker, "The Virgin Mary in the Ministry of Jesus"; Shoemaker, "Georgian *Life of the Virgin*"; Shoemaker, "The Cult of Fashion"; Shoemaker, "The Virgin Mary's Hidden Past"; Shoemaker, "A Mother's Passion"; Shoemaker, "Mary at the Cross";

Shoemaker, "Mother of Mysteries"; Shoemaker, *(Ps?-)Maximus the Confessor, The Life of the Virgin.*
45. Norelli, *Marie des apocryphes*, 134–6.

Chapter 1 A Virgin Unspotted

1. For more detailed analysis of Mary's representation in the New Testament, see in general Brown, *Mary in the New Testament*; and Gaventa, *Mary.*
2. Unless otherwise indicated, all biblical translations are from the New Revised Standard Version.
3. See also Brown, *Mary in the New Testament*, 51–65.
4. See also ibid., 83–97; Gaventa, *Mary*, 29–44.
5. Schüssler Fiorenza, *In Memory of Her*, 326–7.
6. See also Painter, *Just James*, 14–20; Brown, *Mary in the New Testament*, 182–96; Gaventa, *Mary*, 81–9.
7. Brown, *Mary in the New Testament*, 205–16; Gaventa, *Mary*, 89–97.
8. Gaventa, *Mary*, 56.
9. See also Brown, *Mary in the New Testament*, 105–43; Gaventa, *Mary*, 50–9.
10. See also Brown, *Mary in the New Testament*, 143–62; Gaventa, *Mary*, 59–69.
11. See Gaventa, *Mary*, 70, which is also the source of the translation.
12. Delius, *Geschichte*, 28.
13. McGuckin, "Early Cult of Mary," 21 n. 11. See also in this regard Brown, *Mary in the New Testament*, 170–2; Räisänen, *Mutter*, 141–2; Meier, *Marginal Jew*, vol. 3, 70.
14. See also Brown, *Mary in the New Testament*, 173–7; Gaventa, *Mary*, 71–3.
15. See, e.g., Mary Margaret Pazdan, "Mary, Mother of Jesus," in Freedman, ed., *Anchor Bible Dictionary*, vol. 4, 584–6; Meier, *Marginal Jew*, vol. 3, 69–71; Zervos, "Christmas with Salome," 77–8; van den Hengel, "Miriam of Nazareth," 140–5. But see also Painter, *Just James*, esp. 12–13, 20–2; Bauckham, *Jude*, 46–57, esp. 46–8, 56.
16. For more on this, see Harris, *The Tübingen School*, esp. 181–5.
17. A similar argument is advanced in McGuckin, "Early Cult of Mary," 5–6. See also Painter, *Just James*, 58–82; Bauckham, *Jude*, 55–60.
18. See, e.g., Marcus, "Mark—Interpreter of Paul."
19. Crossan, "Mark and the Relatives of Jesus"; Painter, *Just James*, 58–82; McGuckin, "Early Cult of Mary," 5–6.
20. For another possible explanation of this tradition, see Painter, *Just James*, 16–18.
21. As, for instance, Delius assumes: Delius, *Geschichte*, 27–8.
22. Bettiolo and Norelli, eds., *Ascensio Isaiae*, vol. 1, 118–21
23. Norelli, *Marie des apocryphes*, 33–92, esp. 39–47. See also Norelli, *Ascensio Isaiae*, 116–42.
24. See, e.g., von Campenhausen, *Virgin Birth*, 19, 29–30.
25. *Odes of Solomon* 19 (Charlesworth, ed., *Odes of Solomon*, 81–3), translation slightly modified.
26. *Infancy Gospel of Thomas* 14.3, 19 (Burke, ed., *De infantia Iesu*, 328–9, 334–7).
27. Justin Martyr, *Dialogue with Trypho* 43.8, 67.1–2, 68.6, 71.3, 84.1 (Marcovich, ed., *Dialogus cum Tryphone*, 141–2, 184–5, 188, 193, 215); see also *1st Apology* 33 (Minns and Parvis, eds., *Justin*, 172–5).
28. Justin Martyr, *Dialogue with Trypho* 100.4–5 (Marcovich, ed., *Dialogus cum Tryphone*, 242–3).
29. Irenaeus, *Against Heresies* 3.22.4 (Rousseau and Doutreleau, eds., *Irénée de Lyon*, vol. 3.2, 438–45).
30. Reynolds, *Gateway to Heaven*, 111.
31. E. g., Graef, *Mary*, 31. The passage in question is found in Irenaeus, *Against Heresies* 5.19.1 (Rousseau and Doutreleau, eds., *Irénée de Lyon*, vol. 5.2, 248–51).

32. For more on Postel and his translation, see esp. Backus, "Guillaume Postel."
33. For more details, see the discussion of the apocryphon's title in de Strycker, *La forme la plus ancienne*, 208–16.
34. See, e.g., Norelli, *Marie des apocryphes*, 49.
35. See, e.g., Schneemelcher, *New Testament Apocrypha*, vol. 1, 414–38; and Hock, *The Infancy Gospels.*
36. Nonetheless Alexander Toepel recently argues for an understanding of the *Protevangelium* as an aretological text, whose primary purpose is to extol the wondrous deeds of a god, following Helmut Koester primarily. Thus, in this view the *Protevangelium* is primarily about Jesus and should be classed as an Infancy Gospel. See Toepel, *Protevangelium*, 38–41, 269–70.
37. Regarding the definition of Christian apocrypha, see the discussion in Shoemaker, "Early Christian Apocryphal Literature," 528–32.
38. See Ray, "August 15"; Shoemaker, *Ancient Traditions of the Virgin Mary's Dormition*, 81–98.
39. de Strycker, "Die griechischen Handschriften," 585–8.
40. Brown, *Mary in the New Testament*, 248.
41. On the Latin *Protevangelium* and its influence on the Irish traditions, see McNamara et al., *Apocrypha Hiberniae*, 46–52, 671–880, 921–57.
42. The two texts have been published together with extensive commentary in Gijsel and Beyers, eds., *Libri de nativitate mariae.*
43. Regarding the Apocalypse of John, see my forthcoming article, "The Afterlife of the Apocalypse of John in Byzantine Apocalyptic Literature and Commentary." In *The New Testament in Byzantium*, edited by Derek Krueger and Robert S. Nelson, forthcoming. Washington, DC: Dumbarton Oaks, 2016.
44. For more on the *Protevangelium* and other Marian apocrypha as writings that belong more properly to the category of Tradition, see Shoemaker, "Between Scripture and Tradition."
45. *Protevangelium of James* 4.2 (de Strycker, *La forme la plus ancienne*, 80–1).
46. On this topic, see now especially Vuong, *Gender and Purity*, 107–47.
47. *Protevangelium of James* 16.1 (de Strycker, *La forme la plus ancienne*, 138–9).
48. *Protevangelium of James* 17.2 (ibid., 144–5).
49. Schneemelcher, *New Testament Apocrypha*, vol. 1, 424; Elliott, *Apocryphal New Testament*, 49–50.
50. E.g., Ehrman and Pleše, *Apocryphal Gospels*, 34–5; Ehrman, *Forgery*, 487–93.
51. Foskett, "Virginity as Purity," 68. See also Vuong, *Gender and Purity*, 52–7.
52. Gaventa, *Mary*, 109; Hunter, "Helvidius, Jovinian, and the Virginity of Mary," 64.
53. Norelli, *Marie des apocryphes*, 45–6, 70–8.
54. Gaventa, *Mary*, 119.
55. Ibid., 109–10.
56. See, e.g., de Strycker, *La forme la plus ancienne*, 81 n. 3; de Strycker, "Die griechischen Handschriften," 581–2; Hock, *The Infancy Gospels*, 39; Vuong, *Gender and Purity*, 82–3, 167–8; van der Horst, "Sex, Birth, Purity," 59. Gaventa is somewhat indecisive on the question of whether Mary was conceived without intercourse: Gaventa, *Mary*, 111–12. Schmid and following him Toepel accept the perfect reading while understanding the form as a "prophetic perfect" that in fact signals a future event despite its form: Smid, *Protevangelium*, 41; Toepel, *Protevangelium*, 79.
57. See, e.g., Jugie, *L'Immaculée Conception*, 56–63.
58. de Strycker, *La forme la plus ancienne*, 86–9.
59. See van der Horst, "Sex, Birth, Purity," 57–60; and also van der Horst, "Seven Months' Children." See also Toepel, *Protevangelium*, 92–3.
60. *Protevangelium of James* 6 (de Strycker, *La forme la plus ancienne*, 88–97).

61. Gaventa, *Mary*, 120; Foskett, "Virginity as Purity," 75.
62. Gaventa, *Mary*, 118.

Chapter 2 Mother of God and Mother of Mysteries

1. What follows is based on the excellent summary of Tertullian's Marian teaching in Graef, *Mary*, 32–4.
2. E.g., Tertullian, *On the Flesh of Christ* 7; 17; 20 (Mahé, ed., *La chair*, 240–6, 278–82, 290–4).
3. Tertullian, *On the Flesh of Christ* 23.2 (ibid., 302); *On Monogamy* 8.2 (Mattei, ed., *Le mariage*, 164).
4. Tertullian, *On the Flesh of Christ* 7.13 (Mahé, ed., *La chair*, 246); *Against Marcion* 4.26.13 (Braun, ed., *Contre Marcion*, vol. 4, 342–4).
5. Again, for Clement and Origen's Marian doctrine I rely primarily on the summary in Graef, *Mary*, 34–6.
6. Clement of Alexandria, *Miscellanies* 7.16 (Stählin, Früchtel, and Treu, eds., *Clemens Alexandrinus*, vol. 3, 66).
7. Origen of Alexandria, *Homilies on Luke* 14 (Rauer, ed., *Origenes Werke*, vol. 9, 100); *Homilies on Leviticus* 8.2 (Baehrens, ed., *Origenes Werke*, vol. 3, 395).
8. Origen of Alexandria, *Commentary on Matthew* 25 (Klostermann and Benz, eds., *Origenes Werke*, vol. 11, 42–3).
9. Origen of Alexandria, *Homilies on Luke* 7 (Rauer, ed., *Origenes Werke*, vol. 9, 49); *Commentary on Matthew* 10.17 (Klostermann and Benz, eds., *Origenes Werke*, vol. 10, 22).
10. Origen of Alexandria, *Homilies on Luke* 17 (Rauer, ed., *Origenes Werke*, vol. 9, 117).
11. Regarding Origen's possible use of this term, see, e.g., Johnson, "*Sub Tuum Praesidium*," 58.
12. Hunt, Johnson, and Roberts, *Catalogue of the Greek Papyri*, vol. 3, 46–7; Mercenier, "L'antienne."
13. The best reconstruction of the text is found in Stegmüller, "Sub tuum praesidium." See also Giamberardini, *Il culto mariano*, 69–97; Giamberardini, "'Sub tuum praesidium.'"
14. Hunt, Johnson, and Roberts, *Catalogue of the Greek Papyri*, vol. 3, 46; Förster, "Zur ältesten Überlieferung," 185.
15. See e.g., Shoemaker, "Apocrypha and Liturgy"; Mimouni, "La lecture liturgique."
16. As proposed, for instance, by Johnson, "*Sub Tuum Praesidium*," 59–69; and Triacca, "'Sub tuum praesidium.'"
17. Hunt, Johnson, and Roberts, *Catalogue of the Greek Papyri*, vol. 3, 46.
18. For a summary of the different datings, see Förster, "Zur ältesten Überlieferung," 188–9, which has references to the various studies in question. Note also that in this article Förster argues for a redating of the *Sub tuum praesidium* papyrus on the basis of paleography that would place it in the sixth or seventh century, which it just so happens would make it contemporary with another copy of the prayer in the Vienna collection, where Förster works. Nevertheless, Cornelia Römer judges Förster's arguments unpersuasive: Römer, "Christliche Texte II," 138. Likewise, AnneMarie Luijendijk maintains the traditional earlier dating in her recent monograph: Luijendijk, *Forbidden Oracles?*, 30 (and I thank her for directing my attention to both of these references). One of the problems with the argument is that Förster identifies parallels for individual letters in individual texts from later periods, but he is not able to identify any texts from this later period that as a whole have the same style of writing as the papyrus, which would perhaps be more persuasive.
19. Starowieyski, "Le titre θεοτόκος," esp. 237; Stegmüller, "Sub tuum praesidium," 80; Johnson, "*Sub Tuum Praesidium*," 53–9, esp. 58.

20. Cited in Johnson, "*Sub Tuum Praesidium*," 56, which also explains the text further and gives the dating. The translation is taken from Jasper and Cuming, *Prayers of the Eucharist*, 72, with a slight modification.
21. Stegmüller, "Sub tuum praesidium," 78. While Stegmüller proposes a date at the end of the fourth century, the paleographic parallels that he cites belong to this period.
22. Ibid., 80–2.
23. The remainder of this chapter draws often on three earlier articles that I have published. Those interested in more detailed discussion of this topic should consult these articles. Shoemaker, "Rethinking the 'Gnostic Mary'"; Shoemaker, "A Case of Mistaken Identity?"; Shoemaker, "Jesus' Gnostic Mom." See also Shoemaker, "Mother of Mysteries," esp. 15–20.
24. Here I follow especially Brakke, *The Gnostics*; but see also Markschies, *Gnosis*, as well as Shoemaker, *Ancient Traditions of the Virgin Mary's Dormition*, 233–8. Although it is intended primarily as a course textbook, Lewis, *Introduction to Gnosticism* is also an excellent introduction to this topic and many of the individual Nag Hammadi texts as well.
25. See, e.g., Pagels, *Gnostic Gospels*, esp. chap. 3, "God the Father/God the Mother," and also King, ed., *Images of the Feminine*.
26. If these remarks seem unnecessary, I offer them in order to correct in no uncertain terms the potentially defamatory remarks made about me and my scholarship in Kateusz, "Collyridian Déjà Vu," 78 n. 12.
27. See esp. Shoemaker, "Rethinking the 'Gnostic Mary'"; Shoemaker, "A Case of Mistaken Identity?"
28. See, e.g., Baarda, *Gospel quotations of Aphrahat*, 486 n. 27.
29. *Gospel of Mary* 10.1–8 (Parrott, *Nag Hammadi Codices V, 2-5*, 460–1).
30. *Gospel of Mary* 17.7–19.2 (ibid., 466–9)
31. King, for instance, raises doubts about whether it should be designated as Gnostic: King, *What is Gnosticism?*, 151, 163; and it would not fit Brakke's more narrowly defined category. Marjanen, however, does consider the text to be Gnostic: Marjanen, *Woman Jesus Loved*, 94 n. 1. On women's leadership in early Gnostic Christian communities, see, e.g., McGuire, "Women, Gender, and Gnosis."
32. See, e.g., Schüssler Fiorenza, *In Memory of Her*, 304–7, 323–3.
33. See especially Brown, *Mary in the New Testament*, 97–103, 213, 287–8.
34. Gaventa, *Mary*, 49–78, esp. 72.
35. Ibid., 73.
36. So Heikki Räisänen describes Mary of Nazareth's depiction in Acts: as a part of the "Kernbestand der Jerusalemer Gemeinde": Räisänen, *Mutter*, 141.
37. Murray, *Symbols of Church and Kingdom*, 330–1, lists several such instances from the Syrian tradition, including the Syriac *Didascalia*, John Chrysostom, and Severus of Antioch. Jerome, however, without doubting Mary of Nazareth's presence at the cross, carefully distinguishes the Virgin from these other figures, in order to defend her perpetual virginity against the claims of Helvidius, who apparently conflated the different women: Jerome, *Against Helvidius* 13–16 (PL 23, 195–201). See also Setzer, "Excellent Women," 260 n. 6; and Brown, *Mary in the New Testament*, 68–72, who argue on historical-critical grounds against any such identification.
38. Brown, *Mary in the New Testament*, 211–12, 288–9.
39. See Shoemaker, "The Virgin Mary in the Ministry of Jesus," 454–5. This interpretation also seems to be suggested especially by the later traditions of Mary's death at Ephesus, which, on the basis of this incident, suppose her to have accompanied John there as he was spreading the gospel. For more on these traditions, see the discussion in Mimouni, *Dormition*, 585–97. Likewise, in the earliest *Life of the Virgin*, Mary initially sets out with John to help in his evangelism, only to return to Jerusalem at divine command to direct the church and the ministry of the apostles there. See Maximus the Confessor,

The Life of the Virgin 98 (van Esbroeck, ed., *Maxime le Confesseur: Vie de la Vierge*, 127–8 (Geor) and 85–6 (Fr); English trans. Shoemaker, *(Ps?-)Maximus the Confessor, The Life of the Virgin*, 125).

40. King, "Gospel of Mary Magdalene," 618; Marjanen, *Woman Jesus Loved*, 94–5 n. 2; Tuckett, *Gospel of Mary*, 17–18.

41. 1 Cor 15.5–8. See Bovon, "Le privilège pascal," 52, and the response to these in Schüssler Fiorenza, *Jesus*, 119–28.

42. See esp. Murray, *Symbols of Church and Kingdom*, 329–35.

43. On the date of the *Diatessaron*, see Vööbus, *Early Versions of the New Testament*, 1–6; Metzger, *Early Versions of the New Testament*, 30–2; Petersen, "Text of the New Testament," 77–96.

44. See, e.g., Vööbus, *Early Versions of the New Testament*, 22–7.

45. According to a famous passage from Theodoret of Cyrrhus (d. 458), 200 of the 800 churches in his North-Syrian diocese were still using the *Diatessaron* instead of the separate gospels. Theodoret put an end to this by rounding up and destroying these copies of the *Diatessaron* and replacing them with the four gospels. Theodoret of Cyrrhus, *Haereticarum fabularum compendium* 1.20 (PG 83, 372A).

46. Koester, *Introduction to the New Testament*, 207–18.

47. Excepting only the *Pistis Sophia*, whose Egyptian origin seems likely, Marjanen identifies a probable origin for each of these Mary apocrypha in Syria: *Gospel of Thomas*: Marjanen, *Woman Jesus Loved*, 37; *Sophia of Jesus Christ*: 74; *Dialogue of the Savior*: 77–78; *Gospel of Mary*: 99; *First Apocalypse of James*: 127–8; *Gospel of Philip*: 147–8.

48. *Gospel of Thomas* 114 (Layton, ed., *Nag Hammadi Codex II, 2–7*, vol. 1, 92–3).

49. Meyer, "Making Mary Male," 562.

50. *Sophia of Jesus Christ* 98.9–11/89.20–90.1 and 114.8–12/117.12–16 (Parrott, *Nag Hammadi Codices III, 3–4 and V, 1*, 69, 169). Regarding the date, see Marjanen, *Woman Jesus Loved*, 59–60.

51. *Dialogue of the Savior*, passim (Emmel, *Nag Hammadi Codex III, 5: The Dialogue of the Savior*). See also Marjanen, *Woman Jesus Loved*, 77–8, 84.

52. Another apocryphon, the *First Apocalypse of James*, most likely from the third century, mentions Mary among several female disciples. Nevertheless, there is not much further information here, and Mary's close association with Martha certainly brings to mind Mary of Bethany rather than either the Magdalene or the mother of Jesus. *(First) Apocalypse of James*, 40.25 (Parrott, *Nag Hammadi Codices V, 2–5*, 98).

53. *Gospel of Philip* 59.6–11 (Layton, ed., *Nag Hammadi Codex II, 2–7*, vol. 1, 158–9). The translation is my own. For more on the translation of this passage, see Klauck, "Die dreifache Maria," esp. 2356–8.

54. Marjanen, *Woman Jesus Loved*, 160–1; Murray, *Symbols of Church and Kingdom*, 333; Buckley, "Holy Spirit," 105.

55. *Gospel of Philip* 63.33–64.9 (Layton, ed., *Nag Hammadi Codex II, 2–7*, vol. 1, 166–8).

56. *Gospel of Philip* 55.24–36 (ibid., vol. 1, 150–1).

57. Good, "Pistis Sophia," 696, 703–4.

58. *Pistis Sophia* 19 (Schmidt and MacDermot, eds., *Pistis Sophia*, 28); my translation.

59. *Pistis Sophia* 34 (ibid., 56); my translation.

60. Ann Brock argues that, since other women can be called blessed as well, this Mary should still be identified with the Magdalene: Brock, "Setting the Record Straight." Nevertheless, this Mary is not just blessed, but she is blessed among women and in all generations. It is hard to imagine that this characterization would inspire ancient readers and hearers of this text to conclude that this Mary is the Magdalene instead of the Nazarene. See also Shoemaker, "Mother of Mysteries," 18–19.

61. *Pistis Sophia* 36 (Schmidt and MacDermot, eds., *Pistis Sophia*, 58); translation slightly modified.

62. *Pistis Sophia* 59 (ibid., 116).
63. *Pistis Sophia* 59; 62 (ibid., 117, 123).
64. *Pistis Sophia* 72 (ibid., 162).
65. *Pistis Sophia* 83 (ibid., 184). Book 2 explicitly names her Magdalene on the following pages: 185, 189, 199, 201, 203, 218, 233, 237, 244.
66. *Pistis Sophia* 127, 132 (ibid., 319, 338).
67. The difficulties posed by the different Marys provide one of the main reasons given by the text's most recent translator for viewing the different books as compilations from various earlier sources: ibid., XIV
68. See Schneemelcher, *New Testament Apocrypha*, vol. 1, 538.
69. *Gospel (Questions) of Bartholomew* 2.1–22 (Vasiliev, ed., *Anecdota Graeco-Byzantina*, 11–14; Wilmart and Tisserant, "Fragments grecs," 321–5); trans. Schneemelcher, *New Testament Apocrypha*, vol. 1, 543–5, with slight modifications. Regarding the date, see ibid., 540.
70. *Gospel (Questions) of Bartholomew* 4.17 (Vasiliev, ed., *Anecdota Graeco-Byzantina*, 16; trans. Schneemelcher, *New Testament Apocrypha*, vol. 1, 546–7). See also on the status of this passage, Bovon and Geoltrain, eds., *Écrits apocryphes chrétiens*, 282–3 n. 4.17. On the topos of Mary's womb as containing the uncontainable, see, e.g., Reynolds, *Gateway to Heaven*, 16–17, 24.
71. This is, it would seem, the goal of several other scholars working on this subject, including King, Bovon, Marjanen, and Schaberg: see, in addition to the works of the first three cited in the notes above, Schaberg, *Resurrection of Mary Magdalene*, 225–53.
72. See in particular Clark, "Lady Vanishes," where Clark describes the considerable problems with attempting to perceive "real women" through the textual remains of early Christianity: what we find instead is a representation of individual women crafted primarily by the men who controlled the culture.
73. For an excellent, brief discussion of "intertextuality" and a fine example of its application, see Davis, "Crossed Texts, Crossed Sex," esp. 11–14. See also Clark, *History, Theory, Text*, ch. 7.

Chapter 3 Mother of the Great Cherub of Light

1. See esp. Wenger, *L'Assomption*; van Esbroeck, *Aux origines de la Dormition*; Shoemaker, *Ancient Traditions of the Virgin Mary's Dormition*.
2. Shoemaker, "Mother of Mysteries," 30–1.
3. A translation of the complete text including all of these versions can be found in Shoemaker, *Ancient Traditions of the Virgin Mary's Dormition*, 290–50. For the editions, see Arras, *De transitu*, vol. 1; Wright, *Contributions to Apocryphal Literature*, ᴊ-ᴏᴎᴋ (Syr) and 46–8 (Eng); Shoemaker, "New Syriac Dormition Fragments"; and van Esbroeck, "Apocryphes géorgiens".
4. Shoemaker, *Ancient Traditions of the Virgin Mary's Dormition*, 415–18.
5. Abrahà, "La *Dormitio Mariae*," esp. 187.
6. Shoemaker, *Ancient Traditions of the Virgin Mary's Dormition*, 153–61.
7. See ibid., esp. 38–46, 146–68, 232–56.
8. *Book of Mary's Repose* 1 (Arras, *De transitu*, vol. 1, 1 (Eth) and 1 (Lat); trans. Shoemaker, *Ancient Traditions of the Virgin Mary's Dormition*, 290).
9. One should note, however, that some scholars have proposed that this book may be the result of a mistranslation of the Greek original. In all the other narratives of this type, the angel (or in some cases, Christ himself) brings Mary the eponymous palm from the Tree of Life, and the words in Greek for this palm (*brabeion*) and book (*biblion*) are sufficiently similar that the translator or a copyist might have made a mistake here. Nevertheless, even if that is the case, the error must have been generated not only by the

similarity of the two words, but also by the fact that elsewhere in the narrative an important book appears in Mary's possession alongside of the palm. Shoemaker, *Ancient Traditions of the Virgin Mary's Dormition*, 220–6.

10. *Book of Mary's Repose* 1–2 (Arras, *De transitu*, vol. 1, 1–2 (Eth) and 1 (Lat); trans. Shoemaker, *Ancient Traditions of the Virgin Mary's Dormition*, 290–1).

11. See the discussion in Shoemaker, *Ancient Traditions of the Virgin Mary's Dormition*, 212–14, 229–32. Cf. *The Gospel of Truth* 37.37–41.14 (Attridge, ed., *Nag Hammadi Codex I*, vol. 1, 110–15).

12. Shoemaker, *Ancient Traditions of the Virgin Mary's Dormition*, 215–20.

13. Jaroslav Pelikan identifies Arianism as the "final, mighty upheaval" of Angel Christology in early Christianity: Pelikan, *The Christian Tradition*, vol. 1, 197–8. See also Grillmeier, *Christ in Christian Tradition*, vol. 1, 46–51; Shoemaker, *Ancient Traditions of the Virgin Mary's Dormition*, 254.

14. *Book of Mary's Repose* 5–12 (Arras, *De transitu*, vol. 1, 3–7 (Eth) and 2–5 (Lat); trans. Shoemaker, *Ancient Traditions of the Virgin Mary's Dormition*, 292–8). The same episode is also in one of the Georgian fragments: van Esbroeck, "Apocryphes géorgiens," 69–73. See also *Gospel of Ps.-Matthew* 20–1 (Gijsel and Beyers, *Libri de nativitate mariae*, vol. 1, 458–70).

15. *Book of Mary's Repose* 5 (Arras, *De transitu*, vol. 1, 3 (Eth) and 2 (Lat); trans. Shoemaker, *Ancient Traditions of the Virgin Mary's Dormition*, 292).

16. *Book of Mary's Repose* 6 (Arras, *De transitu*, vol. 1, 3–4 (Eth) and 2–3 (Lat); trans. Shoemaker, *Ancient Traditions of the Virgin Mary's Dormition*, 293).

17. Jerome, *Against Helvidius* 19 (PL 23, 213).

18. *Book of Mary's Repose* 6 (Arras, *De transitu*, vol. 1, 4 (Eth) and 3 (Lat); trans. Shoemaker, *Ancient Traditions of the Virgin Mary's Dormition*, 293).

19. Some of the material in this section previously appeared in Shoemaker, "Jesus' Gnostic Mom," where one can find a somewhat fuller discussion of this section of the *Book of Mary's Repose*.

20. *Book of Mary's Repose* 11 (Arras, *De transitu*, vol. 1, 6–7 (Eth) and 4 (Lat); trans. Shoemaker, *Ancient Traditions of the Virgin Mary's Dormition*, 297).

21. *Book of Mary's Repose* 13–16 (Arras, *De transitu*, vol. 1, 7–9 (Eth) and 5–6 (Lat); trans. Shoemaker, *Ancient Traditions of the Virgin Mary's Dormition*, 298–300).

22. See, e.g., the extensive survey of different traditions in Rudolph, *Gnosis*, 171–204, esp. 171–2.

23. See Arras, *De transitu*, vol. 1, 81 (Lat). Examples include *The (First) Apocalypse of James*, 32.28–35.9 (Parrott, ed., *Nag Hammadi Codices V,2–5*, 84–9); *The Books of Jeu*, 33–8, 49–52 (Schmidt and MacDermot, eds., *Books of Jeû*, 83–8, 116–38). For a general discussion, again see Rudolph, *Gnosis*, 172–80, 244. Cf. Irenaeus, *Adversus Haereses*, 1.21.5 (Rousseau and Doutreleau, eds., *Irénée de Lyon*, book 1, vol. 2, 304–8).

24. E.g., *Apocryphon of John* Synopsis 25 (Waldstein and Wisse, eds., *Apocryphon of John*, 60–1; *Pistis Sophia* 30–9, 47–57 (Schmidt and MacDermot, eds., *Pistis Sophia*, 45–63, 86–111, passim); *The Hypostasis of the Archons* 94.17 (Layton, ed., *Nag Hammadi Codex II, 2–7*, vol. 1, 252–3); *On the Origin of the World* 100.7, 26 (ibid., vol. 2, 34–5).

25. *Book of Mary's Repose* 17 (Arras, *De transitu*, vol. 1, 9 (Eth) and 6 (Lat); trans. Shoemaker, *Ancient Traditions of the Virgin Mary's Dormition*, 300).

26. See, e.g., the survey of different traditions in Rudolph, *Gnosis*, 67–113, esp. 76 and 94.

27. *Book of Mary's Repose* 17 (Arras, *De transitu*, vol. 1, 9 (Eth) and 6 (Lat); trans. Shoemaker, *Ancient Traditions of the Virgin Mary's Dormition*, 300).

28. *Book of Mary's Repose* 18 (Arras, *De transitu*, vol. 1, 10 (Eth) and 6 (Lat); trans. Shoemaker, *Ancient Traditions of the Virgin Mary's Dormition*, 300).

29. Regarding the prevalence of these ideas in Gnostic Christianity, see, e.g., Rudolph, *Gnosis*, 88–95.

30. Again, see, e.g., ibid., 109–11, 119–21

31. See also the very helpful comments regarding my earlier position in Norelli, *Marie des apocryphes*, 129–42.

32. *Book of Mary's Repose* 18 (Arras, *De transitu*, vol. 1, 10 (Eth) and 6 (Lat); trans. Shoemaker, *Ancient Traditions of the Virgin Mary's Dormition*, 300).

33. This parable is found in *Book of Mary's Repose* 18–23 (Arras, *De transitu*, vol. 1, 10–12 (Eth) and 7–8 (Lat); Wright, *Contributions to Apocryphal Literature*, ∞ʌ -∞ᴍ (Syr) and 50–1 (Eng); trans. Shoemaker, *Ancient Traditions of the Virgin Mary's Dormition*, 300–3).

34. *Book of Mary's Repose* 24–5 (Arras, *De transitu*, vol. 1, 12–13 (Eth) and 8–9 (Lat); trans. Shoemaker, *Ancient Traditions of the Virgin Mary's Dormition*, 303).

35. For the Rabbinic parallels, see Manns, *Le récit de la Dormition*, 76–7.

36. *Book of Mary's Repose* 24–35 (Arras, *De transitu*, vol. 1, 12–20 (Eth) and 8–13 (Lat); Wright, *Contributions to Apocryphal Literature*, ∞ᴋ-∞ʌ (Syr) and 50–1 (Eng); trans. Shoemaker, *Ancient Traditions of the Virgin Mary's Dormition*, 303–10).

37. Betz, *Greek Magical Papyri*, 331. Note, however, that the second Ethiopic manuscript gives his name as "Merciful."

38. E.g., Rudolph, *Gnosis*, 58. Regarding the "bridal chamber" theme in the ancient gnostic traditions, see ibid., 245–7. On the use of "racial" identity by ancient Gnostics, see ibid., 91–2, and Williams, *Rethinking Gnosticism*, 193–202. The members of this race are hidden to the extent that they themselves do not even recognize their true identity until the Redeemer (Christ in Gnostic Christianity) brings them to knowledge of this fact (Rudolph, *Gnosis*, 119–21).

39. *Book of Mary's Repose* 36–7 (Arras, *De transitu*, vol. 1, 20–1 (Eth) and 13–14 (Lat); Wenger, *L'Assomption*, 214–17; trans. Shoemaker, *Ancient Traditions of the Virgin Mary's Dormition*, 310–12, 356–7).

40. See, e.g., *The Gospel of the Egyptians*, III, 64.22; 66.5; IV, 76.12l; 78.7 (Böhlig and Wisse, eds., *Nag Hammadi Codices III, 2 and IV, 2*, 149–50, 154–5); *The Second Book of Jeu* 42–3 (Schmidt and MacDermot, eds., *Books of Jeû*, 99.15–16, 101.24); *The Untitled Text in the Bruce Codex* 9 (ibid., 241.18); *Pistis Sophia* 55.11 and *passim* (Schmidt and MacDermot, eds., *Pistis Sophia*, 105; see also the entry for παραλήμπτωρ in the index of Greek words, p. 790); *Zostrianos* 47.24 (Sieber, ed., *Nag Hammadi Codex VIII*, 116), and *The Apocryphon of John*, synopsis 69.10 (Waldstein and Wisse, eds., *Apocryphon of John*, 148–9). On the meaning of this term, see esp. the discussion in Böhlig and Wisse, eds., *Nag Hammadi Codices III, 2 and IV, 2*, 194–8.

41. *Book of Mary's Repose* 40 (Arras, *De transitu*, vol. 1, 23 (Eth) and 15 (Lat); van Esbroeck, "Apocryphes géorgiens," 60–1 (Geor) and 65 (Lat); trans. Shoemaker, *Ancient Traditions of the Virgin Mary's Dormition*, 313–14).

42. *Book of Mary's Repose* 40 (Arras, *De transitu*, vol. 1, 23–4 (Eth) and 15–16 (Lat); van Esbroeck, "Apocryphes géorgiens," 61–2 (Geor) and 65 (Lat); trans. Shoemaker, *Ancient Traditions of the Virgin Mary's Dormition*, 314–15).

43. *Book of Mary's Repose* 41 (Arras, *De transitu*, vol. 1, 24–5 (Eth) and 16 (Lat); van Esbroeck, "Apocryphes géorgiens," 61–2 (Geor) and 65 (Lat); trans. Shoemaker, *Ancient Traditions of the Virgin Mary's Dormition*, 314–15). Regarding the question of Mary's sinfulness, see, e.g., Beattie, "Mary in Patristic Theology," 99–102.

44. *Book of Mary's Repose* 44 (Arras, *De transitu*, vol. 1, 27 (Eth) and 17–18 (Lat); trans. Shoemaker, *Ancient Traditions of the Virgin Mary's Dormition*, 316). The same passage occurs identically in the earliest Greek narrative: see Wenger, *L'Assomption*, 220–1; Shoemaker, *Ancient Traditions of the Virgin Mary's Dormition*, 360.

45. Drescher, "A Coptic Amulet," 267.

46. *Book of Mary's Repose* 54–65 (Arras, *De transitu*, vol. 1, 32–9 (Eth) and 21–6 (Lat); English trans., Shoemaker, *Ancient Traditions of the Virgin Mary's Dormition*, 320–4). Paralleled most notably by the earliest Greek narrative (§30, Wenger, *L'Assomption*,

228–9; cf. 251–2), John of Thessalonica's *Homily on the Dormition* 9–11 (Jugie, *Homélies mariales byzantines (II)*, 389–85, 419–23), and Wilmart's Latin *Transitus* 19–21 (Wilmart, *Analecta reginensia*, 338–41). Many of these versions, however, have omitted various portions of the sermon (for instance, although the earliest Greek version published by Wenger mentions the sermon, it omits all of its content). Nevertheless, John of Thessalonica's *Homily on the Dormition* has preserved what is basically a complete version of the sermon as found in the *Book of Mary's Repose*, albeit somewhat altered in the direction of seventh-century orthodoxy. The identity of these two passages and even the nature of John's alterations make it all but certain that this episode as preserved in the *Book of Mary's Repose* belonged to the earliest layer of these traditions.

47. *Book of Mary's Repose* 55 (Arras, *De transitu*, vol. 1, 33 (Eth) and 22 (Lat); English trans., Shoemaker, *Ancient Traditions of the Virgin Mary's Dormition*, 321). Cf. Wenger, *L'Assomption*, 230–1; English trans., Shoemaker, *Ancient Traditions of the Virgin Mary's Dormition*, 364; Jugie, *Homélies mariales byzantines (II)*, 390.

48. Wenger, *L'Assomption*, 230–1; English trans., Shoemaker, *Ancient Traditions of the Virgin Mary's Dormition*, 364; cf. Jugie, *Homélies mariales byzantines (II)*, 390.

49. *Book of Mary's Repose* 57 (Arras, *De transitu*, vol. 1, 33–4 (Eth) and 22 (Lat); English trans., Shoemaker, *Ancient Traditions of the Virgin Mary's Dormition*, 321). See also Wenger's ancient Latin version (L4): "et facta est uox dicens: 'Petre uide ne reuelaris hoc, quia uobis solis datum est hec cognoscere et loqui scientiam.'" (Wenger, *L'Assomption*, 251). John of Thessalonica preserves the same scene, but there the voice only rebukes Peter for speaking in terms that his audience cannot understand, without any mention of secrets: *Homily on the Dormition* 9 (Jugie, *Homélies mariales byzantines (II)*, 390).

50. *Book of Mary's Repose* 66 (Arras, *De transitu*, vol. 1, 39 (Eth) and 26 (Lat); English trans., Shoemaker, *Ancient Traditions of the Virgin Mary's Dormition*, 324–5). Cf. Wenger, *L'Assomption*, 230–1. See also Shoemaker, "Gender at the Virgin's Funeral."

51. How to reconcile this passage with Mary's earlier confession that she had sinned is admittedly not clear.

52. *Book of Mary's Repose* 67–9 (Arras, *De transitu*, vol. 1, 39–41 (Eth) and 26–7 (Lat); English trans., Shoemaker, *Ancient Traditions of the Virgin Mary's Dormition*, 327–8).

53. *Book of Mary's Repose* 72–7 (Arras, *De transitu*, vol. 1, 41–45 (Eth) and 27–30 (Lat); English trans., Shoemaker, *Ancient Traditions of the Virgin Mary's Dormition*, 327–32). See also Shoemaker, "'Let Us Go and Burn Her Body.'"

54. Cf. *Testament of Solomon* 20 (McCown, ed., *The Testament of Solomon*, 60*–63*).

55. *Book of Mary's Repose* 78–84 (Arras, *De transitu*, vol. 1, 45–50 (Eth) and 30–3 (Lat); English trans., Shoemaker, *Ancient Traditions of the Virgin Mary's Dormition*, 332–7); Wright, *Contributions to Apocryphal Literature*, ܣܪܐ (Syr) and 42–4 (Eng); Donahue, *Testament of Mary*, 40–3. The translation of a second early Irish version, without the original text, can be found in Herbert and McNamara, *Irish Biblical Apocrypha*, 125–6. Note that in the Irish version the setting is slightly different: the debate occurs in place of the *Book of Mary's Repose*'s all-night vigil, before Christ's initial appearance and Mary's death.

56. *Book of Mary's Repose* 85–8 (Arras, *De transitu*, vol. 1, 50–2 (Eth) and 33–4 (Lat); English trans., Shoemaker, *Ancient Traditions of the Virgin Mary's Dormition*, 337–40); Wright, *Contributions to Apocryphal Literature*, ܪܠ (Syr) and 44-6 (Eng); Donahue, *Testament of Mary*, 42–5.

57. For more on this particular passage, see Shoemaker, "Asceticism," where these points are discussion in more detail.

58. See Luedemann, *Opposition to Paul*, esp. 197.

59. Hunter, *Marriage, Celibacy, and Heresy*, 113–15; Brown, *Body and Society*, 138–9.

60. Hunter, "Helvidius, Jovinian, and the Virginity of Mary." See now also Hunter, *Marriage, Celibacy, and Heresy*, esp. 130–42. Both Helvidius and Jovinian are discussed in relation to Marian piety in chapter 5.

61. Gribomont, "Le plus ancien Transitus," 246.

62. *Book of Mary's Repose* 90–100 (Arras, *De transitu*, vol. 1, 53–9 (Eth) and 35–38 (Lat); Wright, *Contributions to Apocryphal Literature*, ∞-∞< (Syr) and 47–8 (Eng); English trans., Shoemaker, *Ancient Traditions of the Virgin Mary's Dormition*, 341–6); Donahue, *Testament of Mary*, 52–5; Herbert and McNamara, *Irish Biblical Apocrypha*, 130; Wenger, *L'Assomption*, 258–9.

63. Bauckham, "Four Apocalypses of the Virgin," 360; Norelli, *Marie des apocryphes*, 134–5; Grypeou and Monferrer-Sala, "Tour of the Other World," 122.

64. Bauckham, "Four Apocalypses of the Virgin," 344–6; Shoemaker, *Ancient Traditions of the Virgin Mary's Dormition*, 42–6; and Cothenet, "Marie dans les Apocryphes," 127–9.

65. *Book of Mary's Repose* 99 (Arras, *De transitu*, vol. 1, 58 (Eth) and 38 (Lat); English trans., Shoemaker, *Ancient Traditions of the Virgin Mary's Dormition*, 345). The interval is given in the *Book of Mary's Repose* as nine hours by one manuscript and three days by the other. The Latin and Irish both have three hours, which is likely the original reading.

66. Cothenet, "Marie dans les Apocryphes," 127.

67. Clayton, "Transitus Mariae," 93; Norelli, *Marie des apocryphes*, 132–6.

68. BL Syr. Add. 17,137, f. 9a, second column. On the manuscript's date and condition, see Wright, *Catalogue of Syriac Manuscripts*, vol. 1, 369. The upper text is written across the lower in the same direction, greatly impeding reading. The fragment has now been published in Shoemaker, "New Syriac Dormition Fragments," 260–3, 267.

69. A Jerusalemite origin is of course central to the (rather dubious) hypotheses of Bagatti, Testa, and Manns, concerning the genesis of these traditions among the Jewish-Christians of the Holy Land. There is, however, fairly widespread agreement concerning the emergence of these traditions in Palestine, despite, as noted above, some rather striking differences otherwise concerning the nature of the corpus of early traditions. See, e.g., Baldi and Mosconi, "Atti del congresso nazionale mariano," 114, 125; Cothenet, "Marie dans les Apocryphes," 144–6; Jugie, *La mort et l'assomption*, 85–92; van Esbroeck, "Les textes littéraires," 276–85; Mimouni, *Dormition et Assomption*, 371–585; Daley, *On the Dormition of Mary*, 7; Shoemaker, *Ancient Traditions of the Virgin Mary's Dormition*, esp. 78–141. See now also esp. Shoemaker, "Epiphanius of Salamis," which argues that Epiphanius seems to have been aware of the nascent Dormition traditions (and the Six Books apocryphon in particular) while he was still in Palestine in the mid-fourth century.

Chapter 4 A Cult Following

1. Some portions of this chapter also appear in Shoemaker, "Ancient Dormition Apocrypha."

2. Shoemaker, "Apocrypha and Liturgy."

3. There is still no proper critical edition of this extremely popular and widely transmitted text, and the standard edition remains Tischendorf, *Apocalypses apocryphae*, 95–110. Ps.-John's dependence on the earlier *Six Books* narrative has been compellingly demonstrated by Bonnet, "Die ältesten Schriften." See also van Esbroeck, "Les textes littéraires," 269–75; Cothenet, "Marie dans les Apocryphes," 119. Simon Mimouni is undecided: Mimouni, *Dormition et Assomption*, 122–3. Regarding the liturgical usage of the Ps.-John *Transitus*, see Mimouni, "La lecture liturgique."

4. Wenger, *L'Assomption*, 17; van Esbroeck, "Les textes littéraires," 266–9; de Santos Otero, *Die handschriftliche Überlieferung*, vol. 2, 161–95

5. Ewald, "Review of 'The departure of my lady Mary,'" 1022–3; cited in the translation from Smith Lewis, *Apocrypha Syriaca*, xvi.

6. Davies, *Heinrich Ewald*, 22–3. Ewald, likewise, was not one to mince words: he was twice forced from his position at Göttingen for public remarks against the king and toward the end of his life was jailed for libel against Otto von Bismarck.

7. Smith Lewis, *Apocrypha Syriaca*, xvi. See also Wright, *Contributions to Apocryphal Literature*, 9–10.

8. Ewald dates the text to the second half of the fourth century at the latest, based on reference to a tradition from the *Testament of Adam* in book 3 and a reference to convents at the end of book 4: Ewald, "Review of 'The departure of my lady Mary,'" 1020. Nevertheless, the final Christian redaction of *Testament of Adam* belongs to the third century, although its traditions are considerably earlier: Charlesworth, ed., *Old Testament Pseudepigrapha*, vol. 1, 990. Moreover, the mention of "convents" in Wright's text is entirely absent from the sixth-century Göttingen MS (syr 10, 33a) and the Sinai palimpsest fragments from the later fifth century: Smith Lewis, *Apocrypha Syriaca*, ܡܒ; trans. Shoemaker, *Ancient Traditions of the Virgin Mary's Dormition*, 372. The lacunae in the Sinai MS are not sufficient to have included the reading from Wright's text.

9. Bonnet, "Die ältesten Schriften," 244–5.

10. Shoemaker, *Ancient Traditions of the Virgin Mary's Dormition*, 46–51; Shoemaker, "New Syriac Dormition Fragments."

11. On the fourth-century date of this apocryphon, see also Shoemaker, "Epiphanius of Salamis," 398–401; Shoemaker, "A Peculiar Version of the *Inventio crucis*," which updates and corrects Shoemaker, *Ancient Traditions of the Virgin Mary's Dormition*, 286–7; Shoemaker, "Death and the Maiden"; Bauckham, *Fate of the Dead*, 358–60; van Esbroeck, "Some Earlier Features."

12. In regard to the True Cross traditions of the *Six Books Apocryphon*, see Shoemaker, "A Peculiar Version of the *Inventio crucis*"; and on the apocalypse, Bauckham, *Fate of the Dead*, 358–60.

13. *Six Books Dormition Apocryphon A* 1.1–5 (Wright, "Departure of my Lady Mary," ܣ-ܠ (Syr) and 129–30 (Eng); cf. Smith Lewis, *Apocrypha Syriaca*, ܚܒ-ܗ (Syr) and 12–15 (Eng)). Note that we distinguish in the notes between versions A and B. Version A designates the version in the sixth-century manuscripts published by Wright and in Göttingen, and the section numbers correspond to the edition of this text that I have prepared for publication. Version B designates the version in the fifth-century palimpsest published by Smith Lewis. Version B will require slightly different section numbers. In the near future I will publish an edition of both versions in the Corpus Christianorum Series Apocryphorum (Brepols): the project is delayed awaiting access to important palimpsest manuscripts from Sinai. Although I give reference to Wright's translation and edition, the translations in the text are my own, based on my revision of Wright's earlier version.

14. *Six Books Dormition Apocryphon A* 1.9 (Wright, "Departure of my Lady Mary," ܙ-ܝ (Syr) and 132 (Eng); cf. Smith Lewis, *Apocrypha Syriaca*, ܝܚ (Syr) and 18 (Eng)).

15. In Syriac: BL syr. add. 14,484, fols. 9–11 (Wright, *Contributions to Apocryphal Literature*, ܠ-ܡ (Syr) and 18–24 (Eng)); and Dam. Patr. 12/17 and 12/18 (I know this version only through its Karshuni apograph at St. Mark's Church in Jerusalem). In Ethiopic: BL Orient. 604, BL Orient. 605, and BL Orient. 606: Wright, *Catalogue of the Ethiopic Manuscripts*, 142, 144–6; Paris Abbadie 128: Chaîne, *Catalogue des manuscrits*; EMML Pr. No. 543: Macomber and Getatchew, *Catalogue of Ethiopian Manuscripts*, vol. 2, 278–81; EMML Pr. No. 744: ibid., vol. 3, 51; Ṭānāsee/Kebrān 45: Hammerschmidt, *Äthiopische Handschriften vom Ṭānāsee 1*, 189–90. In each of these manuscripts, this invention narrative is preceded by an "epitome" of the *Six Books* and followed by a fuller account of the *Six Books* (which itself is abbreviated in comparison with the fifth- and sixth-century Syriac manuscripts). It is not certain which of the two narratives the monk's story is to be associated with, but inasmuch as they present essentially the same

text at different lengths, perhaps it is to be understood that the story applies to both versions. Budge has published a translation (without original text) of all three narratives from BL Orient. 604 in Budge, *Legends of Our Lady Mary*, 143–201. Here, Budge alters the order of presentation in the manuscript so that it appears as if the story of discovery is a preface to the *Six Books* epitome, when in fact it falls in between the epitome (which comes first) and the fuller version (which is the last of the three narratives). This more extensive version of the *Six Books* has been published from two different manuscripts in Chaîne, *Apocrypha de Beata Maria*, 21–49 (Eth) and 17–42 (Lat); English trans. in Shoemaker, *Ancient Traditions of the Virgin Mary's Dormition*, 375–96. The epitome has been published from the British Library MSS in Arras, *De transitu*, vol. 1, 85–100 (Eth) and 55–66 (Lat). The version published by Chaîne is essentially identical to the version translated by Budge. Note, however, that the MSS published in Chaîne's edition do not include the invention story, and one (BN éthiop. 53) includes neither the discovery story nor the epitome. Arabic: Enger, *Ioannis Apostoli de Transitu* is based on only one manuscript. At present, the Dormition narratives of the Arabic (and Karshuni) tradition are largely unknown although vast in number. See now, however, González Casado, *La dormición de la Virgen*; González Casado, "Los relatos árabes apócrifos"; and González Casado, "Textos árabes cristianos," which make something of a start.

16. See Chitty, *The Desert a City*, 168–9.
17. *Six Books Dormition Apocryphon A* 2.8 (Wright, "Departure of my Lady Mary," ܚ (Syr) and 136 (Eng)).
18. *Six Books Dormition Apocryphon A* 2.13 (ibid., ܠ (Syr) and 138 (Eng); cf. Smith Lewis, *Apocrypha Syriaca*, ܙ (Syr) and 48 (Eng)).
19. *Six Books Dormition Apocryphon A* 3.22 (Wright, "Departure of my Lady Mary," ܠ (Syr) and 146 (Eng); cf. Smith Lewis, *Apocrypha Syriaca*, ܛ (Syr) and 48 (Eng)).
20. *Six Books Dormition Apocryphon A* 4.3 (Wright, "Departure of my Lady Mary," ܕ (Syr) and 150–1 (Eng); cf. Smith Lewis, *Apocrypha Syriaca*, ܒ ܨ-ܐ ܨ (Syr) and 54–5 (Eng)).
21. *Six Books Dormition Apocryphon A* 3.1 (Wright, "Departure of my Lady Mary," ܪ (Syr) and 141 (Eng)).
22. *Six Books Dormition Apocryphon A* 5.4 (ibid., ܡܛ-ܡܛ (Syr) and 157–8 (Eng); cf. Smith Lewis, *Apocrypha Syriaca*, ܡܚ-ܡܘ)).
23. *Six Books Dormition Apocryphon A* 6.3 (Wright, "Departure of my Lady Mary," ܠܗ (Syr) and 159 (Eng)).
24. *Six Books Dormition Apocryphon A* 4.6 (ibid., ܠܐ-ܠ (Syr) and 151 (Eng); cf. Smith Lewis, *Apocrypha Syriaca*, ܐ ܨ-ܠ ܨ (Syr) and 56 (Eng)).
25. *Six Books Dormition Apocryphon A* 4.7 (Wright, "Departure of my Lady Mary," ܠܒ (Syr) and 152 (Eng)).
26. *Six Books Dormition Apocryphon A* 3.1–2 (ibid., ܕܒ-ܪ (Syr) and 141 (Eng); cf. Smith Lewis, *Apocrypha Syriaca*, ܠ (Syr) and 33–4 (Eng)).
27. *Six Books Dormition Apocryphon A* 3.3 (Wright, "Departure of my Lady Mary," ܕܒ-ܓܒ (Syr) and 142 (Eng); cf. Smith Lewis, *Apocrypha Syriaca*, ܠܒ (Syr) and 35 (Eng)).
28. *Six Books Dormition Apocryphon A* 3.22–3 (Wright, "Departure of my Lady Mary," ܠ-ܠܐ (Syr) and 146–7 (Eng); cf. the much longer account in Smith Lewis, *Apocrypha Syriaca*, ܡܘ-ܡܚ (Syr) and 46–9 (Eng)).
29. *Six Books Dormition Apocryphon A* 3.24–5 (Wright, "Departure of my Lady Mary," ܠܒ-ܠܐ (Syr) and 147–8 (Eng); cf. Smith Lewis, *Apocrypha Syriaca*, ܡܛ-ܡܚ (Syr) and 49–50 (Eng)).
30. *Six Books Dormition Apocryphon A* 3.26 (Wright, "Departure of my Lady Mary," ܠܒ-ܠܡ (Syr) and 148–9 (Eng)).
31. *Six Books Dormition Apocryphon A* 1.4 (ibid., ܐ (Syr) and 130 (Eng); cf. Smith Lewis, *Apocrypha Syriaca*, ܒ-ܒܚ (Syr) and 14 (Eng)).

32. *Six Books Dormition Apocryphon A* 1.9 (Wright, "Departure of my Lady Mary," ـ-ـ (Syr) and 132 (Eng), trans. slightly modified; cf. Smith Lewis, *Apocrypha Syriaca*, ـ (Syr) and 18 (Eng)).

33. *Six Books Dormition Apocryphon A* 3.2 (Wright, "Departure of my Lady Mary," ـ-ـ (Syr) and 141 (Eng); cf. Smith Lewis, *Apocrypha Syriaca*, ـ (Syr) and 33–4 (Eng)).

34. *Six Books Dormition Apocryphon A* 4.6 (Wright, "Departure of my Lady Mary," ـ-ـ (Syr) and 151–2 (Eng); cf. Smith Lewis, *Apocrypha Syriaca*, ـ-ـ (Syr) and 56–7 (Eng)).

35. *Six Books Dormition Apocryphon A* 4.11–13 (Wright, "Departure of my Lady Mary," ـ-ـ (Syr) and 152–3 (Eng); MS Göttingen Syr. 10, fol. 30b–31a; cf. Smith Lewis, *Apocrypha Syriaca*, ـ-ـ (Syr) and 59–61 (Eng)).

36. *Six Books Dormition Apocryphon A* 4.14 (Wright, "Departure of my Lady Mary," ـ-ـ (Syr) and 153 (Eng)).

37. MS Göttingen Syr. 10, fol. 31: "And the apostles ordered that there will be a commemoration of the blessed one in these three months, so that people will be delivered from hard afflictions and a plague of wrath will not come upon the earth and its inhabitants. And the apostles ordered that offerings that have been made to the blessed one should not remain overnight, but in the evening let flour of the finest wheat flour come to the church and be placed before the altar. And the priests will make the offering and set up censers of incense and light the lights. And the entire evening service [vespers] will concern these offerings. And when the service is finished, let everyone take his offering to his house. Because as soon as the priests pray and say the prayer of my master Mary, the Theotokos, 'Come to us and help the people who call upon you,' and with the priest's word of blessing, my master Mary comes and blesses these offerings. And as soon as everyone takes his offering and goes to his house, great aid and the blessing of my master Mary will enter his dwelling and sustain it forever."

38. Smith Lewis, *Apocrypha Syriaca*, ـ-ـ (Syr) and 59–61 (Eng). Note that although this section appears in Smith Lewis's edition and translation, here and elsewhere Smith Lewis has filled in the gaps in the fifth-century manuscript using a codex from the nineteenth century. Although the sections from this modern manuscript are typeset differently in both the Syriac and the translation, it is important to distinguish material from the two manuscripts. Although they are often remarkably close, they are sufficiently different in places that we cannot simply assume, as Smith Lewis appears to, that the modern version can be used to supply the missing sections of the fifth-century manuscript. See also the passages from Smith Lewis's edition indicated in the notes above.

39. Ibid., ـ-ـ, ـ-ـ; trans. Shoemaker, *Ancient Traditions of the Virgin Mary's Dormition*, 372; Shoemaker, "New Syriac Dormition Fragments," 270–2.

40. The topics addressed in this section have been examined in more detail in my previous article, Shoemaker, "Epiphanius of Salamis," which one should consult for a more thorough presentation and argument.

41. Epiphanius, *Panarion* 79.1.7 (Holl and Dummer, eds., *Epiphanius*, vol. 3, 476).

42. Epiphanius, *Panarion* 78.23.3 (ibid., vol. 3, 473).

43. It is true that the *Six Books* account of Mary's three annual feasts and their observance is exceptional in this era, and I know of no other saint for whom we have such a detailed liturgical program. Nevertheless, one should also note that the *Six Books Apocryphon* is equally exceptional in this regard in relation to other witnesses to early Marian piety.

44. See Shoemaker, "Epiphanius of Salamis," 376–83; see also Shoemaker, "Marian Liturgies and Devotion"; Shoemaker, "Cult of the Virgin in the Fourth Century."

45. Epiphanius, *Panarion* 78.23.5, 79.5.1–4 (Holl and Dummer, eds., *Epiphanius*, vol. 3, 473, 479–80).

46. Epiphanius, *Panarion* 79.4.4–5 (ibid., vol. 3, 479); Fragments 7–10 (Holl, *Gesammelte Aufsatze*, vol. 3, 358). On Epiphanius's iconoclastic writings, see Quasten, *Patrology*, vol. 3, 390–3; and Clark, *Origenist Controversy*, 103–4.
47. Epiphanius, *Panarion* 79.9.3 (Holl and Dummer, eds., *Epiphanius*, vol. 3, 484; trans. Williams, *Panarion*, vol. 2, 628).
48. Eire, *War Against the Idols*, 4–7.
49. See, e.g., Brown, *Cult of the Saints*, 1–22; Bradshaw, *Search for the Origins of Christian Worship*, 21–3, 213–21, 229–30.
50. See also Shoemaker, "Epiphanius of Salamis," 387–96.
51. Epiphanius, *Panarion* 78.23.9 (Holl and Dummer, eds., *Epiphanius*, vol. 3, 473; trans. Williams, *Panarion*, vol. 2, 619).
52. Epiphanius, *Panarion* 79.5.1–4 (Holl and Dummer, eds., *Epiphanius*, vol. 3, 479–80; trans. Williams, *Panarion*, vol. 2, 624–5, slightly modified).
53. Davis, *Cult of Saint Thecla*, 4; and see also chapter 5 in this book.
54. Epiphanius, *Panarion* 79.5.2 (Holl and Dummer, eds., *Epiphanius*, vol. 3, 479).
55. Epiphanius, *Panarion* 79.5.3 (ibid., vol. 3, 480).
56. Kaestli, "Le rôle des textes bibliques," esp. 329–30. See also Schneemelcher, *New Testament Apocrypha*, vol. 2, 161–3, 204–5.
57. E.g., Dölger, "Die eigenartige Marienverehrung"; Benko, *Virgin Goddess*, 170–95.
58. Grant and Menzies, eds., *Joseph's Bible Notes*, 1–4, 14–16.
59. *Hypomnestikon of Joseph* 140 (ibid., 290–305).
60. *Hypomnestikon of Joseph* 140.49 (ibid., 300).
61. See ibid., where phrasing derived from Epiphanius—in the authors' judgment—is set in bold type. See also Moreau, "Observations," esp. 246–9; Goranson, "Joseph of Tiberias Episode," 152–60; Mimouni, "L'Hypomnesticon" (2011), 262–4; originally published as Mimouni, "L'Hypomnesticon" (1997); Grant and Menzies, eds., *Joseph's Bible Notes*, 9–12.
62. On the *Epitome*, see, e.g., Williams, *Panarion*, vol. 1 (2nd ed.), xxii. Concerning Augustine's use of the *Epitome*, see Bardy, "Le 'de haeresibus' et ses sources"; Altaner, "Augustinus und Epiphanius von Salamis." Regarding the relationship between *Joseph's Bible Notes* and Epiphanius's writings, see Grant and Menzies, eds., *Joseph's Bible Notes*, 9–12; and Goranson, "Joseph of Tiberias Episode," 158.
63. Goranson, "Joseph of Tiberias Episode," 144–60; Mimouni, "L'Hypomnesticon" (2011), 264–71. See also Goranson, "Joseph of Tiberias Revisited."
64. For more on this topic, see the discussions in Grant and Menzies, eds., *Joseph's Bible Notes*, 16–20, 23; and Moreau, "Observations," esp. 246–9.
65. Grant and Menzies, eds., *Joseph's Bible Notes*, 20–3, where the issue of likely interpolations is also addressed.
66. Ibid., 23–7
67. On Epiphanius's role as the first patristic witness to traditions concerning Mary's Dormition and Assumption, see, e.g., Shoemaker, *Ancient Traditions of the Virgin Mary's Dormition*, 11–15; Shoemaker, "Epiphanius of Salamis," 389–97; cf. Mimouni, "L'Hypomnesticon" (2011), 272–3.
68. Shoemaker, "Epiphanius of Salamis," 285.
69. Kateusz, "Collyridian Déjà Vu."
70. Particularly troubling in this regard is the argument's reliance on Hans Förster's proposal that a Coptic fragment that he published preserves a Dormition narrative that should be dated to the second century: Förster, *Transitus Mariae*. This dating is extremely improbable, and the fragment is almost certainly an early medieval text. See Shoemaker, "A New Dormition Fragment in Coptic." Further doubt has now been added by Alin Suciu, who has identified additional fragments of the text edited by Förster, which show that the fragment is most likely part of an otherwise unidentified

homily on the Dormition: see A. Suciu, "About Some Coptic Fragments on the Dormition of the Virgin," http://alinsuciu.com/2011/09/15/coptic-fragments-on-the-dormition-of-the-virgin/ (posted on September 15, 2011; accessed January 3, 2012).

71. Tertullian of Carthage, *Prescription against Heretics* 41.5 (Refoulé and Labriolle, eds., *Traité de la prescription*, 147).
72. Smith Lewis, *Apocrypha Syriaca*, ܐ (Syr) and 48 (Eng).
73. Ibid., ܕ-ܡܚ (Syr) and 47-8 (Eng).
74. Ibid., ܘ (Syr) and 34 (Eng).
75. *Six Books Apocryphon A* 3.2 (Wright, "Departure of my Lady Mary," ܗܒ-ܪܐ (Syr) and 141 (Eng); Smith Lewis, *Apocrypha Syriaca*, ܘ (Syr) and 34 (Eng)); Kateusz, "Collyridian Déjà Vu," 83). Note that the verb in question, ܣܐܡ, can also mean "to make the sign of the cross," in which case Mary would simply make the sign of the cross over these women to heal them.
76. Smith Lewis, *Apocrypha Syriaca*, ܡܚ (Syr) and 32 (Eng); Kateusz, "Collyridian Déjà Vu," 80.
77. Kateusz, "Collyridian Déjà Vu," 87–91.
78. See Shoemaker, "Epiphanius of Salamis," 375–85, 399–400.
79. *Six Books Dormition Apocryphon A* 4.14 (Wright, "Departure of my Lady Mary," ܡ-ܪܚ (Syr) and 153 (Eng); Göttingen MS syr. 10, fol. 31b).
80. McGuckin, *Encyclopedia of Eastern Orthodox*, vol. 1, 53–4.
81. The name was presumably invented from their practice of offering a *kollyris*, a loaf of bread, to the Virgin.

Chapter 5 The Memory of Mary

1. See, e.g., Johnson, *Praying and Believing*, 73–88.
2. Peter of Alexandria, *On Easter to Tricenius* (PG 18, 517B); Alexander of Alexandria, *Letter to Alexander of Thessalonica* (PG 18, 568).
3. E.g., Pelikan, *Mary through the Centuries*, 57–8; Johnson, *Praying and Believing*, 68–73; Graef, *Mary*, 38–9; Price, "The Theotokos," 90.
4. For more on the Mariology of the Cappadocian Fathers, see, e.g., Graef, *Mary*, 49–53.
5. Julian the Apostate, *Against the Galileans* 262 D (Wright, ed., *The Works of the Emperor Julian*, vol. 3, 398–9).
6. See, e.g., Johnson, "*Sub Tuum Praesidium*," 66–7; Cameron, "Early Cult of the Virgin," 8.
7. Graef, *Mary*, 45–9.
8. E.g., ibid., 38–78; Beattie, "Mary in Patristic Theology"; Reynolds, *Gateway to Heaven*; and even Gambero, *Mary and the Fathers of the Church*, 95–230, which should be used with some caution since it adopts a very confessionally Catholic point of view.
9. John Chrysostom, *Homilies on John* 21.2 (PG 59, 129–32); *Homilies on Matthew* 4.4 (PG 58, 44).
10. Graef, *Mary*, 58–60.
11. Brakke, *Athanasius*, 52–4, 70–3, 165, 169, 254, 268, 276–9.
12. Ambrose of Milan, *On Virgins* 2.6–16 (Gori, *Verginità e vedovanza*, vol. 1, 168–79). See also Pelikan, *Mary through the Centuries*, 116–22.
13. Jerome, *Against Helvidius* (PL 23, 183–306). See also Hunter, "Helvidius, Jovinian, and the Virginity of Mary," 48–50.
14. Published in Morin, "Pages inédites," 297–301, although I owe my knowledge of this text to Burrus, "Word and Flesh." I thank Julie Kelto Lillis for pointing me toward the relevant part of this article.
15. Morin, "Pages inédites," 298.
16. Hunter, "Helvidius, Jovinian, and the Virginity of Mary," 51–61.

17. Davis, *Cult of Saint Thecla*, 4.
18. Ibid., 87, 94, 95–103.
19. Mossay, ed., *Grégoire de Nazianze: Discours 24–26*, 9–27.
20. Gregory Nazianzus, *Oration 24*, 9–11 (ibid., 54–61). English translation in Gambero, *Mary and the Fathers of the Church*, 166–7.
21. Mossay, ed., *Grégoire de Nazianze: Discours 24–26*, 25; Stegmüller, "Sub tuum praesidium," 78; Peltomaa, *Image of the Virgin Mary*, 75.
22. McGuckin, *Gregory of Nazianzus*, 252.
23. Gregory of Nyssa, *Life of Gregory Thaumaturgus* (Heil, Cavarnos, and Lendle, eds., *Gregorii Nysseni Opera, vol. 10.1*, 16–18; trans. Gambero, *Mary and the Fathers of the Church*, 93–4).
24. Starowieyski, "La plus ancienne description d'une mariophane."
25. Kelly, *Early Christian Doctrines*, 498.
26. Constas, *Proclus of Constantinople*, 246.
27. Sozomen, *Ecclesiastical History* 7.5.1–3 (Bidez and Hansen, eds., *Sozomenus: Kirchengeschichte*, 306; trans. Schaff and Wace, eds., *Nicene and Post-Nicene Fathers, Second Series*, vol. 2, 378–9).
28. Carter, "Chronology," 6–7, 17.
29. Severian of Gabala, *Homily 6 on Creation of the World* 10 (PG 56, 498).
30. Reynolds, *Gateway to Heaven*, 162–3.
31. Carter, "Chronology," 12–17.
32. Severian of Gabala, *Homily on the Legislator* 7 (PG 56, 409–10).
33. Cameron, "Virgin's Robe," 42.
34. In some places this section reproduces material from my previous articles: Shoemaker, "Marian Liturgies and Devotion"; and Shoemaker, "Cult of the Virgin in the Fourth Century."
35. Athanasius of Alexandria, *Letter to Epictetus* 4 (PG 26,1056–7; trans. from Pelikan, *Mary through the Centuries*, 60).
36. Athanasius of Alexandria, *Letter to Maximus* 3 (PG 26, 1088: trans. from Pelikan, *Mary through the Centuries*, 60).
37. See, e.g., McGuckin, "Early Cult of Mary," 9–10; Pelikan, *Mary through the Centuries*, 55–65; Mathews and Muller, "Isis and Mary"; Giamberardini, *Il culto mariano*.
38. As both Pelikan and Johnson also conclude: Pelikan, *Mary through the Centuries*, 59–61; and Johnson, *Praying and Believing*, 85–6. See also Mimouni, "Genèse et évolution," 123–33, esp. 127 n. 243.
39. Proclus of Constantinople, *Homily I: On the Holy Virgin Theotokos* (Constas, ed., *Proclus of Constantinople*, 128–56)
40. Ibid., 128.
41. See ibid., 31–5, 56–9; Constas, "Weaving the Body of God," 172–6.
42. See Baldovin, *Urban Character of Christian Worship*, 105–226; Michel van Esbroeck, "Le culte de la Vierge."
43. See Shoemaker, "(Re?)Discovery of the Kathisma Church"; and Shoemaker, *Ancient Traditions of the Virgin Mary's Dormition*, 78–141.
44. Note that while there is evidence for the celebration of the feast of the Presentation (Hypapante) in the later fourth century from Egeria's pilgrimage account, there is no indication that by this time the feast had any specific Marian associations, such as it would develop in later years to come.
45. Renoux, *Le codex arménien Jérusalem 121*, vol. 2, 354–7; regarding the date, see vol. 1, pp. 166–72.
46. *Protevangelium of James* 17.1.3 (de Strycker, ed., *La forme la plus ancienne*, 144–7).
47. Ray, "August 15"; Capelle, "La fête de la Vierge"; some rather different speculations on the origin of the feast, which also connect it with the birth of Christ, are offered in

Verhelst, "Le 15 août." The site's excavator, Rina Avner, rejects any early association with the Nativity, although the argument is not very persuasive. The argument is based primarily on Joan Taylor's critique of the Jerusalem Franciscan School's scholarship. Nevertheless, Taylor's argument against the idea that an early Jewish Christian community in Jerusalem accurately preserved the memory of where the events of the New Testament actually took place is not especially relevant to this question. Whether or not the tradition is accurate, there is no denying that the *Protevangelium* and Justin Martyr, both from the second century (and both of which Avner mentions), attest to a tradition identifying the location of the Kathisma church with the Nativity. The additional evidence in the articles referenced above makes such a connection rather compelling, as do the readings assigned for the Kathisma in the early liturgical sources. See Avner, "Initial Tradition," 17–19.

48. In general regarding the Kathisma church, see Shoemaker, *Ancient Traditions of the Virgin Mary's Dormition*, 81–98; and Shoemaker, "(Re?)Discovery of the Kathisma Church," 23–36.

49. Jodi Magness, in an important, more recent study of the excavations at Ramat Rahel, largely confirms the dating of the original excavators, adding further precision by identifying pottery from the second half of the fifth century in the church, which means it must have been in use by that time at the latest: Magness, *Jerusalem Ceramic Chronology*, 107, 116–17.

50. Theodore of Petra, *The Life of Theodosius* (Usener, ed., *Der heilige Theodosius*, 13–14). See also Mimouni, *Dormition et Assomption*, 522; and Milik, "Notes d'épigraphie," 571.

51. Cyril of Scythopolis, *The Life of Theodosius* (Schwartz, ed., *Kyrillos von Skythopolis*, 236).

52. Garitte, ed., *Le Calendrier palestino-géorgien*, 84, 108, 301, 401.

53. The site's excavator, Rina Avner, maintains that the large octagonal church should be identified as both the Old and New Kathisma and that the reference to the Old Kathisma refers not to a second church but to its run-down state by the early sixth century and its renovation at this time. Excavation of the site does show new construction in the early sixth century, but I remain unpersuaded by this solution, partly because it requires, as Avner concludes, that the first church of the Kathisma was built only in 455 by Ikelia. Yet there must have been a church at this site before 439, the latest possible date of the *Armenian Lectionary*, and even before 428, the time of Hesychius's homily (discussed below), in order to observe the feast of the Memory of Mary there. It is extremely unlikely that this feast would have been observed without a church and an altar at the site. Avner additionally proposes that the indication of a second dedication date for this church in the Georgian lectionary (which reflects liturgical practice in Jerusalem during the later sixth and early seventh centuries) confirms her hypothesis. She rejects Walter Ray's suggestion that this second date instead corresponds with Ikelia's new construction in the fifth century on the grounds that it "is not supported by the archaeological evidence." Nevertheless, I see no problem at all in squaring this with the archaeological evidence at all, if the smaller church and monastery, which were built before the *Armenian Lectionary*, are the Old Kathisma, while the large octagonal church that Ikelia built is the New Kathisma. Both churches would presumably have two different dedication dates, and this would be fully consistent with the archaeological, literary, and liturgical evidence. More problematic, in my view, is that Avner's interpretation of the archaeological evidence contradicts both the literary and liturgical evidence. See Avner, "Initial Tradition," esp. 14–17. See also Avner, "Recovery of the Kathisma Church."

54. Hesychius of Jerusalem, *Homily VI* (Aubineau, ed., *Les homélies festales*, vol. 1, 117–205; see also Mimouni, *Dormition et Assomption*, 392–5.

55. Pétré, ed., *Éthérie*. On the date, see Devos, "Le date du voyage d'Égérie"; Devos, "Égérie à Bethléem"; Baldovin, *Urban Character of Christian Worship*, 55–7; Wilkinson, *Egeria's Travels*, 169–71.

56. Egeria, *Travels* (Pétré, ed., *Éthérie*). On the date, see Devos, "Le date du voyage d'Égérie"; and Devos, "Égérie à Bethléem."
57. Ray, "August 15," 6.
58. Baldovin, *Urban Character of Christian Worship*, 94.
59. Shoemaker, *Ancient Traditions of the Virgin Mary's Dormition*, 98–107.
60. A similar version of the material in this section should appear in the proceedings of the Fifth International Symposium of the International Centre for Christian Studies at the Orthodox Church of Georgia: "The Tradition of the Theotokos's Adoration in the Orthodox Church," Tbilisi, Georgia, 12–19 May 2014. Also, a much longer discussion of the chantbook and its significance will be published as "Sing, O Daughter(s) of Zion: Public Worship in the Melanias' Jerusalem." To appear in *Melania: Early Christianity in the Life of One Family*, edited by Catherine M. Chin and Caroline T. Schroeder.
61. Edited by Metreveli, Čankievi, and Xevsuriani, უძველსი იადგარი (*Uzvelesi iadgari*). See also Jeffery, "Sunday Office"; Jeffery, "Earliest Christian Chant Repertory"; Jeffery, "Earliest Octōēchoi"; Frøyshov, "Early Development"; Frøyshov, "Georgian Witness."
62. The hymns of the Georgian Lectionary were studied in Leeb, *Die Gesänge*, a work that appeared before the editions of the Georgian Chantbook.
63. Jeffery, "Sunday Office," 54, 58.
64. Métrévéli, "Les manuscrits liturgiques," 47. See also Péradzé, "Les monuments liturgiques"; Renoux, *Les hymnes de la Résurrection I*, 85–6; Frøyshov, "Early Development"; Frøyshov, "Georgian Witness," 233–8; see also Wade, "The Oldest Iadgari: The Jerusalem Tropologion, V–VIII c.," 451.
65. Metreveli, Čankievi, and Xevsuriani, უძველსი იადგარი, 7–333.
66. Jeffery, "Sunday Office," 57. See also Jeffery, "Earliest Christian Chant Repertory," 14.
67. Metreveli, Čankievi, and Xevsuriani, უძველსი იადგარი, 334–66; Jeffery, "Sunday Office," 55, 57. See also Jeffery, "Earliest Christian Chant Repertory," 14
68. Metreveli, Čankievi, and Xevsuriani, უძველსი იადგარი, 367–512.
69. The first and most important of these translations and studies is Renoux, *Les hymnes de la Résurrection I*. The project has now been completed with the recent publication of Renoux, *Les hymnes de la Résurrection II*; and Renoux, *Les hymnes de la Résurrection III*. Renoux has also translated the festal hymns from Lazarus Saturday through Pentecost from the oldest manuscript (which reflects a monastic setting): Renoux, *L'hymnaire de Saint-Sabas*. Another important set of German translations has been published by Hans-Michael Schneider, which translates hymns from the beginning of the festal collection: those for the Annunciation, the Nativity and its Octave, and Epiphany and its Octave. See Schneider, *Lobpreis im rechten Glauben*.
70. Renoux, *Les hymnes de la Résurrection I*, 30–64; see also the very brief summary of some of these points in Frøyshov, "Early Development," 165–8; and Frøyshov, "Georgian Witness," 237. On the differences in the manuscripts, see Renoux, *Les hymnes de la Résurrection III*, 325–6, which gives a good summary, and also Renoux, *Les hymnes de la Résurrection I*, 10–13.
71. Frøyshov, "Early Development," 164–9, 171–3.
72. Translations of these hymns have been published in Renoux, *Les hymnes de la Résurrection II*; and Renoux, *Les hymnes de la Résurrection III*.
73. Renoux, *Les hymnes de la Résurrection II*, 20–1; Métrévéli, Tchankieva, and Khevsouriani, "Le plus ancien tropologion," 60–1; Jeffery, "Sunday Office," 58.
74. Renoux, *Les hymnes de la Résurrection II*, 21–2.
75. Metreveli, Čankievi, and Xevsuriani, უძველსი იადგარი, 439, lines 27–31; trans. Renoux, *Les hymnes de la Résurrection II*, 160; cf. Constas, ed., *Proclus of Constantinople*, 136, lines 18–22 (cf. PG 65, 681B).
76. Metreveli, Čankievi, and Xevsuriani, უძველსი იადგარი, 399, lines 10–13; Renoux, *Les hymnes de la Résurrection II*, 122.

77. Renoux, *Les hymnes de la Résurrection II*, 22–3.
78. As a quick glance at "ἀσυγχύτος/ἀσυγχύτως" in G. W. H. Lampe, *A Patristic Greek Lexicon* (Oxford: Clarendon Press, 1961), or a search in the TLG readily demonstrates. Elsewhere, Renoux reaches the same conclusion regarding the use of the term უქცევეⴓად (ἀτρέπτως), which, despite its association with Chalcedon, was well in use before the Fourth Council: Renoux, *Les hymnes de la Résurrection II*, 285 n. 8.
79. E.g., Renoux, *Les hymnes de la Résurrection I*, 60–2, 98, 100–1, 104–5, 109, etc.
80. Metreveli, Čankievi, and Xevsuriani, ⴓძველისი იადგარი, 372, line 4–5.
81. In addition to the passage considered above from the "Praises to the Holy Theotokos," see also one other possible example, ibid., 479, line 1; Renoux, *Les hymnes de la Résurrection II*, 285 n. 8. Here the hymn uses the term უქცევეⴓად (ἀτρέπτως), which, as Renoux notes, despite its association with Chalcedon, was commonly used well before the Fourth Council. On the Armenian hymns, see Renoux, *Les hymnes de la Résurrection I*, 52–4.
82. E.g., Renoux, *Les hymnes de la Résurrection I*, 54, 62, 109, 111,116, 117, etc.
83. Ibid., 60–2.
84. See, e.g., Shoemaker, "Marian Liturgies and Devotion"; Shoemaker, "Epiphanius of Salamis"; Shoemaker, "Cult of the Virgin in the Fourth Century"; Shoemaker, "Apocrypha and Liturgy."
85. See Jensen, *Understanding*, 9–20.
86. See, e.g., Salgado, "Le culte rendu."
87. Grabar, *Christian Iconography*, 9; see also Parlby, "Origins of Marian Art."
88. Peppard, "Illuminating the Dura-Europos Baptistery," 544–54. A more extended argument regarding the interpretation of this figure and the Annunciation will appear in Peppard's forthcoming book, *The World's Oldest Church: Bible, Art, and Ritual at Dura-Europos, Syria*. In the final chapter of the book, which focuses on the woman at the well, Peppard surveys a number of ancient representations of the Annunciation. The earliest is on a fourth-century sarcophagus from Syracuse, and there is also a fifth-century ivory book cover in Milan. Peppard identifies numerous other examples dating more generally to the fifth and sixth centuries. I thank Prof. Peppard for sharing parts of this manuscript with me. For these two early depictions of the Annunciation, see Schiller, *Iconography*, vol. 1, nos. 53, 57.
89. Johnson, "*Sub Tuum Praesidium*," 64–5.
90. Vopel, *Die altchristlichen Goldgläser*, 24; see also Wellen, *Theotokos*, 166. On the date of Santa Maria Maggiore, see Belting, *Likeness and Presence*, 34. The best recent discussion of these objects can be found in Rubery, "From Catacomb to Sanctuary."
91. Davis, *Cult of Saint Thecla*, 117 n. 15.
92. Kondakov, Иконографія Богоматери, vol. 1, 82–4. See also Wellen, *Theotokos*, 76.
93. Wellen, *Theotokos*, 166; Davis, *Cult of Saint Thecla*, 156–7.
94. Effenberger, "Maria als Vermittlerin," 54–5, 58–61, 99–102.
95. Kateusz, "Ascension of Christ."
96. Ibid., 287–92.
97. de Bruyn, "Greek Amulets." The papyrus cited above is *P.Bon.* I 9 (Vogliano, "Papiri Bolognesi," 229). I also wish to thank Prof. de Bruyn for sharing his forthcoming work on "Appeals to the Intercessions of Mary in Greek Liturgical and Paraliturgical Texts from Egypt."
98. For text, translation, and commentary, see Horsley, "New Documents Illustrating Early Christianity," vol. 2, 141–6.
99. Luijendijk, *Forbidden Oracles*, 13–14, 30–2, 44–7, 72.
100. Papaconstantinou, "Les sanctuaires de la Vierge," 84.
101. Shoemaker, "The Cult of Fashion," 56–61. For more on this church, see also the following chapter.

102. Shoemaker, *Ancient Traditions of the Virgin Mary's Dormition*, 107–15; Rahmani, "Two Early Christian Ampullae"; Grabar and Fourmont, *Ampoules*, 43–4.
103. Davis, *Cult of Saint Thecla*, 117–20, 129, 154–6, 172, although it is certainly possible that I may have missed something.
104. Ibid., 156-7, 172–4.
105. Ibid., 201–8.
106. This was determined through a quick search of papyri.info, which "aggregates material from the Advanced Papyrological Information System (APIS), Duke Databank of Documentary Papyri (DDbDP), Heidelberger Gesamtverzeichnis der griechischen Papyrusurkunden Ägyptens (HGV), Bibliographie Papyrologique (BP)," in August of 2013. A more refined search would perhaps yield even more examples.
107. Bagnall, "Religious Conversion," 110

Chapter 6 The Scepter of Orthodoxy

1. Especially Holum, *Theodosian Empresses*; Limberis, *Divine Heiress*; Constas, *Proclus of Constantinople*. See also Fassler, "First Marian Feast," 31–46.
2. Angelidi, *Pulcheria*; Price, "Marian Piety." James, *Empresses and Power*, 14, 39, seems to support the interpretation offered by Holum and Limberis. Yet several years later she takes a very different tack in James, "The Empress and the Virgin," 146–8.
3. Kate Cooper has argued in favor of a more limited role for Pulcheria in these events, and her case is somewhat persuasive: see Cooper, "Constesting the Nativity"; Cooper, "Empress and *Theotokos*." The same is also true of Lena Mari Peltomaa, who accepts in the main Holum's reconstruction, although she disagrees with some occasional over-statements: Peltomaa, *Image of the Virgin Mary*, e.g., 51 n. 10, 57 n. 52. See also McGuckin, *Cyril of Alexandria*, 40–1, 90, who also understands Pulcheria as playing a pivotal role in the events of the council.
4. One of the weaknesses of Angelidi's interpretation of Pulcheria is that much of her argumentation rests on an assumption, which we have noted is fairly common, that Marian cult did not originate until after the Council of Ephesus: e.g., Angelidi, *Pulcheria*, 121–2.
5. See, e.g., Graef, *Mary*, 80–2; Price, "Marian Piety," 31, 37–8.
6. Socrates Scholasticus, *Ecclesiastical History* 7.32 (Hansen and Širinjan, *Sokrates Kirchengeschichte*, 380; trans. Schaff and Wace, eds., *Nicene and Post-Nicene Fathers, Second Series*, vol. 2, 170, slightly modified).
7. Proclus of Constantinople, *Homily 1: On the Theotokos* 9 (Constas, ed., *Proclus of Constantinople*, 146–7). See also ibid., 56–9, 65–8.
8. Schwartz, ed., *Acta conciliorum oecumenicorum*, I.5.1, 37–9.
9. Frend, "Popular Religion," 19–22.
10. The arguments in this section were presented at the 2014 Byzantine Studies Conference in Vancouver, BC, and I thank the participants, and especially David Olster, George Bevan, and Adam Schor, for their questions and criticisms.
11. *Letter to Cosmas* 8 (Nau, ed., *Documents*, 279; trans. Price, "Marian Piety," 32–3).
12. E.g., Nau, ed., *Documents*, 273–4; for doubts regarding specific elements, see Abramowski, *Untersuchungen*, 15–20.
13. Price, "Marian Piety," 33.
14. *Letter to Cosmas* 5–7 (Nau, ed., *Documents*, 278).
15. Price, "Marian Piety," 34.
16. Barhadbeshabba 'Arbaya *Ecclesiastical History* 27 (Nau, ed., *La seconde partie*, 565–6).
17. Nestorius, *The Bazaar of Heracleides* (Bedjan, ed., *Le livre d'Héraclide*, 148; trans. Driver and Hodgson, *The Bazaar of Heracleides*, 96–7).
18. Price, "Marian Piety," 34.

19. As Price himself must acknowledge: Price, "The Theotokos," 92.
20. Price, "Marian Piety," 33. The reference is to Schwartz, ed., *Acta conciliorum oecumenicorum*, I.5.1, 40, ll. 13–14.
21. Price, "Marian Piety," 33–4.
22. "Puto enim quod nunc non satis curet sanctissimo vestro frater Cyrilo": Mansi, ed., *Sacrorum conciliorum*, vol. 5, 988 A.
23. Gregory, *Vox Populi*, 112; Holum, *Theodosian Empresses*, 176.
24. So also Holum concludes: Holum, *Theodosian Empresses*, 179–83. See also Gregory, *Vox Populi*, 113;
25. Holum, *Theodosian Empresses*, 163–4; emphasis in the original.
26. Ibid., 159–65 and esp. 163 n. 86; Schwartz, ed., *Acta conciliorum oecumenicorum*, II.4.12.15, 37; John Rufus, *Plerophories* 3 (Nau, ed., *Plérophories*, 14–15).
27. Another serious weakness in Angelidi's arguments about Pulcheria is that for some inconceivable reason her study overlooks Proclus almost completely. He is mentioned seemingly only once in his role as bishop of Constantinople—after the Council of Ephesus: Angelidi, *Pulcheria*, 78. In this respect and others Constas, *Proclus of Constantinople*, is an important corrective to Angelidi's study of Pulcheria, providing us with a much better basis for understanding her role in the controversy. The same is also true of James, "The Empress and the Virgin," which mentions neither Proclus nor Constas's important study.
28. Constas, "Weaving the Body of God," 171–2.
29. Gennadius of Marseilles, *On Famous Men* 52 (Bernoulli, ed., *Hieronymus*, 79; trans. Holum, *Theodosian Empresses*, 138).
30. Atticus of Constantinople, *Homily on the Nativity* 2 (Thomson, "Slavonic Translation" 18–19; see also Brière, "Une homélie inédite," 181).
31. See also on this point Holum, *Theodosian Empresses*, 138–40.
32. Constas, *Proclus of Constantinople*, 35–7; McGuckin, "Nestorius and the Political Factions," 8.
33. Holum, *Theodosian Empresses*, 137.
34. Proclus of Constantinople, *Homily 12: On the Resurrection* (PG 65, 788–9; trans. Holum, *Theodosian Empresses*, 137).
35. Constas, *Proclus of Constantinople*, 193–5.
36. Shoemaker, "The Cult of Fashion," 60–2. Here I note (n. 42) Pentcheva's suggestion that the passage from Theodore Anagnostes's early sixth-century *Ecclesiastical History* identifying Pulcheria as the foundress of Blachernai and Chalkoprateia is likely a later interpolation: Pentcheva, *Icons and Power*, 120. Nevertheless, upon further consideration, I am not persuaded that her reasoning for this conclusion is sound. It is true that the passage in question is only in thirteenth-century manuscripts and not in some of the earlier witnesses, as she observes. Nevertheless, all of the manuscripts for this text are partial, and all the earlier manuscripts alleged by Pentcheva to omit the passage in question do not—they simply are not extant for this section! We have no idea whether or not the passage was included, but in any case, there is *no* evidence that it was not present in these earlier manuscripts. Therefore it seems a bit misguided to rely on the missing sections of these manuscripts as evidence that this passage was absent from some earlier version of the *Ecclesiastical History*. Furthermore, Hansen's stemma indicates that this tradition must have been a part of the textual tradition at least by the year 700, when he dates the archetype of MSS P & V: Hansen, ed., *Theodoros Anagnostes*, XXXV, 102.
37. Shoemaker, "The Cult of Fashion," 62 n.42.
38. See, for instance, Price, "Marian Piety," 31–2; Price, "The Theotokos," 89–93, both of which lay out this divide fairly well.
39. Constas, *Proclus of Constantinople*, 245–8, 258–61; translation slightly modified.
40. E.g., Gregory, *Vox Populi*, 106–7; Holum, *Theodosian Empresses*, 164.

41. Shoemaker, *Ancient Traditions of the Virgin Mary's Dormition*, 74–6.
42. Gregory, *Vox Populi*, 107, 125 n. 140.
43. Karwiese, "The Church of Mary."
44. Holum, *Theodosian Empresses*, 164. See also McGuckin, *Cyril of Alexandria*, 40–1.
45. Schwartz, ed., *Acta conciliorum oecumenicorum*, I.1.2, 102.
46. Ibid., I.1.1, 118; trans. Gregory, *Vox Populi*, 104, slightly modified.
47. See, e.g., Frend, "Popular Religion," 22; Holum, *Theodosian Empresses*, 166 and n. 99; McGuckin, *Cyril of Alexandria*, 90–1.
48. *The Coptic Acts of the Council of Ephesus* 39 (Bouriant, ed., *Actes du concile*, 50–2).
49. See also Cooper, "Contesting the Nativity," 43.

Conclusions

1. Baun, "Apocalyptic *Panagia*," 202. With respect to the Christian West, see, e.g., Madigan, *Medieval Christianity*, 341–2.
2. Ibid., 204.
3. "Assumption of Our Lady, The," in O'Carroll, *Theotokos*, 55–8, 56.
4. http://www.fifthmariandogma.com/petition-in-english/, accessed on 14 April 2014.
5. See, e.g., Calkins, "Pope John Paul II's Teaching."

Bibliography

Abbreviations

CCSA   Corpus Christianorum Series Apocryphorum
CSCO   Corpus Scriptorum Christianorum Orientalium
CSEL   Corpus Scriptorum Ecclesiasticorum Latinorum
GCS   Die griechischen christlichen Schriftstellern der ersten drei Jahrhunderte
JECS   *Journal of Early Christian Studies*
NHS   Nag Hammadi Studies; Nag Hammadi and Manichaean Studies
PG   *Patrologia Graeca*, ed. J. P. Migne, et al. (Paris, 1857–)
PL   *Patrologia Latina*, ed. J. P. Migne, et al. (Paris, 1844–)
PO   Patrologia Orientalis
SC   Sources chrétiennes
SH   Subsidia Hagiographica

Biblical and Rabbinic texts are cited according to the list of abbreviations given in Patrick H. Alexander, *The SBL Handbook of Style for Ancient Near Eastern, Biblical, and Early Christian Studies*. Peabody, Mass.: Hendrickson Publishers, 1999.

Primary Sources

Dormition and Assumption Narratives

The Book of Mary's Repose (*Obsequies of the Virgin*). Complete Ethiopic version edited by Victor Arras. *De transitu Mariae apocrypha aethiopice*. 2 vols., CSCO 342–3, 351–2. Louvain: Secrétariat du CSCO, 1973. Georgian fragments edited by Michel van Esbroeck. "Apocryphes géorgiens de la Dormition." *Analecta Bollandiana* 92 (1973): 55–75. Syriac fragments edited by Wright, William. *Contributions to the Apocryphal Literature of the New Testament*. London: Williams and Norgate, 1865; and also by Stephen J. Shoemaker. "New Syriac Dormition Fragments from Palimpsests in the Schøyen Collection and the British Library: Presentation, Edition and Translation." *Le Muséon* (2011): 259–78. English translation in Stephen J. Shoemaker, *Ancient Traditions of the Virgin Mary's Dormition and Assumption*, Oxford Early Christian Studies. Oxford: Oxford University Press, 2002, 290–350.

The Earliest Greek Dormition Narrative. Edited by Antoine Wenger. *L'Assomption de la T.S. Vierge dans la tradition byzantine du VIe au Xe siècle; études et documents*, Archives de l'Orient chrétien, 5. Paris: Institut français d'études byzantines, 1955.

John of Thessalonica. *Homily on the Dormition*. Edited by Martin Jugie. *Homélies mariales byzantines (II)*, PO 19.3. Paris: Librairie de Paris/Firmin-Didot et Cie, 1926.

Latin Transitus W (L2). Edited by André Wilmart. *Analecta reginensia: Extraits des manuscrits latins de la reine Christine conservés au Vatican*, Studi e Testi, 59. Città del Vaticano: Biblioteca apostolica Vaticana, 1933.

The "Archaic" Latin Transitus (L4). Edited by Antoine Wenger. *L'Assomption de la T.S. Vierge dans la tradition byzantine du VIe au Xe siècle; études et documents*, Archives de l'Orient chrétien, 5. Paris: Institut français d'études byzantines, 1955.

The Old Irish Dormition Narratives. Edited by C. Donahue. *The Testament of Mary: The Gaelic Version of the Dormitio Mariae together with an Irish Latin Version*. New York: Fordham University Press, 1942. Translation of a second manuscript in Máire Herbert and Martin McNamara. *Irish Biblical Apocrypha: Selected Text in Translation*. Edinburgh: T & T Clark, 1989.

Ps-John Transitus Mariae. Edited by Constantin Tischendorf. *Apocalypses apocryphae Mosis, Esdrae, Pauli, Johannis, item Mariae dormito: additis evangeliorum et actuum apocryphorum supplementis. Maiximam partem nunc primum*. Leipzig: H. Mendelssohn, 1866.

The Six Books Dormition Apocryphon. Complete Syriac version edited by Wright, William. "The Departure of My Lady Mary from This World." *The Journal of Sacred Literature and Biblical Record* 6–7 (1865): 417–48 and 108–60. Syriac fragments also edited by Agnes Smith Lewis. *Apocrypha Syriaca*, Studia Sinaitica 11. London: C. J. Clay and Sons, 1902. Also edited by Stephen J. Shoemaker. "New Syriac Dormition Fragments from Palimpsests in the Schøyen Collection and the British Library: Presentation, Edition and Translation." *Le Muséon* (2011): 259–78. Arabic version edited by Maximilian Enger. اخبار يوحنّا اسليح في نقلة امّ المسيح *(Akhbâr Yûhannâ as-salîh fi naqlat umm al-masîh) id est Joannis apostoli de transitu Beatae Mariae Virginis liber*. Elberfeld: R. L. Friderichs, 1854. Ethiopic version edited by Marius Chaîne. *Apocrypha de Beata Maria Virgine*. 2 vols., CSCO 39–40, Scriptores Aethiopici, 22–3. Louvain: L. Durbecq, 1955. Also edited by E. A. Wallis Budge. *Legends of Our Lady Mary the Perpetual Virgin and her Mother Hannâ*. London: Oxford University Press, 1933.

Other Primary Sources

Alexander of Alexandria, *Letter to Alexander of Thessalonica*. PG 18, 547–72.

Ambrose of Milan, *On Virgins*. Edited by Franco Gori. *Verginità e vedovanza*. 2 vols., Sancti Ambrosii episcopi Mediolandensis opera 14. Milan Biblioteca Ambrosiana, 1989.

The (First) Apocalypse of James. Edited by Douglas M. Parrott. *Nag Hammadi Codices V, 2–5 and VI with Papyrus Berolinensis 8502, 1 and 4*, NHS 11. Leiden: E. J. Brill, 1979.

The Apocryphon of John. Edited by Michael Waldstein and Frederic Wisse. *The Apocryphon of John: A Synopsis of Nag Hammadi Codices II,1, III,1, and IV,1 with BG 8502,2*, NHS 33. New York: E. J. Brill, 1995.

The Ascension of Isaiah. Edited by Paolo Bettiolo and Enrico Norelli. *Ascensio Isaiae*. 2 vols., CCSA 7–8. Turnhout: Brepols, 1995.

Athanasius of Alexandria. *Letter to Epictetus*. PG 26, 1049–70.

———. *Letter to Maximus* 3. PG 26, 1085–90.

Atticus of Constantinople. *Homily on the Nativity*. Edited by Maurice Brière. "Une homélie inédite d'Atticus, Patriarche de Constantinople." Revue de l'Orient chrétien 29 (1933–4): 160-86. Also edited by Francis J. Thomson, "The Slavonic Translation of the Hitherto Untraced Greek *Homilia in Nativitatem Domini Nostri Jesu Christi* by Atticus of Constantinople." *Analecta Bollandiana* 118 (2000): 5–36.

Augustine of Hippo. *Against Faustus the Manichaean*. Edited by Joseph Zycha. *Sancti Aureli Augustini De utilitate credendi*. CSEL 25.1. Vienna: F. Tempsky, 1891.

———. *Questions on the Heptateuch*. Edited by Joseph Zycha. *Sancti Aureli Augustini Quaestionum in Heptateuchum libri VII*. CSEL 28.2. Vienna: F. Tempsky, 1895.

———. *City of God*. Edited by Bernhard Dombart, Alfons Kalb, and Johannes Divjak. *Sancti Aurelii Augustini episcopi De civitate Dei libri XXII*, 5th ed., 2 vols. Stuttgart: B. G. Teubner, 1981.

Barhadbeshabba 'Arbaya. *Ecclesiastical History*. Edited by François Nau. *La seconde partie de l'Histoire de Barhadbešabba 'Arbaïa : et Controverse de Théodore de Mopsueste avec les macédoniens : texte syriaque*, PO 9.5. Paris: Firmin-Didot, 1913.

The Book of the Nativity of Mary. Edited by Jan Gijsel and Rita Beyers. *Libri de nativitate mariae*. 2 vols., CCSA, 9–10. Turnhout: Brepols, 1997.

The Books of Jeu. Edited by Carl Schmidt and Violet MacDermot. *The Books of Jeû and the Untitled Text in the Bruce Codex*, NHS 13. Leiden: E. J. Brill, 1978.

Clement of Alexandria, *Miscellanies*. Edited by Otto Stählin, Ludwig Früchtel, and Ursula Treu. *Clemens Alexandrinus*. 3 vols., GCS 52 (15), 17. Berlin: Akademia-Verlag, 1960.

The Coptic Acts of the Council of Ephesus. Edited by U. Bouriant. *Actes du concile d'Ephèse: Texte copte publié et traduit*, Mémoires publiés par la Mission archéologique française au Caire 8.1. Paris: Leroux, 1892.

Cyril of Scythopolis. *The Life of Theodosius*. Edited by Eduard Schwartz. *Kyrillos von Skythopolis*. Edited by Eduard Schwartz, Texte und Untersuchungen 49.2. Leipzig: J. C. Hinrichs, 1939.

Dialogue of the Savior. Edited by Stephen Emmel. *Nag Hammadi Codex III, 5: The Dialogue of the Savior*, NHS 26. Leiden: E. J. Brill, 1984.

Egeria. *Travels*. Edited by Hélène Pétré. *Éthérie: Journal de voyage*, SC 21. Paris: Éditions du Cerf, 1971.

Epiphanius of Salamis. *Fragments*. Edited by Karl Holl. *Gesammelte Aufsätze zur Kirchengeschichte*. 3 vols. Tübingen: J. C. B. Mohr (Paul Siebeck), 1928–32.

———. *Panarion*. Edited by Karl Holl and Jürgen Dummer, eds. *Epiphanius*. 2nd ed. 3 vols., GCS 25, 31, 37. Leipzig; Berlin: J. C. Hinrichs; Akademie-Verlag, 1915, 1980, 1985. Translated by Frank Williams. *The Panarion of Epiphanius of Salamis*. 2 vols., NHS 35–6. Leiden: E. J. Brill, 1987, 1994; and idem. *The Panarion of Epiphanius of Salamis. Book I (sects. 1–46)*. 2nd ed, NHS 63. Leiden: Brill, 2009.

Gennadius of Marseilles, *On Famous Men*. Edited by Carl Albrecht Bernoulli. *Hieronymus und Gennadius: De viris inlustribus*. Freiburg i.B., Leipzig,: Mohr, 1895.

The Gospel (Questions) of Bartholomew. Edited by A. Vasiliev. *Anecdota Graeco-Byzantina, Pars Prior*. Moscow: Universitas Caesareae, 1893. Also edited by Andre Wilmart and Eugene Tisserant. "Fragments grecs et latins de l'Évangile de Barthélemy." *Revue Biblique* 10 (1913): 161–90; 321–68.

The Gospel of Mary. Edited by Douglas M. Parrott. *Nag Hammadi Codices V, 2–5 and VI with Papyrus Berolinensis 8502, 1 and 4*, NHS 11. Leiden: E. J. Brill, 1979.

The Gospel of Ps.-Matthew. Edited by Jan Gijsel and Rita Beyers. *Libri de nativitate mariae*. 2 vols, CCSA, 9–10. Turnhout: Brepols, 1997.

The Gospel of Philip. Edited by Bentley Layton. *Nag Hammadi Codex II, 2–7*. 2 vols., NHS 20. Leiden: E. J. Brill, 1989.

The Gospel of the Egyptians. Edited by Alexander Böhlig and Frederik Wisse. *Nag Hammadi Codices III, 2 and IV, 2: The Gospel of the Egyptians*, NHS 4. Grand Rapids MI: Eerdmans, 1975.

The Gospel of Thomas. Edited by Bentley Layton. *Nag Hammadi Codex II, 2–7*. 2 vols, NHS 20. Leiden: E. J. Brill, 1989.

The Gospel of Truth. Edited by Harold. W. Attridge. *Nag Hammadi Codex I (The Jung Codex)*. 2 vols., NHS 22–3. Leiden: E. J. Brill, 1985.

Gregory of Nazianzus. *Oration 24*. Edited by Justin Mossay. *Grégoire de Nazianze: Discours 24–26*, SC 284. Paris: Les Éditions du Cerf, 1981.

Gregory of Nyssa, *Life of Gregory Thaumaturgus*. Edited by Gunterus Heil, Johannes P. Cavarnos, and Otto Lendle. *Gregorii Nysseni Opera*. Vol. 10.1, *Gregorii Nysseni Sermones, Pars II*. Leiden: E. J. Brill, 1990.

Hesychius of Jerusalem. *Homilies*. Edited by Michel Aubineau. *Les homélies festales d'Hésychius de Jérusalem*. 2 vols., SH 59. Brussels: Société des Bollandistes, 1978.

The Hypomnestikon of Joseph. Edited by Robert M. Grant and Glen W. Menzies. *Joseph's Bible Notes (Hypomnestikon)*, Society of Biblical Literature Texts and Translations, Early Christian Series 41. Atlanta: Scholars Press, 1996.

The Hypostasis of the Archons. Edited by Bentley Layton. *Nag Hammadi Codex II, 2–7*. 2 vols., NHS 20. Leiden: E. J. Brill, 1989.

The Infancy Gospel of Jesus. Edited by Tony Burke. *De infantia Iesu Evangelium Thomae Graecae*, CCSA 17. Turnhout: Brepols, 2010.

Irenaeus of Lyon. *Against Heresies*. Edited by Adelin Rousseau and Louis Doutreleau. *Irénée de Lyon: Contre les hérésies*. 9 vols., SC 100, 152–3, 210–11, 263–4, 293–4. Paris: Les Éditions du Cerf, 1969–82.

Jerome. *Against Helvidius*. PL 23, 183–206.

———. *Against Jovinian*. PL 23, 211–338.

The Jerusalem Armenian Lectionary. Edited by A. Renoux. *Le codex arménien Jérusalem 121*. 2 vols, PO 35.1 and 36.2. Turnhout: Brepols, 1971.

The Jerusalem Georgian Calendar. Edited by Gérard Garitte. *Le Calendrier palestino-géorgien du Sinaiticus 34 (Xe siècle)*, SH 30. Bruxelles: Société des Bollandistes, 1958.

The Jerusalem Georgian Chantbook. Edited by El. Metreveli, C'. Čankievi, and L. Xevsuriani. უძველესი იადგარი (Uzvelesi iadgari (The Oldest Chantbook)), Żveli k'art'uli mcerlobis żeglebi 2. Tibilisi: Mec'niereba, 1980.

John Chrysostom, *Homilies on John*. PG 59.

———. *Homilies on Matthew*. PG 57–8.

John Rufus, *Plerophories*. Edited by François Nau. *Jean Rufus, évêque de Maïouma. – Plérophories : témoignages et révélations contre le Concile de Chalcédoine*, PO 8.1. Paris: Firmin-Didot, 1912.

Julian the Apostate. *Against the Galileans*. Edited by Wilmer Cave France Wright. *The Works of the Emperor Julian*. 3 vols., The Loeb Classical Library 13, 29, 157. Cambridge: Harvard University Press, 1913.

Justin Martyr, *Dialogue with Trypho*. Edited by Miroslav Marcovich. *Dialogus cum Tryphone*, Patristische Texte und Studien 47. Berlin; New York: Walter de Gruyter, 1997.

The Letter to Cosmas. Edited by François Nau. *Documents pour servir à l'histoire de l'Èglise nestorienne: textes syriaques*, PO 13.2. Paris: Firmin-Didot, 1919.

Maximus the Confessor. *The Life of the Virgin*. Edited by Michel van Esbroeck. *Maxime le Confesseur: Vie de la Vierge*. 2 vols., CSCO 478–9, Scriptores Iberici, 21–2. Lovanii: E. Peeters, 1986. Translated by Stephen J. Shoemaker. *Maximus the Confessor, The Life of the Virgin: Translated, with an Introduction and Notes*. New Haven and London: Yale University Press, 2012.

Nestorius. *The Bazaar of Heracleides*. Edited by Paul Bedjan. *Le livre d'Héraclide de Damas*. Paris: O. Harrassowitz, 1910. Translated by Godfrey Rolles Driver and Leonard Hodgson. *The Bazaar of Heracleides*. Oxford: Clarendon Press, 1925.

The Odes of Solomon. Edited by James H. Charlesworth. *The Odes of Solomon: The Syriac Texts*, Texts and Translations 13, Pseudepigrapha Series 7. Missoula, MT: Scholars Press, 1978.

On the Origin of the World. Edited by Bentley Layton. *Nag Hammadi Codex II, 2–7*. 2 vols., NHS 20. Leiden: E. J. Brill, 1989.

Origen of Alexandria. *Commentary on Matthew*. Edited by Klostermann, Erich, and Ernst Benz, eds. *Origenes Werke*. 12 vols. Vol. 10–11, *Origenes Matthäuserklärung I & II. Die lateinische Übersetzung der Commentariorum series*, GCS 38 and 40. Leipzig: J. C. Henrichs, 1933–5.

———. *Homilies on Luke*. Edited by Max Rauer. *Origenes Werke*. 12 vols. Vol. 9, *Die Homilien zu Lukas in der Übersetzung des Hieronymus und die griechischen Reste der Homilien und des Lukas-Kommentars*, GCS 35. Berlin: J. C. Hinrichs, 1930.

———. *Homilies on Leviticus*. Edited by W. A. Baehrens. *Origenes Werke*. 12 vols. Vol. 3, *Homillien zum Hexateuch in Rufins Übersetzung*. GCS 6. Leipzig: J. C. Hinrichs, 1899.

Peter of Alexandria, *On Easter to Tricenius*. PG 18, 512–20.

The Pistis Sophia. Edited by Carl Schmidt and Violet MacDermot. *Pistis Sophia*, NHS 9. Leiden: E. J. Brill, 1978.

The Protevangelium of James. Edited by Émile de Strycker. *La forme la plus ancienne du Protévangile de Jacques*, SH 33. Bruxelles: Société des Bollandistes, 1961.

Proclus of Constantinople, *Homilies*. Edited by Nicholas Constas. *Proclus of Constantinople and the Cult of the Virgin in Late Antiquity: Homilies 1–5, Texts and Translations*, Supplements to Vigiliae Christianae 66. Leiden: Brill, 2003. Also edited in PG 65, 679–850.

Severian of Gabala, *Homily 6 on Creation of the World*. PG 56, 484–500.

———. *Homily on the Legislator*. PG 56, 397–410.

Socrates Scholasticus. *Ecclesiastical History*. Edited by Günther Christian Hansen and Manja Širinjan. *Sokrates Kirchengeschichte*, GCS, n. F. 1. Berlin: Akademie Verlag, 1995.

The Sophia of Jesus Christ. Edited by Douglas M. Parrott. *Nag Hammadi Codices III, 3–4 and V, 1*, NHS 27. Leiden: E. J. Brill, 1991.

Sozomen. *Ecclesiastical History*. Edited by Joseph Bidez and Günther Christian Hansen. *Sozomenus: Kirchengeschichte*. 2nd ed, GCS, n.F. 4. Berlin: Akademie Verlag, 1995.

Tertullian of Carthage. *Prescription against Heretics*. Edited by François Refoulé and Pierre de Labriolle. *Traité de la prescription contre les hérétiques*, SC 46. Paris: Éditions du Cerf, 1957.

———. *Against Marcion*. Edited by René Braun. *Contre Marcion*. 5 vols., SC 365, 368, 399, 456, 483. Paris: Éditions du Cerf, 1990.

———. *On Monogamy*. Edited by Paul Mattei. *Le mariage unique = De monogamia*, SC 343. Paris: Éditions du Cerf, 1988.

———. *On the Flesh of Christ*. Edited by Jean-Pierre Mahé. *La chair du Christ*. 2 vols., SC 216–17. Paris: Éditions du Cerf, 1975.

The Testament of Solomon. Edited by C. C. McCown. *The Testament of Solomon, Edited from Manuscripts at Mount Athos, Bologna, Holkham Hall, Jerusalem, London, Milan, Paris and Vienna*. Leipzig: J. C. Hinrichs, 1922.

Theodore Anagnostes. *Ecclesiastical History*. Edited by Günther Christian Hansen. *Theodoros Anagnostes Kirchengeschichte*. 2nd ed., GCS, n.F. 3 Berlin: Akademie-Verlag, 1995.

Theodore of Petra. *The Life of Theodosius*. Edited by H. Usener. *Der heilige Theodosius, Schriften des Theodoros und Kyrillos*. Leipzig: Teubner, 1890.

Theodoret of Cyrrhus. *Compendium of Heretical Tales*. PG 83, 335–556.

The Untitled Text in the Bruce Codex. Edited by Carl Schmidt and Violet MacDermot. *The Books of Jeû and the Untitled Text in the Bruce Codex*, NHS 13. Leiden: E. J. Brill, 1978.

Zostrianos. Edited by John H. Sieber. *Nag Hammadi Codex VIII*, NHS 31. Leiden: E. J. Brill, 1991.

Secondary Sources

Abrahà, Tedros. "La *Dormitio Mariae* in Etiopia." In *Il dogma dell'assunzione de Maria: problemi attuali e tentativi de ricomprensione. Atti del XVII Simposio Internazionale Mariologico (Roma, 6–9 ottobre 2009)*, edited by Ermanno M. Toniolo, 167–200. Rome: Edizioni Marianum, 2010.

Abramowski, Luise. *Untersuchungen zum Liber Heraclidis des Nestorius*, CSCO 242, Subsidia 22. Louvain: Secrétariat du CSCO, 1963.

Altaner, Berthold. "Augustinus und Epiphanius von Salamis." In *Mélanges J. De Ghellinck*, 2 vols., vol. 1, 265–75. Gembloux: Duculot, 1951.

Angelidi, Christine. *Pulcheria: la castità al potere (c. 399–c. 455)*, Donne d'Oriente e d'Occidente 5. Milan: Jaca book, 1998.

Avner, Rina. "The Recovery of the Kathisma Church and Its Influence on Octagonal Buildings." In *One Land – Many Cultures: Archaeological Studies in Honor of Stanislao Loffreda, O.F.M.*, edited by G. C. Bottini, L. D. Segni and D. Chrupcala, 173–88. Studium Biblicum Franciscanum Collectio major 41. Jerusalem: Franciscan Printing Press, 2003.

———. "The Initial Tradition of the Theotokos at the Kathisma: Earliest Celebrations and the Calendar." In *The Cult of the Mother of God in Byzantium: Texts and Images*, edited by Leslie Brubaker and Mary B. Cunningham, 9–29. Aldershot: Ashgate, 2011.

Baarda, Tjitze. *The Gospel quotations of Aphrahat the Persian Sage*. 2 vols. Vol. 1, *Aphrahat's Text of the Fourth Gospel*. Amsterdam: Vrije Universiteit, 1975.

Backus, Irene. "Guillaume Postel, Théodore Bibliander et le Protévangile de Jacques. Introduction historique, édition et traduction française du MS Londres, British Library, Sloane 1411, 260r–267r." *Apocrypha* 6 (1995): 7–65.

Bagnall, Roger. "Religious Conversion and Onomastic Change in Byzantine Egypt." *Bulletin of the American Society of Papyrologists* 19 (1982): 105–24.

Baldi, Donato, and Anacleto Mosconi. "L'Assunzione di Maria SS. negli apocrifi." In *Atti del congresso nazionale mariano dei Fratei Minori d'Italia (Roma 29 aprile–3 maggio 1947)*, 75–125. Studia Mariana 1. Rome: Commissionis Marialis Franciscanae, 1948.

Baldovin, John Francis. *The Urban Character of Christian Worship: The Origins, Development, and Meaning of Stational Liturgy*, Orientalia Christiana Analecta, 228. Roma: Pont. Institutum Studiorum Orientalium, 1987.

Bardy, Gustave. "Le 'de haeresibus' et ses sources." In *Miscellanea agostiniana*, 2 vols., vol. 2, 395–416. Rome: Tipografia poliglotta vaticana, 1930–1.

Barker, Margaret. *The Mother of the Lord*. Vol. 1, *The Lady of the Temple*. London; New York: Bloomsbury T & T Clark, 2012.

Bauckham, Richard. *Jude and the Relatives of Jesus in the Early Church*. Edinburgh: T & T Clark, 1990.

———. "The Four Apocalypses of the Virgin Mary." In *The Fate of the Dead: Studies on Jewish and Christian Apocalypses*, 332–62. Supplements to Novum Testamentum 93. Leiden: Brill, 1998.

———. *The Fate of the Dead: Studies on Jewish and Christian Apocalypses*, Supplements to Novum Testamentum, 93. Leiden: Brill, 1998.

Baun, Jane. "Apocalyptic *Panagia*: Some Byways of Marian Revelation in Byzantium." In *The Cult of the Mother of God in Byzantium: Texts and Images*, edited by Leslie Brubaker and Mary B. Cunningham, 199–218. Aldershot: Ashgate, 2011.

Beattie, Tina. "Mary in Patristic Theology." In *Mary: The Complete Guide*, edited by Sarah Jane Boss, 75–105. London: Continuum, 2007.

Belting, Hans. *Likeness and Presence: A History of the Image Before the Era of Art*. Chicago: University of Chicago Press, 1994.

Benko, Stephen. *The Virgin Goddess: Studies in the Pagan and Christian Roots of Mariology*, Studies in the History of Religions 59. Leiden: E. J. Brill, 1993.

Betz, Hans Dieter. *The Greek Magical Papyri in Translation, Including the Demotic Spells*. 2nd ed. Chicago: University of Chicago Press, 1992.

Blancy, Alain, Maurice Jourjon, and Groupe des Dombes. *Mary in the Plan of God and in the Communion of the Saints: Toward a Common Christian Understanding*. Translated by Matthew J. O'Connell. New York: Paulist Press, 2002.

Bonnet, Maximilian. "Die ältesten Schriften von der Himmelfahrt Mariä." *Zeitschrift für Wissenschaftliche Theologie* 23 (1880): 227–47.

Bovon, François. "Le privilège pascal de Marie-Madeleine." *New Testament Studies* 30 (1984): 50–62.

Bovon, François, and Pierre Geoltrain, eds. *Écrits apocryphes chrétiens*. Vol. 1, Bibliothèque de la Pléiade 442. Paris: Gallimard, 1997.

Braaten, Carl E., and Robert W. Jenson, eds. *Mary, Mother of God*. Grand Rapids, Mich.: W. B. Eerdmans Pub. Co., 2004.

Bradshaw, Paul F. *The Search for the Origins of Christian Worship: Sources and Methods for the Study of Early Liturgy*. 2nd ed. Oxford: Oxford University Press, 2002.

Brakke, David. *Athanasius and the Politics of Asceticism*, Oxford Early Christian Studies. Oxford: Oxford University Press, 1995.

———. *The Gnostics: Myth, Ritual, and Diversity in Early Christianity*. Cambridge, Mass.: Harvard University Press, 2010.

Brock, Ann Graham. "Setting the Record Straight – The Politics of Identification: Mary Magdalene and Mary the Mother in *Pistis Sophia*." In *Which Mary?: The Marys of Early Christian Tradition*, edited by F. Stanley Jones, 43–52. Atlanta: Society of Biblical Literature, 2002.

Brown, Peter. *The Cult of the Saints: Its Rise and Function in Latin Christianity*, The Haskell Lectures on History of Religions, New Series, 2. Chicago: University of Chicago Press, 1981.

———. *The Body and Society: Men, Women, and Sexual Renunciation in Early Christianity*, Lectures on the History of Religions, New Series 13. New York: Columbia University Press, 1988.

Brown, Raymond E., et al. *Mary in the New Testament: A Collaborative Assessment by Protestant and Roman Catholic Scholars*. New York: Paulist Press, 1978.

Buckley, Jorunn Jacobson. "'The Holy Spirit' Is a Double Name." In *Female Fault and Fulfilment in Gnosticism*. Chapel Hill: The University of North Carolina Press, 1986.

Burrus, Virginia. "Word and Flesh: The Bodies and Sexuality of Ascetic Women in Christian Antiquity." *Journal of Feminist Studies in Religion* 10 (1994): 27–51.

Calkins, Arthur Burton. "Pope John Paul II's Teaching on Marian Coredemption." In *Mary: Coredemptrix, Mediatrix, Advocate: Theological Foundations II: Papal, Pneumatological, Ecumenical*, edited by Mark I. Miravalle, 113–47. Santa Barbara: Queenship Publications, 1996.

Cameron, Averil. "The Theotokos in Sixth-Century Constantinople." *Journal of Theological Studies* N.S. 29 (1978): 79–108.

———. "The Virgin's Robe: An Episode in the History of Early Seventh-Century Constantinople." *Byzantion* 49 (1979): 42–56.

———. "Virginity as Metaphor: Women and the Rhetoric of Early Christianity." In *History as Text: The Writing of Ancient History*, edited by Averil Cameron, 184–205. London: Duckworth, 1989.

———. *Christianity and the Rhetoric of Empire: The Development of Christian Discourse*, Sather Classical Lectures 55. Berkeley: University of California Press, 1991.

———. *The Mediterranean World in Late Antiquity, A.D. 395–600*. London: Routledge, 1993.

———. "The Early Cult of the Virgin." In *Mother of God: Representations of the Virgin in Byzantine Art*, edited by Maria Vassilaki, 3–15. Milan: Skira, 2000.

———. "The Cult of the Virgin in Late Antiquity: Religious Development and Myth-Making." In *The Church and Mary*, edited by R. N. Swanson, 1–21. Studies in Church History 39. Suffolk: The Boydell Press, 2004.

———. "Introduction." In *Images of the Mother of God: Perceptions of the Theotokos in Byzantium*, edited by Maria Vassilaki, xxvii–xxxii. Aldershot: Ashgate, 2005.

———. "Introduction – The Mother of God in Byzantium: Relics, Icons, Texts." In *The Cult of the Mother of God in Byzantium*, edited by Leslie Brubaker and Mary Cunningham, 1–5. Aldershot: Ashgate, 2011.

Capelle, Bernard. "La fête de la Vierge à Jérusalem au Ve siècle." *Le Muséon* 56 (1943): 1–33.

Carroll, Michael P. *The Cult of the Virgin Mary: Psychological Origins.* Princeton: Princeton University Press, 1986.

Carter, Robert E. "The Chronology of Twenty Homilies of Severian of Gabala." *Traditio* 55 (2000): 1–17.

Chaîne, Marius. *Catalogue des manuscrits éthiopiens de la collection Antoine d'Abbadie.* Paris: Imprimerie nationale, 1912.

Charlesworth, James H., ed. *The Old Testament Pseudepigrapha.* 2 vols. Garden City, NY: Doubleday, 1983.

Chitty, Derwas J. *The Desert a City: An Introduction to the Study of Egyptian and Palestinian Monasticism under the Christian Empire.* Oxford: Blackwell, 1966.

Clark, Elizabeth A. *The Origenist Controversy: The Cultural Construction of an Early Christian Debate.* Princeton: Princeton University Press, 1992.

———. "The Lady Vanishes: Dilemmas of a Feminist Historian after the 'Linguistic Turn'." *Church History* 67 (1998): 1–31.

———. *History, Theory, Text: Historians and the Linguistic Turn.* Cambridge: Harvard University Press, 2004.

———. *Founding the Fathers: Early Church History and Protestant Professors in Nineteenth-Century America*, Divinations: Rereading Late Ancient Religion. Philadelphia: University of Pennsylvania Press, 2011.

Clayton, Mary. "The Transitus Mariae: The Tradition and Its Origins." *Apocrypha* 10 (1999): 74–98.

Constas, Nicholas. "Weaving the Body of God: Proclus of Constantinople, the Theotokos, and the Loom of the Flesh." *JECS* 3 (1995): 169–94.

———. *Proclus of Constantinople and the Cult of the Virgin in Late Antiquity: Homilies 1–5, Texts and Translations*, Supplements to Vigiliae Christianae 66. Leiden: Brill, 2003.

Cooper, Kate. "Contesting the Nativity: Wives, Virgins, and Pulcheria's *imitatio Mariae*." *Scottish Journal of Religious Studies* 19 (1998): 31–43.

———. "Empress and *Theotokos*: Gender and Patronage in the Christological Controversy." In *The Church and Mary*, edited by R. N. Swanson, 39–51. Suffolk: Boydell & Brewer, 2004.

Cothenet, Édouard. "Marie dans les Apocryphes." In *Maria: études sur la Sainte Vierge*, edited by Hubert Du Manoir de Juaye, 7 vols. Vol. 6, 71–156. Paris: Beauchesne, 1952.

Crisafulli, Virgil S., John W. Nesbitt, and John F. Haldon. *The Miracles of St. Artemios: A Collection of Miracle Stories by an Anonymous Author of Seventh Century Byzantium*, The Medieval Mediterranean 13. Leiden: E. J. Brill, 1997.

Crossan, John Dominic. "Mark and the Relatives of Jesus." *Novum Testamentum* 15 (1973): 81–113.

Cunningham, Lawrence S. *Mother of God.* 1st ed. San Francisco: Harper & Row, 1982.

———. *A Brief History of Saints*, Blackwell Brief Histories of Religion. Oxford: Blackwell Publishing, 2005.

Daley, Brian E. *On the Dormition of Mary: Early Patristic Homilies.* Crestwood, NY: St. Vladimir's Seminary Press, 1998.

Davies, T. Witton. *Heinrich Ewald, Orientalist and Theologian 1803–1903: A Centenary Appreciation.* London: T. Fisher Unwin, 1903.

Davis, Stephen J. *The Cult of Saint Thecla: A Tradition of Women's Piety in Late Antiquity*, Oxford Early Christian Studies. Oxford: Oxford University Press, 2001.

———. "Crossed Texts, Crossed Sex: Intertextuality and Gender in Early Christian Legends of Holy Women Disguised as Men." *JECS* 10 (2002): 1–36.

273

de Bruyn, Theodore. "Greek Amulets from Egypt Invoking Mary as Expressions of 'Lived Religion.'" *Journal of the Canadian Society for Coptic Studies* 3–4 (2012): 55–69.

de Santos Otero, Aurelio. *Die handschriftliche Überlieferung der altslavischen Apokryphen.* 2 vols., Patristische Texte und Studien 20 and 23. Berlin: Walter de Gruyter, 1978–81.

de Strycker, Émile. *La forme la plus ancienne du Protévangile de Jacques*, SH 33. Bruxelles: Société des Bollandistes, 1961.

———. "Die griechischen Handschriften des Protevangeliums Iacobi." In *Griechische Kodikologie und Textüberlieferung*, edited by Dieter Harlfinger, 577–612. Darmstadt: Wissenschaftliche Buchgesellschaft, 1980.

Delehaye, Hippolyte. *Sanctus: essai sur le culte des saints dans l'antiquité*, SH 17. Bruxelles: Société des Bollandistes, 1927.

———. *Les origines du culte des martyrs.* 2nd ed, SH 20. Bruxelles: Bureaux de la Société des Bollandistes, 1933.

Delius, Walter. *Geschichte der Marienverehrung.* München: E. Reinhardt, 1963.

Devos, Paul. "Le date du voyage d'Égérie." *Analecta Bollandiana* 85 (1967): 165–94.

———. "Égérie à Bethléem; Le 40ᵉ jour après Paques à Jérusalem, en 383." *Analecta Bollandiana* 56 (1968): 87–108.

Dölger, Franz J. "Die eigenartige Marienverehrung der Philomarianiten oder Kollyridianer in Arabia." *Antike und Christentum* 1 (1929): 107–42.

Drescher, James. "A Coptic Amulet." In *Coptic Studies in Honor of Walter Ewing Crum*, edited by Michel Malinine, 265–70. Bulletin of the Byzantine Institute of America, vol. 2. Boston: Byzantine Institute, 1950.

Effenberger, Arne. "Maria als Vermittlerin und Fürbitterin: Zum Marienbild in der spätantiken und frühbyzantinischen Kunst Ägyptens." In *Presbeia Theotokou, The Intercessory Role of Mary across Times and Places in Byzantium (4th–9th century)*, edited by Leena Mari Peltomaa, Pauline Allen and Andreas Külzer, 49–108. Vienna: Austrian Academy of Sciences, 2015.

Ehrman, Bart D. *Forgery and Counterforgery: The Use of Literary Deceit in Early Christian Polemics.* New York: Oxford University Press, 2014.

Ehrman, Bart D., and Zlatko Pleše. *The Apocryphal Gospels: Texts and Translations.* New York: Oxford University Press, 2011.

Eire, Carlos M. N. *War Against the Idols: The Reformation of Worship from Erasmus to Calvin.* Cambridge: Cambridge University Press, 1986.

Elliott, J. K. *The Apocryphal New Testament: A Collection of Apocryphal Christian Literature in an English Translation.* Oxford: Clarendon Press, 1993.

Ewald, Heinrich. "Review of 'The departure of my lady Mary from this world. Edited from two Syriac MSS. in the British Museum, and translated by W. Wright'." *Göttingische gelehrte Anzeigen* 26 (1865): 1018–31.

Fassler, Margot. "The First Marian Feast in Constantinople and Jerusalem: Chant Texts, Readings, and Homiletic Literature." In *The Study of Medieval Chant: Paths and Bridges, East and West*, edited by Peter Jeffery, 25–88. Suffolk: Boydell, 2001.

Fehlner, Peter Damian M., F.F.I. "Immaculata Mediatrix: Toward a Dogmatic Definition of the Coredemption." In *Mary: Coredemptrix, Mediatrix, Advocate: Theological Foundations II: Papal, Pneumatological, Ecumenical*, edited by Mark I. Miravalle, 259–329. Santa Barbara: Queenship Publications, 1996.

Förster, Hans. "Zur ältesten Überlieferung der marianischen Antiphon '*Sub tuum praesidium*'." *Biblos: Österreichische Zeitschrift für Buch- und Bibliothekwesen, Dokumentation, Bibliographie, und Bibliophilie* 44, no. 2 (1995): 183–92.

———. *Transitus Mariae: Beiträge zur koptischen Überlieferung mit einer Edition von P. Vindob. K 7589, Cambridge Add 1876 8 und Paris BN Copte 129¹⁷ ff. 28 und 29*, Neutestamentliche Apokryphen 2. Berlin; New York: Walter de Gruyter, 2006.

Foskett, Mary F. *A Virgin Conceived: Mary and Classical Representations of Virginity.* Bloomington: Indiana University Press, 2002.

———. "Virginity as Purity in the *Protevangelium of James*." In *A Feminist Companion to Mariology*, edited by Amy-Jill Levine, 67–76. London: T & T Clark, 2005.

Freedman, David Noel, ed. *The Anchor Bible Dictionary*. 6 vols. New York: Doubleday, 1992.

Frend, W. H. C. "Popular Religion and Christological Controversy in the Fifth Century." *Studies in Church History* 8 (1972): 19–29.

Frøyshov, Stig. "The Early Development of the Liturgical Eight-Mode System in Jerusalem." *St. Vladimir's Theological Quarterly* 51 (2007): 139–78.

———. "The Georgian Witness to the Jerusalem Liturgy: New Sources and Studies." In *Inquiries into Eastern Christian Worship. Selected Papers of the Second International Congress of the Society of Oriental Liturgies, Rome, 17–21 September 2008*, edited by B. Groen, S. Hawkes-Teeples and S. Alexopoulos, 227–67. Leuven: Peeters, 2012.

Fulton, Rachel. *From Judgment to Passion: Devotion to Christ and the Virgin Mary, 800–1200*. New York: Columbia University Press, 2002.

Gambero, Luigi. *Mary and the Fathers of the Church*. Translated by Thomas Buffer. San Francisco: Ignatius Press, 1999.

———. "Patristic Intuitions of Mary's Role as Mediatrix and Advocate: The Invocation of the Faithful for Her Help." *Marian Studies* 52 (2001): 78–101.

Gaventa, Beverly Roberts. *Mary: Glimpses of the Mother of Jesus*, Studies on Personalities of the New Testament. Columbia, SC: University of South Carolina Press, 1995.

Gaventa, Beverly Roberts, and Cynthia L. Rigby, eds. *Blessed One: Protestant Perspectives on Mary*. 1st ed. Louisville, Ky.: Westminster John Knox Press, 2002.

Geffcken, Johannes. *The Last Days of Greco-Roman Paganism*, Europe in the Middle Ages. New York: North Holland Publishing, 1978.

Giamberardini, Gabriele. "Il 'Sub tuum praesidium' e il titolo 'Theotokos' nella tradizione egiziana." *Marianum* 31 (1969): 324–62.

———. *Il culto mariano in Egitto*. 3 vols, Pubblicazioni dello Studium Biblicum Franciscanum, Analecta 6–8. Jerusalem: Franciscan Printing Press, 1974–5.

———. *Il culto mariano in Eggito*. 2nd ed. 3 vols. Vol. 1 Sec. I–VI, Pubblicazioni dello Studium Biblicum Franciscanum, Analecta 6. Jerusalem: Franciscan Printing Press, 1975.

González Casado, Pilar. "Los relatos árabes apócrifos de la dormición de la virgen: narrativa popular religiosa cristiana." *Ilu* 3 (1998): 91–108.

———. "Textos árabes cristianos sobre la dormición de la Virgen." *Ilu: Revista de Ciencias de las Religiones* 4 (2001): 75–95.

———. *La dormición de la Virgen: Cinco relatos árabes*. Madrid: Editorial Trotta, 2002.

Good, Deirdre. "Pistis Sophia." In *Searching the Scriptures*, edited by Elisabeth Schüssler Fiorenza, 2 vols. Vol. 2, *A Feminist Commentary*, 678–707. New York: Crossroad, 1993–94.

Goranson, Stephen C. "The Joseph of Tiberias Episode in Epiphanius: Studies in Jewish and Chistian Relations." Ph.D. dissertation, Duke University, 1990.

———. "Joseph of Tiberias Revisited: Orthodoxies and Heresies in Fourth-Century Galilee." In *Galilee through the Centuries: Confluence of Cultures*, edited by Eric M. Meyers, 335–43. Winona Lake, Ind.: Eisenbrauns, 1999.

Grabar, André. *Christian Iconography: A Study of its Origins*, Bollingen Series 35, The A. W. Mellon Lectures in the Fine Arts 10. Princeton: Princeton University Press, 1968.

Grabar, André, and Denise Fourmont. *Ampoules de Terre Sainte (Monza, Bobbio)*. Paris: C. Klincksieck, 1958.

Graef, Hilda C. *Mary: A History of Doctrine and Devotion*. Repr. ed. Notre Dame, IN: Christian Classics, 2009.

Gregory, Timothy E. *Vox Populi: Popular Opinion and Violence in the Religious Controversies of the Fifth Century A.D.* Columbus: Ohio State University Press, 1979.

Gribomont, Jean. "Le plus ancien Transitus Marial et l'encratisme." *Augustinianum* 23 (1983): 237–47.

Grillmeier, Alois. *Christ in Christian Tradition.* Translated by John Bowden. 2nd, rev. ed. Vol. 1, *From the Apostolic Age to Chalcedon (451).* Atlanta: John Knox Press, 1975.

Grypeou, Emmanouela, and Juan Pedro Monferrer-Sala. "'A Tour of the Other World': A Contribution to the Textual and Literary Criticism of the 'Six Books Apocalypse of the Virgin'." *Collectanea Christiana Orientalia* 6 (2009): 115–66.

Hammerschmidt, Ernst. *Äthiopische Handschriften vom Ṭānāsee 1.* Wiesbaden: Franz Steiner Verlag, 1973.

Harris, Horton. *The Tübingen School.* Oxford: Clarendon Press, 1975.

Hock, Ronald F. *The Infancy Gospels of James and Thomas: With Introduction, Notes, and Original Text Featuring the New Scholars Version Translation,* Scholars Bible. Santa Rosa, Calif.: Polebridge Press, 1995.

Holum, Kenneth G. *Theodosian Empresses: Women and Imperial Dominion in Late Antiquity.* Berkeley and Los Angeles: University of California Press, 1982.

Horsley, G. H. R. "New Documents Illustrating Early Christianity." North Ryde, N. S. W.: Ancient History Documentary Research Centre, Macquarie University, 1981.

Hunt, Arthur S., John de Monins Johnson, and Colin H. Roberts. *Catalogue of the Greek Papyri in the John Rylands Library, Manchester.* 4 vols. Manchester: University Press, 1911–52.

Hunter, David G. "Helvidius, Jovinian, and the Virginity of Mary in Late Fourth-Century Rome." *JECS* 1 (1993): 47–71.

———. *Marriage, Celibacy, and Heresy in Ancient Christianity: The Jovinianist Controversy,* Oxford Early Christian Studies. Oxford: Oxford University Press, 2007.

Jaeger, Werner. *Early Christianity and Greek Paideia.* Cambridge: Belknap Press of Harvard University Press, 1961.

James, Liz. *Empresses and Power in Early Byzantium,* Women, Power, and Politics. London: Leicester University Press, 2001.

———. "The Empress and the Virgin in Early Byzantium: Piety, Authority, and Devotion." In *Images of the Mother of God: Perceptions of the Theotokos in Byzantium,* edited by Maria Vassilaki, 145–52. Aldershot: Ashgate, 2005.

Jasper, Ronald Claud Dudley, and G. J. Cuming. *Prayers of the Eucharist: Early and Reformed Texts.* 3rd, rev. ed. Collegeville, MN: Liturgical Press, 1987.

Jeffery, Peter. "The Sunday Office of Seventh-Century Jerusalem in the Georgian Chantbook (Iadgari): A Preliminary Report." *Studia Liturgica* 21 (1991): 52–75.

———. "The Earliest Christian Chant Repertory Recovered: The Georgian Witnesses to Jerusalem Chant." *Journal of the American Musicological Society* 47 (1994): 1–38.

———. "The Earliest Octōēchoi: The Role of Jerusalem and Palestine in the Beginnings of Modal Ordering." In *The Study of Medieval Chant, Paths and Bridges, East and West. In Honor of Kenneth Levy,* edited by Peter Jeffery, 147–209. Woodbridge: The Boydell Press, 2001.

Jensen, Robin Margaret. *Understanding Early Christian Art.* New York: Routledge, 2000.

Johnson, Elizabeth A. *Truly Our Sister: A Theology of Mary in the Communion of Saints.* New York: Continuum, 2003.

Johnson, Maxwell E. "*Sub Tuum Praesidium*: The *Theotokos* in Christian Life and Worship before Ephesus." *Pro Ecclesia* 17, no. 1 (2008): 52–75.

———. *Praying and Believing in Early Christianity: The Interplay between Christian Worship and Doctrine.* Collegeville, Minn.: Liturgical Press, 2013.

Johnson, Scott Fitzgerald. *The Life and Miracles of Thekla: A Literary Study,* Hellenic Studies 13. Washington, D.C.: Center for Hellenic Studies, 2006.

Jugie, Martin. *La mort et l'assomption de la Sainte Vierge, étude historico-doctrinale,* Studi e testi 114. Vatican City: Biblioteca Apostolica Vaticana, 1944.

———. *L'Immaculée Conception dans l'Ecriture sainte et dans la tradition orientale,* Collectio Edita Cura Academiae Marianae Internationalis, Textus et Disquisitiones, Bibliotheca

Immaculatae Conceptionis, 3. Rome: Academia Mariana/Officium Libri Catholici, 1952.

Kaestli, Jean-Daniel. "Le rôle des textes bibliques dans la genèse et le développement des légendes apocryphes. Le cas du sort final de l'apôtre Jean." *Augustinianum* 23 (1983): 319–36.

Karwiese, Stefan. "The Church of Mary and the Temple of Hadrian Olympios." In *Ephesos, Metropolis of Asia: An Interdisciplinary Approach to its Archaeology, Religion, and Culture*, edited by Helmut Koester, 311–19. Harvard Theological Studies. Valley Forge, Penn.: Trinity Press International, 1995.

Kateusz, Ally. "Collyridian Déjà Vu: The Trajectory of Redaction of the Markers of Mary's Liturgical Leadership." *Journal of Feminist Studies in Religion* 29 (2013): 75–92.

———. "Ascension of Christ or Ascension of Mary?: Reconsidering a Popular Early Iconography." *JECS* 23 (2015): 273–303.

Kearns, Cleo McNelly. *The Virgin Mary, Monotheism, and Sacrifice.* Cambridge: Cambridge University Press, 2008.

Kelly, J. N. D. *Early Christian Doctrines.* rev. ed. New York: Harper & Row, 1978.

King, Karen L. "The Gospel of Mary Magdalene." In *Searching the Scriptures*, edited by Elisabeth Schüssler Fiorenza, 2 vols. Vol. 2, *A Feminist Commentary*. New York: Crossroad, 1993–94.

———. *What is Gnosticism?* Cambridge: Harvard University Press, 2003.

———, ed. *Images of the Feminine in Gnosticism*, Studies in Antiquity and Christianity. Philadelphia: Fortress Press, 1988.

Klauck, Hans-Josef. "Die dreifache Maria: Zur Rezeption von Joh 19.25 in EvPhil 32." In *The Four Gospels 1992. Festschrift Frans Neirynck*, edited by et al. F. van Segbroeck, 3 vols. Leuven: Leuven University Press, 1992.

Koester, Helmut. *Introduction to the New Testament.* Vol. 2, *History and Literature of Early Christianity.* New York: Walter de Gruyter, 1982.

Kondakov, Nikodim Pavlovich. Иконографія Богоматери *(Ikonografiia bogomateri).* 2 vols. St. Petersburg: Tipografiia imperatorskoĭ akademīi nauk, 1914.

Leeb, Helmut. *Die Gesänge im Gemeindegottesdienst von Jerusalem. (Vom 5. bis 8. Jh.)*, Wiener Beiträge zur Theologie 28. Vienna: Herder, 1970.

Lewis, Nicola Denzey. *Introduction to Gnosticism: Ancient Voices, Christian Worlds.* New York: Oxford University Press.

Limberis, Vasiliki. *Divine Heiress: The Virgin Mary and the Creation of Christian Constantinople.* London: Routledge, 1994.

Luedemann, Gerd. *Opposition to Paul in Jewish Christianity.* Translated by M. Eugene Boring. Minneapolis: Fortress Press, 1989.

Luijendijk, AnneMarie. *Forbidden Oracles?: The Gospel of the Lots of Mary*, Studien und Texte zu Antike und Christentum 89. Tübingen: Mohr Siebeck, 2014.

MacCulloch, Diarmaid. *A History of Christianity: The First Three Thousand Years.* New York: Viking, 2009.

Macomber, William F., and Haile Getatchew. *A Catalogue of Ethiopian Manuscripts Microfilmed for the Ethiopian Manuscript Microfilm Library, Addis Ababa, and for the Monastic Manuscript Microfilm Library, Collegeville.* 10 vols. Collegeville, Minn.: Hill Monastic Manuscript Library/St. John's Abbey and University, 1975–.

Madigan, Kevin. *Medieval Christianity: A New History* (New Haven: Yale University Press, 2015).

Magness, Jodi. *Jerusalem Ceramic Chronology circa 200–800 CE*, JSOT/ASOR Monograph Series, 9. Sheffield: JSOT Press, 1993.

Manns, Frédéric. *Le récit de la Dormition de Marie (Vatican grec 1982): contribution à l'étude des origines de l'exégèse chrétienne*, Studium Biblicum Franciscanum, Collectio Maior, 33. Jerusalem: Franciscan Printing Press, 1989.

Mansi, Giovan Domenico, ed. *Sacrorum conciliorum, nova, et amplissima collectio*. Editio novissima ed. 54 vols. Florentiæ: Expensis Antonii Zatta, 1759–1827.

Maraval, Pierre. *Lieux saints et pèlerinages d'orient: Histoire et géographie des origines à la conquête arabe*. 2nd ed. Paris: Les Éditions du Cerf, 2004.

Marcus, Joel. "Mark—Interpreter of Paul." *New Testament Studies* 46 (2000): 1–15.

Marianus, Congressus Mariologicus. *De primordiis cultus Mariani: Acta Congressus Mariologici-Mariani Internationalis in Lusitania anno 1967 celebrati*. 6 vols. Rome: Pontificia Academia Mariana Internationalis, 1970.

Marjanen, Antti. *The Woman Jesus Loved: Mary Magdalene in the Nag Hammadi Library and Related Documents*, NHS 40. Leiden: E. J. Brill, 1996.

Markschies, Christoph. *Gnosis: An Introduction*. Translated by John Bowden. London: T & T Clark, 2003.

Mathews, Thomas F., and Normak Muller. "Isis and Mary in Early Icons." In *Images of the Mother of God: Perceptions of the Theotokos in Byzantium*, edited by Maria Vassilaki, 3–11. Aldershot: Ashgate, 2005.

Maunder, Chris, ed. *Origins of the Cult of the Virgin Mary*. London; New York: Burns & Oates, 2008.

McGuckin, John A. *St. Cyril of Alexandria: The Christological Controversy: Its History, Theology, and Texts*, Supplements to Vigiliae Christianae 23. Leiden: E. J. Brill, 1994.

———. "Nestorius and the Political Factions of 5th Century Byzantium: Factors in his Downfall." *Bulletin of the John Rylands University Library* 78, no. 3 (1996): 7–21.

———. *Saint Gregory of Nazianzus: An Intellectual Biography*. Crestwood, NY: St Vladimir's Seminar Press, 2001.

———. "The Early Cult of Mary and Inter-Religous Contexts in the Fifth-Century Church." In *The Origins of the Cult of the Virgin*, edited by Chris Maunder, 1–22. London: Burns & Oates, 2008.

McGuckin, John A., ed. *The Encyclopedia of Eastern Orthodox Christianity*. 2 vols. Chichester, West Sussex, U.K.; Malden, MA: Wiley-Blackwell, 2011.

McGuire, Anne. "Women, Gender, and Gnosis in Gnostic Texts and Traditions." In *Women & Christian Origins*, edited by Ross Shepard Kraemer and Mary Rose D'Angelo, 257–99. New York; Oxford: Oxford University Press, 1999.

McNamara, Martin, Jean-Daniel Kaestli, and Rita Beyers. *Apocrypha Hiberniae*. Vol. 1, *Evangelia infantiae*, CCSA 13–14. Turnhout: Brepols, 2001.

Meier, John P. *A Marginal Jew: Rethinking the Historical Jesus*. 5 vols. Vol. 1, *The Roots of the Problem and the Person*. New York: Doubleday, 1991.

———. *A Marginal Jew: Rethinking the Historical Jesus*. 5 vols. Vol. 3, *Companions and Competitors*. New York: Doubleday, 2001.

Mercenier, F. "L'antienne mariale grecque la plus ancienne." *Le Muséon* 52 (1939): 229–33.

Métrévéli, Hélène. "Les manuscrits liturgiques géorgiens des IXe–Xe siècles et leur importance pour l'étude de l'hymnographie byzantine." *Bedi Karlisa* 36 (1978): 43–8.

Métrévéli, Hélène, Ts. Tchankieva, and L. Khevsouriani. "Le plus ancien tropologion géorgien." *Bedi Kartlisa: Revue de Kartvélologie* 39 (1981): 54–62.

Metzger, Bruce M. *The Early Versions of the New Testament: Their Origin, Transmission, and Limitations*. Oxford: Clarendon Press, 1977.

Meyer, Marvin W. "Making Mary Male: The Categories 'Male' and 'Female' in the Gospel of Thomas." *New Testament Studies* 31 (1985): 554–70.

Milik, J. T. "Notes d'épigraphie et de topographie palestiniennes." *Revue Biblique* 67 (1960): 550–97.

Mimouni, Simon C. "Genèse et évolution des traditions anciennes sur le sort final de Marie: Etude de la tradition littéraire copte." *Marianum* 42 (1991): 69–143.

———. "La lecture liturgique et les apocryphes du Nouveau Testament: Le cas de la Dormitio grecque du Pseudo-Jean." *Orientalia Christiana Periodica* 59 (1993): 403–25.

278

————. *Dormition et Assomption de Marie: Histoire des traditions anciennes*, Théologie Historique, 98. Paris: Beauchesne, 1995.

————. "L'Hypomnesticon de Joseph de Tibériade : une œuvre du IVe siècle?" *Studia Patristica* 32 (1997): 346–57.

————. "L'Hypomnesticon de Joseph de Tibériade : une œuvre du IVe siècle?" In *Les traditions anciennes sur la Dormition et l'Assomption de Marie*, 257–73. Supplements to Vigiliae Christianae 104. Leiden: Brill, 2011.

Minns, Denis, and P. M. Parvis, eds. *Justin, Philosopher and Martyr: Apologies*, Oxford Early Christian Texts. Oxford; New York: Oxford University Press, 2009.

Moreau, Jacques. "Observations sur l'*Hypomnestikon Biblion Ioseppou*." *Byzantion* 25–7 (1955–57): 241–76.

Morin, G. "Pages inédites de deux Pseudo-Jérômes des environs de l'an 400." *Revue bénédictine* 40 (1928): 289–318.

Murray, Robert. *Symbols of Church and Kingdom: A Study in Early Syriac Tradition*. London: Cambridge University Press, 1975.

Norelli, Enrico. *Ascensio Isaiae. Commentarius*, CCSA 8. Turnhout: Brepols, 1995.

————. *Marie des apocryphes: enquête sur la mère de Jésus dans le christianisme antique*, Christianismes antiques. Genève: Labor et Fides, 2009.

O'Carroll, Michael. *Theotokos: A Theological Encyclopedia of the Blessed Virgin Mary*. Revised ed. Wilmington, Del.: M. Glazier, 1983.

Pagels, Elaine H. *The Gnostic Gospels*. New York: Random House, 1979.

Painter, John. *Just James: The Brother of Jesus in History and Tradition*, Studies on Personalities of the New Testament. Columbia: University of South Carolina Press, 1997.

Papaconstantinou, Arietta. "Les sanctuaires de la Vierge dans l'Égypte byzantine et omeyyade. L'apport des textes documentaires." *Journal of Juristic Papyrology* 30 (2000): 81–94.

Parlby, Geri. "The Origins of Marian Art in the Catacombs and the Problem of Identification." In *The Origins of the Cult of the Virgin Mary*, edited by Chris Maunder, 41–56. London: Burns & Oates, 2008.

Pelikan, Jaroslav. *The Christian Tradition: A History of the Development of Doctrine*. Vol. 1, *The Emergence of the Catholic Tradition (100–600)*. Chicago: University of Chicago Press, 1971.

————. *Mary through the Centuries: Her Place in the History of Culture*. New Haven and London: Yale University Press, 1996.

Peltomaa, Leena Mari. *The Image of the Virgin Mary in the Akathistos Hymn*, The Medieval Mediterranean 35. Leiden: Brill, 2001.

————. "Towards the Origins of the History of the Cult of Mary." *Studia Patristica* 40 (2006): 75–86.

Pentcheva, Bissera. *Icons and Power: The Mother of God in Byzantium*. University Park: Pennsylvania State University Press, 2006.

Peppard, Michael. "Illuminating the Dura-Europos Baptistery: Comparanda for the Female Figures." *JECS* 20 (2012): 543–74.

————. *The World's Oldest Church: Bible, Art, and Ritual at Dura-Europos, Syria*. New Haven and London: Yale University Press, 2016.

Péradzé, G. "Les monuments liturgiques prébyzantins en langue géorgienne." *Le Muséon* 45 (1932): 255–72.

Petersen, William L. "The Diatessaron of Tatian." In *The Text of the New Testament in Contemporary Research: Essays on the Status Quaestionis*, edited by Bart D. Ehrman and Michael W. Holmes. Grand Rapids, MI: Eerdmans, 1995.

Price, Richard M. "Marian Piety and the Nestorian Controversy." In *The Church and Mary*, edited by R. N. Swanson, 31–8. Studies in Church History 39. Suffolk: Boydell & Brewer, 2004.

———. "Martyrdom and the Cult of the Saints." In *The Oxford Handbook of Early Christian Studies*, edited by Susan Ashbrook Harvey and David G. Hunter, 808–25. Oxford: Oxford University Press, 2008.

———. "The Theotokos and the Councl of Ephesus." In *The Origins of the Cult of the Virgin*, edited by Chris Maunder, 89–103. London: Burns & Oates, 2008.

Quasten, Johannes. *Patrology*. 3 vols. Westminister, Md.: Newman Press, 1950–53.

Rahmani, L. Y. "Two Early Christian Ampullae." *Israel Exploration Journal* 16 (1966): 71–4.

Räisänen, Heikki. *Die Mutter Jesu im Neuen Testament*. 2nd ed., Suomalaisen Tiedeakatemian toimituksia Sarja B 247. Helsinki: Suomalainen Tiedeakatemis, 1989.

Rauer, Max, ed. *Origenes Werke*. 12 vols. Vol. 9, *Die Homilien zu Lukas in der Übersetzung des Hieronymus und die griechischen Reste der Homilien und des Lukas-Kommentars*, GCS 35. Berlin: J.C. Hinrichs, 1930.

Ray, Walter D. "August 15 and the Development of the Jerusalem Calendar." Ph.D. diss., University of Notre Dame, 2000.

Renoux, Charles. *Les hymnes de la Résurrection I. Hymnographie liturgique géorgienne : textes du Sinaï 18.*, Sources liturgiques 3. Paris: Cerf, 2000.

———. *L'hymnaire de Saint-Sabas (Ve–VIIe siècle): le manuscrit géorgien H 2123. I. Du samedi de Lazare à la Pentecôte*, PO 50.3. Turnhout: Brepols, 2008.

———. *Les hymnes de la Résurrection II. Hymnographie liturgique géorgienne, texte des manuscrits Sinaï 40, 41 et 34*, PO 52.1. Turnhout: Brepols, 2010.

———. *Les hymnes de la Résurrection III. Hymnographie liturgique géorgienne, introduction, traduction, annotation des manuscrits Sinaï 26 et 20 et index analytique des trois volumes*, PO 52.2. Turnhout: Brepols, 2010.

Reynolds, Brian. *Gateway to Heaven: Marian Doctrine and Devotion, Image and Typology in the Patristic and Medieval Periods*. Hyde Park, NY: New City Press, 2012.

Römer, Cornelia. "Christliche Texte II." *Archiv für Papyrusforschung* 44 (1998): 129–39.

Rubery, Eileen. "From Catacomb to Sanctuary: The Orant figure and the Cults of the Mother of God and S. Agnes in Early Christian Rome, with Special Reference to Gold Glass." *Studia Patristica* 73 (2014): 129–74.

Rubin, Miri. *Mother of God: A History of the Virgin Mary*. New Haven: Yale University Press, 2009.

Rudolph, Kurt. *Gnosis: The Nature and History of Gnosticism*. Translated by Robert McLachlan Wilson. San Francisco: Harper & Row, 1987.

Salgado, Jean-Marie, O.M.I. "Le culte rendu à la Très Sainte Vierge Marie durant les premiers siècles à la lumière des fresques de la catacombe de Priscille." In *De primordiis cultus Mariani; Acta Congressus Mariologici-Mariani Internationalis in Lusitania anno 1967 celebrati*, edited by Congressus Mariologicus Marianus, 6 vols., vol. 5, 43–62. Rome: Pontificia Academia Mariana Internationalis, 1970.

Schaberg, Jane. *The Resurrection of Mary Magdalene: Legends, Apocrypha, and the Christian Testament*. New York: Continuum, 2002.

Schaff, Philip, and Henry Wace, eds. *A Select Library of Nicene and Post-Nicene Fathers of the Christian Church. Second Series*. 14 vols. New York: The Christian Literature Company, 1891.

Schiller, Gertrud. *Iconography of Christian Art*. Translated by Janet Seligman. 2 vols. Greenwich, Conn.: New York Graphic Society, 1971.

Schneemelcher, Wilhelm, ed. *New Testament Apocrypha*. Translated by R. McL. Wilson. rev. ed. 2 vols. Louisville, Ky.: Westminster/John Knox Press, 1991–2.

Schneider, Hans-Michael. *Lobpreis im rechten Glauben: die Theologie der Hymnen an den Festen der Menschwerdung der alten Jerusalemer Liturgie im georgischen Udzvelesi Iadgari*, Hereditas. Studien zur alten Kirchengeschichte. Bonn: Borengässer, 2004.

Schüssler Fiorenza, Elisabeth. *In Memory of Her: A Feminist Theological Reconstruction of Christian Origins*. New York: Crossroad, 1983.

———. *Jesus: Miriam's Child, Sophia's prophet: Critical Issues in Feminist Christology*. New York: Continuum, 1994.

Schwartz, Eduard, ed. *Acta conciliorum oecumenicorum*. 4 vols. Berlin: W. de Gruyter, 1914–40.

Setzer, Claudia. "Excellent Women: Female Witness to the Resurrection." *Journal of Bibilical Literature* 116 (1997): 259–72.

Shoemaker, Stephen J. "'Let Us Go and Burn Her Body': The Image of the Jews in the Early Dormition Traditions." *Church History* 68.4 (1999): 775–823.

———. "Rethinking the 'Gnostic Mary': Mary of Nazareth and Mary of Magdala in Early Christian Tradition." *JECS* 9, no. 4 (2001): 555–95.

———. "The (Re?)Discovery of the Kathisma Church and the Cult of the Virgin in Late Antique Palestine." *Maria: A Journal of Marian Studies* 2 (2001): 21–72.

———. "Gender at the Virgin's Funeral: Men and Women as Witnesses to the Dormition." *Studia Patristica* 34 (2001): 552–8.

———. *Ancient Traditions of the Virgin Mary's Dormition and Assumption*, Oxford Early Christian Studies. Oxford: Oxford University Press, 2002.

———. "A Case of Mistaken Identity?: Naming the Gnostic Mary." In *Which Mary?: The Marys of Early Christian Tradition*, edited by F. Stanley Jones, 5–30. Society of Biblical Literature Symposium Series 19. Atlanta: Society of Biblical Literature, 2002.

———. "Jesus' Gnostic Mom: Mary of Nazareth and the Gnostic Mary Traditions." In *Mariam, the Magdalen, and the Mother*, edited by Deirdre Good, 153–83. Bloomington: Indiana University Press, 2005.

———. "The Virgin Mary in the Ministry of Jesus and the Early Church according to the Earliest *Life of the Virgin*." *Harvard Theological Review* 98, no. 4 (2005): 441–67.

———. "Death and the Maiden: The Early History of the Dormition and Assumption Apocrypha." *St Vladimir's Theological Quarterly* 50 (2006): 59–97.

———. "A Peculiar Version of the *Inventio crucis* in the Early Syriac Dormition Traditions." *Studia Patristica* 41 (2006): 75–81.

———. "The Georgian *Life of the Virgin* attributed to Maximus the Confessor: Its Authenticity(?) and Importance." In *Mémorial R.P. Michel van Esbroeck, S.J.*, edited by Alexey Muraviev and Basil Lourié, 307–28. Scrinium 2. St. Petersburg: Vizantinorossika, 2006.

———. "Marian Liturgies and Devotion in Early Christianity." In *Mary: The Complete Resource*, edited by Sarah Jane Boss, 130–45. London: Continuum Press, 2007.

———. "Early Christian Apocryphal Literature." In *Oxford Handbook of Early Christian Studies*, edited by Susan Ashbrook Harvey and David G. Hunter, 521–48. Oxford: Oxford University Press, 2008.

———. "The Cult of the Virgin in the Fourth Century: A Fresh Look at Some Old and New Sources." In *The Origins of the Cult of the Virgin Mary*, edited by Chris Maunder, 71–87. London: Burns & Oates, 2008.

———. "Between Scripture and Tradition: The Marian Apocrypha of Early Christianity." In *The Reception and Interpretation of the Bible in Late Antiquity*, edited by Lorenzo DiTommaso and Lucian Turcescu, 491–510. Bible in Ancient Christianity 6. Leiden: Brill, 2008.

———. "The Cult of Fashion: The Earliest *Life of the Virgin* and Constantinople's Marian Relics." *Dumbarton Oaks Papers* 62 (2008): 53–74.

———. "Epiphanius of Salamis, the Kollyridians, and the Early Dormition Narratives: The Cult of the Virgin in the Later Fourth Century." *JECS* 16 (2008): 369–99.

———. "The Virgin Mary's Hidden Past: From Ancient Marian Apocrypha to the Medieval *vitae Virginis*." *Marian Studies* 60 (2009): 1–30.

———. "Asceticism in the Early Dormition Narratives." *Studia Patristica* 44 (2010): 509–13.

———. "Apocrypha and Liturgy in the Fourth Century: The Case of the 'Six Books' Dormition Apocryphon." In *Jewish and Christian Scriptures: The Function of 'Canonical' and 'Non-canonical' Religious Texts*, edited by James H. Charlesworth and Lee Martin McDonald, 153–63. London: T & T Clark, 2010.

———. "Mary at the Cross, East and West: Maternal Compassion and Affective Piety in the Earliest Life of the Virgin and the High Middle Ages." *Journal of Theological Studies* 62 (2011): 570–606.

———. "A Mother's Passion: Mary's Role in the Crucifixion and Resurrection in the Earliest Life of the Virgin and its Influence on George of Nicomedia's Passion Homilies." In *The Cult of the Mother of God in Byzantium*, edited by Leslie Brubaker and Mary Cunningham 53–67. Aldershot: Ashgate, 2011.

———. "A New Dormition Fragment in Coptic: P. Vindob. K 7589 and the Marian Apocryphal Tradition." In *Bibel, Byzanz und Christlicher Orient. Festschrift für Stephen Gerö zum 65. Geburtstag*, edited by D. Bumazhnov, E. Grypeou, T. B. Sailors and A. Toepel, 203–29. Orientalia Lovaniensia Analecta 187. Louvain: Peeters, 2011.

———. "From Mother of Mysteries to Mother of the Church: The Institutionalization of the Dormition Apocrypha." *Apocrypha* 22 (2011): 11–47.

———. "The Ancient Dormition Apocrypha and the Origins of Marian Piety: Early Evidence of Marian Intercession from Late Ancient Palestine." In *Presbeia Theotokou, The Intercessory Role of Mary across Times and Places in Byzantium (4th–9th century)*, edited by Leena Mari Peltomaa, Pauline Allen and Andreas Külzer, 23–39. Vienna: Austrian Academy of Sciences, 2015.

Smid, Harm Reinder. *Protevangelium Jacobi; A Commentary*. Assen: Van Gorcum, 1965.

Smith, Jonathan Z. *Drudgery Divine: On the Comparison of Early Christianities and the Religions of Late Antiquity*, Jordan Lectures in Comparative Religion, 14. Chicago: University of Chicago Press, 1990.

Starowieyski, M. "La plus ancienne description d'une mariophane par Grégoire de Nysse." In *Studien zu Gregor von Nyssa und der christlichen Spätantike*, edited by H. Drobner and C. Klock, 245–53. Leiden: Brill, 1990.

Starowieyski, Marek. "Le titre Θεοτόκος avant le concile d'Ephèse." *Studia Patristica* 19 (1989): 236–42.

Stegmüller, Otto. "Sub tuum praesidium: Bemerkungen zur ältesten Überlieferung." *Zeitschrift für katholische Theologie* 74 (1952): 76–82.

Talbot, Alice-Mary, and Scott Fitzgerald Johnson. *Miracle Tales from Byzantium*, Dumbarton Oaks Medieval Library. Cambridge: Harvard University Press, 2012.

Tavard, George H. *The Thousand Faces of the Virgin Mary*. Collegeville, Minn.: Liturgical Press, 1996.

Toepel, Alexander. *Das Protevangelium des Jakobus: Ein Beitrag zur neueren Diskussion um Herkunft, Auslegung und theologische Einordnung*, Frankfurter theologische Studien 71. Münster: Aschendorff, 2014.

Triacca, Achille M. "'Sub tuum praesidium': nella 'lex orandi' un'anticipata presenza della 'lex credendi.' La 'teotocologia' precede la 'mariologia'?" In *La mariologia nella catechesi dei padri (età prenicena). Convegno di studio e aggiornamento, Facoltà di Lettere cristiane e classiche (Pontificium Institutum Altioris Latinitatis), Roma, 10–11 marzo 1989,* edited by S. Felici, 183–205. Biblioteca di scienze religiose 95. Rome: LAS, 1989.

Tsironis, Niki. "From Poetry to Liturgy: The Cult of the Virgin in the Middle Byzantine Period." In *Images of the Mother of God: Perceptions of the Theotokos in Byzantium*, edited by Maria Vassilaki, 91–102. Aldershot: Ashgate, 2005.

Tuckett, C. M. *The Gospel of Mary*, Oxford Early Christian Gospel Texts. Oxford: Oxford University Press, 2007.

van den Hengel, John. "Miriam of Nazareth: Between Symbol and History." In *A Feminist Companion to Mariology*, edited by Amy-Jill Levine, 130–46. London: T & T Clark, 2005.

van der Horst, Pieter W. "'Seven Months' Children in Jewish and Christian Literature from Antiquity." *Ephemerides Theologicae Lovanienses* 54 (1978): 346–60.

———. "Sex, Birth, Purity, and Asceticism in the *Protevangelium Jacobi*." In *A Feminist Companion to Mariology*, edited by Amy-Jill Levine, 56–66. London: T & T Clark, 2005.

van Esbroeck, Michel. "Les textes littéraires sur l'assomption avant le Xe siècle." In *Les actes apocryphes des apôtres*, edited by François Bovon, 265–85. Geneva: Labor et Fides, 1981.

———. *Aux origines de la Dormition de la Vierge: Etudes historique sur les traditions orientales*. Brookfield, VT: Variorum, 1995.

———. "Some Earlier Features in the Life of the Virgin." *Marianum* 63 (2001): 297–308.

Verhelst, Stéphane. "Le 15 août, le 9 av et le kathisme." *Questions liturgiques* 82 (2001): 161–91.

Vogliano, A. "Papiri Bolognesi." *Acme* 1 (1948): 195–231.

von Campenhausen, Hans. *The Virgin Birth in the Theology of the Ancient Church*. Translated by Frank Clarke, Studies in Historical Theology, 2. London: SCM Press, 1964.

Vööbus, Arthur. *Early Versions of the New Testament: Manuscript Studies*, Papers of the Estonian Theological Society in Exile, 6. Stockholm: Estonian Theological Society in Exile, 1954.

Vopel, Hermann. *Die altchristlichen Goldgläser: ein Beitrag zur altchristlichen Kunst- und Kulturgeschichte*, Archäologische Studien zum christlichen Altertum und Mittelalter 5. Freiburg I. B.: J. C. B. Mohr, 1899.

Vuong, Lily C. *Gender and Purity in the Protevangelium of James*, Wissenschaftliche Untersuchungen zum Neuen Testament 2 Reihe 358. Tübingen: Mohr Siebeck.

Wade, Andrew. "The Oldest Iadgari: The Jerusalem Tropologion, V–VIII c." *Orientalia Christiana Periodica* 50 (1984): 451–6.

Warner, Marina. *Alone of All Her Sex: The Myth and the Cult of the Virgin Mary*. 1st American ed. New York: Knopf, 1976.

Wellen, Gerard. *Theotokos: eine ikonographische Abhandlung über das Gottesmutterbild in früh-christlicher Zeit*. Utrecht: Het Spectrum, 1961.

Wenger, Antoine. *L'Assomption de la T.S. Vierge dans la tradition byzantine du VIe au Xe siècle; études et documents*, Archives de l'Orient chrétien, 5. Paris: Institut français d'études byzantines, 1955.

Wilkinson, John. *Egeria's Travels: Newly Translated with Supporting Documents and Notes*. 3rd ed. Warminster, England: Aris & Phillips, 1999.

Williams, Michael A. *Rethinking Gnosticism: An Argument for Dismantling a Dubious Category*. Princeton: Princeton University Press, 1996.

Wright, William. *Catalogue of Syriac Manuscripts in the British Museum Acquired since the Year 1838*. 3 vols. London: British Museum, 1870–2.

———. *Catalogue of the Ethiopic Manuscripts in the British Museum Acquired Since the Year 1847*. London: British Museum, 1877.

Zervos, George T. "Christmas with Salome." In *A Feminist Companion to Mariology*, edited by Amy-Jill Levine, 77–98. London: T & T Clark, 2005.

Index

Abraham, 128, 137
Acts of the Apostles, 39, 81
Acts of Paul and Thecla, 17–19, 200
Acts of Thomas, 72
Adam, 4, 46, 112–13
Affective piety, 21
Agnes, Saint, 197
Akathist hymn, 178, 191
Alexander of Alexandria, 166, 169
Alexandria, 66, 135, 155, 173, 202, 204, 208, 233, 236
Ambrose of Milan, 169–70, 172
Anaphora of Egyptian Basil, 71, 231
Andrew, 77–8, 123, 126
Angel Christology, 24, 104–7, 110–15, 117, 231; and Angel of Death, 117; as Great Cherub of Light, 120, 129, 231
Anna, 49, 51, 56, 58–9
Annunciation, 4, 35–6, 38, 45, 59, 83, 168, 195–6
Antioch, 41, 44, 168, 176, 202, 208
Antionë, 198
Apocryphon of John, 112
Apocalypse of Paul, 126–7
Apocalypse of the Virgin, 126
Apostles, 24–5, 40, 71, 77–83, 94, 99, 101, 104–5, 110–11, 114–17, 119, 121–8, 137, 139–41; conflict with Mary, 77–8, 87–92, 96; Mary of Magdala as apostle to, 80; miraculous journey to the

Dormition, 104, 120, 136; veneration of Mary, 136–7
Arabia, 152
Arcadius, Emperor, 219
Artemius, St., 17–19
Artoklasia (Breaking of bread), service of, 161
Ascension, 198–9
Ascension of Isaiah, 43–4, 55
Asceticism, 14, 21, 124–5, 169–73, 203; as form of Marian devotion, 172–3
Asia Minor, 61
Assumption: see Dormition
Assumption Dogma, 239
Asynchytos/asynchytōs, 191
Athanasius, 166–7, 169–70, 173, 178–80, 202–4
Athens, 138
Atticus of Constantinople, 180, 219, 221, 223
Augustine, 57
Avars, 177–8

El-Bagawat, 198, 200–1
Balaam, 196
Baldovin, John, 185
Barhadbeshabba 'Arbaya, 213, 217
Bartholomew, 93–5
Basil the Great, 167
Bauckham, Richard, 134
Baun, Jane, 238

Baur, F. C., 41
Bazaar of Heracleides, 213–14
Beloved Disciple, 35, 82–3
Bethany, 181
Bethlehem, 20, 49, 52, 130, 136–9, 141, 181–2; Dormition narratives, 130
Blachernai, Church of St. Mary at, 200, 220–1
Bonnet, Max, 132–3
Book of Mary's Repose, 24–5, 71, 100–29, 132, 134, 136–8, 144, 152, 163–4, 231–2, 237, 240; book of mysteries in, 104, 117, 120; date, 103, 106, 109, 119, 124–6; esoteric/secret knowledge in, 104–5, 110–18, 121, 123–4, 231; Ethiopic translation, 102–3, 108; intercessions of Mary in, 121; manuscripts, 101–2; secret prayer of ascent, 110–12, 114, 120, 231. See also Angel Christology
Book of the Nativity of Mary, 50
Brakke, David, 169, 173
Bread offerings, 134, 143, 145, 147–54, 156–7, 160–4, 202, 232–3; distinct from Eucharistic offerings, 161. See also Kollyridians; the *Six Books Dormition Apocryphon*
Brothers and sisters of Jesus, 31, 40, 42–3, 66, 80–1, 168, 170. See also James the brother of Jesus
Brown, Peter, 2, 13

Cameron, Averil, 5, 14, 16–18
Cana, wedding at, 33–4, 82–3, 168
Cappadocia, 167, 174–5
Catacombs, Roman, 26, 195–6, 204, 234
Celsus, 54
Chalcedon, Council of, 3, 186, 191–2
Chalkoprateia, Church of St. Mary at, 220–1
Christmas: see Nativity, Feast of
Clayton, Mary, 127
Clement of Alexandria, 66–7, 96
Constantine, 134, 194
Constantinople, 3, 17, 20, 27–9, 174–7, 179–81, 190–1, 193, 198, 200, 202, 204–9, 211, 215–16, 218–23, 226–7, 233–4, 236
Constas, Nicholas, 175, 180, 220
Cooper, Kate, 222
Co-Redemptrix, 239
Cosmas and Damian, Sts., 17–19
Cyprian of Antioch (in Pisidia), 174

Cyprian of Carthage, 174
Cyril of Alexandria, 208, 216–18, 220, 224–6

Daley, Brian, 4
David, 128, 137, 143
Davis, Stephen, 173, 194, 197, 200–1
Dead Sea Scrolls, 73
Deborah, 177
Delius, Walter, 38
Dialogue of the Savior, 88
Diatessaron: see Tatian
Docetism, 172, 178–9
Dormition, 121–8; accounts of, 1, 6, 23–6, 50, 78, 99–101, 186, 193, 202; and Mary's intercessions, 177–8; women as original witnesses to, 122
Dura-Europos, 196

Effenberger, Arne, 198, 201
Egeria, 184–5, 202
Egypt, 17, 23, 27, 61, 68–9, 71–3, 86, 117, 135, 140, 178–80, 193, 198–202, 227; Flight into, 33, 107, 110, 119
Eire, Carlos, 147
Elijah, 59, 150–1, 165
Elizabeth, 36, 52–3, 91, 128
Enoch, 128
Ephesus, 135, 141, 224–5, 227; Council of, 3–4, 7–8, 16, 18, 25–7, 29, 155, 175, 184, 186, 189, 191, 193, 197–9, 200, 202, 204–6, 209, 215–16, 218, 224–5, 227–8, 234–5; church of the Virgin Mary at, 18, 200, 224–5
Ephrem the Syrian, 167
Epiphanius of Salamis, 25–6, 134, 145–56, 159–65, 232–3; knowledge of the *Six Books Dormition Apocryphon*, 151–2, 164–5; opposition to veneration of saints, 145–7, 150–1, 165; profession of Mary's Dormition and Assumption, 150–1; and traditions of the end of Mary's life, 149–50, 156, 161–2, 164
Esoteric Christianity, 66, 73, 78, 103, 105–7, 112, 114–15, 118, 203, 230–1, 237. See also the *Book of Mary's Repose*, esoteric/secret knowledge in; and Gnostic Christianity
Eternal Feminine, 11
Ethiopia, 24, 103
Eucharist, 13, 71, 159–63, 188, 211–12, 214

Eudoxia, Empress, 218
Eve, 4, 45–6, 62, 111, 167, 229
Ewald, Heinrich, 131–2
Exodus, 117
Ezekiel, 120

Feasts, Marian: see Mary: commemorations of
Fiorenza, Elisabeth Schüssler, 34
Förster, Hans, 69
Forty Martyrs of Sebaste, 219
Foskett, Mary, 54, 59
Frend, W. H. C., 210

Gabriel, 35–6, 137
Gaul, 197
Gaventa, Beverly Roberts, 7, 39, 55
Gehenna: see Hell
Gelasian Decree, 49
Gennadius of Marseilles, 219
Gnostic Christianity, 45, 66, 72–3, 78, 86, 88–9, 98, 105–6, 112–13, 115. 117–18. See also Esoteric Christianity
Goddesses: see Mary and goddess traditions
Good, Deirdre, 90
Goranson, Stephen, 154
Gospel (Questions) of Bartholomew, 93–5
Gospel of the Lots of Mary, 200
Gospel of Mary, 74–87, 91–2, 112
Gospel of Philip, 88–90, 98
Gospel of Ps.-Matthew, 50, 107, 110
Gospel of Thomas, 87–9
Gospel of Truth, 105
Göttingen, 133, 143–4
Graef, Hilda, 10
Great Angel: see Angel Christology
Gregory of Nazianzus, 167, 174–6
Gregory of Nyssa, 167, 174–6
Gregory the Wonderworker, 175
Gribomont, Jean, 125

Hannah, 36
Hell, tour of, 25, 94–5, 126–8, 137
Helvidius, 125, 170–2
Herod, 48, 53
Hesychius of Jerusalem, 184–5, 190
Hodegoi, Church of St. Mary at, 220
Holum, Ken, 211, 220, 222, 224
Hymns, Marian, 189–94, 204. See also Akathist hymn; Ephrem the Syrian; Jerusalem Georgian

Chantbook; Magnificat; Sub tuum praesidium
Hypomnestikon of Joseph: see Joseph's Bible Notes

Iadgari: see the Jerusalem Georgian Chantbook
Ignatius of Antioch, 44
Ikelia, 183
Immaculate Conception, 57–8, 119
Infancy Gospel of Thomas, 44
Intercession, of angels, 126–8, 164; of the apostles, 127–8, 164; of Mary, 1, 9, 15, 18, 23, 25, 34–5, 44, 46, 68–9, 71–2, 96, 99, 104, 121, 126–8, 134, 137–42, 148, 163–4, 167, 174–8, 190, 192, 197, 199, 202–4, 207, 231–3, 237; and Mary's Dormition and Assumption, 177–8; of the saints, 19–20; orans as symbolic of, 197
Irenaeus of Lyons, 44–7, 62, 119, 229
Isaac, 58, 128, 137
Isaiah, 32, 45, 196
Italy, 173

Jacob, 128, 137, 196
Jael, 177
James the brother of Jesus, 40–2, 47, 135
Jeffery, Peter, 188
Jerome, 170, 172–3
Jerusalem, 17–18, 20, 27, 37, 40–2, 49, 52, 82, 105, 129, 135–6, 139–40, 152, 173, 178–9, 181–95, 197, 200, 202, 204, 233, 236
Jerusalem Armenian Lectionary, 181, 183–7
Jerusalem Georgian Calendar, 183
Jerusalem Georgian Chantbook, 27, 187–94, 233
Jerusalem Georgian Lectionary, 186–7
Jewish Christianity, 105
Jews and Judaism, 41, 52, 58, 66, 105–6, 220; accusations against Mary's virginity, 45, 54; as opponents of Mary, 101, 122–3, 136, 139–41
Joachim, 49, 51, 56, 59
John, 35, 41, 82–3, 119–20, 123, 126, 135–6, 141, 146, 150–1, 165, 175, 224, 229; Gospel of, 32–5, 40, 42–3, 79–80, 82–7
John the Baptist, 36, 48, 53, 60
John Chrysostom, 66, 168, 176–7, 218
John Paul II, Pope, 239

John Rufus, 218
Johnson, Maxwell, 196
Joseph, 32, 37, 52–3, 55, 59–60, 62, 66–7, 107–10, 119, 128, 170–1; children of, 107–9, 119; as model of male continence, 109
Joseph (Patriarch), 117
Joseph of Tiberias, 154
Joseph's Bible Notes, 152–6, 164
Jovinian, 125, 171–2
Judges, 177
Julian the Apostate, 155, 167
Justin Martyr, 44–5, 47, 62, 229
Juvenal of Jerusalem, 186

Kateusz, Ally, 157–60, 198–9
Kathisma, church of, 20, 182–4, 200
Kollouthos, Saint, 198
Kollyridians, 25, 134, 145–65, 232–3; connection with Dormition and Assumption traditions, 149–56, 164, 232; worship of Mary as a "goddess," 145–8, 153, 155, 161–63. See also Bread offerings; Women's ecclesiastical leadership
Kondakov, N. P., 197

Leo of Rome, 218
Letter to Cosmas, 211–12, 217
Levi: see Matthew
Lex orandi, developing ahead of *lex credendi*, 70, 194, 236, 238–40
Liber requiei Mariae: see the *Book of Mary's Repose*
Life and Miracles of Thecla, 17–18
Limberis, Vasiliki, 211, 220, 222
Luke, Gospel of, 32–3, 35–40, 43, 52, 59–60, 62, 66, 79–83, 91, 229. See also: Acts of the Apostles

Magi, 33, 60, 195
Magnificat, 36, 81
Mango, Cyril, 220–1
Manichaeans, 172
Mariam/Mariamme, 76, 78, 91
Marianites: see Kollyridians
Mark, Gospel of, 30–2, 35, 37–8, 40, 42–3, 66, 79–81, 83
Martyrs, veneration of, 19–20, 28
Mary: agricultural associations, 142–5, 148; apparitions, 25, 140, 164, 175–6, 232–3; ascetic devotion to, 172–3; birth after seven months, 51, 58; churches dedicated to, 18–20, 178–86, 195, 197, 200, 220–1, 224–5, 233, 236; commemorations of, 9, 18, 25, 27, 134, 141–5, 147–54, 156–7, 160–4, 167, 178–86, 190, 202–4, 206, 209, 220, 223, 232–4, 236; composite identity in apocrypha, 87–93, 97–8, 231; in conflict with the apostles, 77–8, 87–92, 96; coronation of, 135, 199; at the Crucifixion, 34–5, 37, 67, 80, 82–3; as disciple of Jesus, 35–9, 62, 80–3; doubts of, 67, 104, 119; in early Christian doctrine, 2, 7, 10–11, 166, 168; fear at dying, 104, 118–19; and female ascetic devotion, 172–3; as first witness to the Resurrection, 84–6; as general, 177–8; and goddess traditions, 11–15, 29, 142, 145–8, 153, 155, 161, 163; and "heterodox" traditions, 6, 23–6, 72, 74–99, 129, 132–3, 165, 203, 230–3, 236–7, 240; intimacy with her son, 16, 84; as liturgical leader, 157–63; in material culture, 18, 26, 194–203, 233–4, 236; in medieval and modern periods, 2, 15–16, 21–2, 29; miracles of, 18, 25, 104, 138–41, 148, 164, 204, 232; miraculous conception of, 55–7, 60; as model of virginity, 4, 109, 125, 169–73, 203, 219, 225, 233–4, 236; namesakes of, 201; as New Eve, 4, 44–6, 62, 66, 167, 177, 229; nursing, 198; painless birthing, 44; as prophet, 36, 81; as Queen, 190; relation to Jesus' movement, 31–5, 37–40, 42–3, 66, 80–3, 97–8, 168; relics, 20, 123, 200; silence of early church fathers, 4, 6, 68, 70, 96–7, 129, 132–3, 232, 236–40; and sin, 104, 119, 122, 128; sword, soul pierced by, 37, 67, 149; as teacher of the mysteries, 6, 23–4, 77–8, 88, 90–7, 111, 128, 164, 230–1, 237; Temple, early years in, 49, 51, 59–60, 197. See also Dormition; Hymns; Intercession; Maternity, Divine; Perpetual Virginity; Theotokos; Virginal Conception/Birth; Virginity *in partu*
Mary of Bethany, 76, 90, 98
Mary of Magdala, 12, 74–93, 97–8; as first witness to the Resurrection, 79–80, 84–6
Maternity, Divine, 1, 94–5, 166–7, 179–81, 192, 199, 203, 206, 232
Matins, 161, 188–90, 192

Matthew, 77–8; Gospel of, 32–3, 35, 37–8, 40, 43, 52, 79, 110
McGuckin, John, 38
Mediatrix of all Graces, 239
Memory of Mary, 178, 180–2, 184–5, 193, 204
Menas, St., 17–19
Meyer, Marvin, 87, 89
Michael, 122, 126–8, 137
Mimouni, Simon, 154
Mount of Olives, 94, 105–7, 123
Mount Sinai, 133, 135–6, 188–9

Nag Hammadi Library, 73–4. 103
Nativity, Feast of, 13, 20; of Jesus, 32–3, 35–7, 48–50, 52–3, 60, 181–2; of Mary, 47, 49, 51
Nazareth, 37
Nestorius, 3–4, 27–8, 155, 168, 177, 180–1, 205–28, 234
Noah, 128
Norelli, Enrico, 25, 43, 55, 127

Obsequies of the Virgin, 101
Odes of Solomon, 44, 46
Oktoechos, 189
Origen of Alexandria, 66–8, 71, 96
Orthros: see Matins
Oxyrhynchus, 200

Paganism, 13–14
Palestine, 129, 144, 149, 152, 154, 186, 200
Palm of the Tree of Life (and Palm Dormition narratives), 101, 104, 122–3
Paradise, 101, 104, 110, 121, 125, 137, 142, 177; tour of, 128, 137
Paralēmptōr, 118
Paul, 16, 18, 20, 30–1, 35, 37, 39–43, 46, 84, 105, 120–1, 123–5, 135, 140, 197
Peltomaa, Leena Mari, 12
Peppard, Michael, 196
Perpetual Virginity, 66–7, 109, 168–73
Peter, 20, 39–41, 76–8, 84, 87, 91–2, 94, 121, 123–4, 126, 135, 140–1, 197
Peter of Alexandria, 166
Philip of Side, 208
Pistis Sophia, 74, 90–3
Pleroma, 113, 118
Postel, Guillaume, 47
Presentation in the Temple, 37
Price, Richard, 212–16, 218
Priests, Jewish, 51, 59–60, 122

Proclus of Constantinople, 180–1, 190–1, 208–10, 218–21, 223–4, 227, 234
Protestantism, 6–8, 11, 13–14, 38, 235, 240
Protevangelium of James, 5, 9, 18, 22–4, 47–63, 66, 70, 94–5, 108, 128, 130, 163, 182, 197, 199–200, 203, 229–31, 235, 237, 240; as apocryphon, 48–51; apologetic elements, 54; influence on later tradition, 48–51; as liturgical reading, 49–50; Mary's sacred purity in, 55, 57, 60, 62, 108; miraculous conception of Mary in, 55–7, 60; purpose of glorifying Mary, 54–5; title, 47–8
Proto-orthodox, 4, 25, 64–5, 73–4, 78, 96, 129, 133, 203, 229, 232, 237
Ps.-John Dormition of Mary, 130–1, 135–6
Psychoanalysis, 11
Pulcheria, Empress, 28, 200, 205–6, 210–22, 224, 226–7, 234.

Rachael, 117
Ray, Walter, 185
Renoux, Charles (Athanase), 188, 190–3
Reynolds, Brian, 11, 46, 177
Roman Catholicism, 2, 6–8, 10, 13, 15, 46, 57, 71, 195, 239–40; anti-Catholicism, 8, 131–2
Rome, 18, 26, 135, 138, 140, 181, 195–8, 200–1, 204
Ruler (the Demiurge), 112–13, 118

Sacrifice, anthropology of, 11–12
Saints, cult of, 2, 12–16, 19–21, 27–9, 146–8, 150–1, 162, 165, 174, 223–4, 235–6
Salome, 53, 54, 60
Santa Maria Maggiore, 18, 197
Sarah, 51
Satan (Beliar), 94–5, 120, 174, 178
Schmidt, Carl, 93
Scythia, 152
Second Vatican Council, 8
Seleucia, 17, 202
Severian of Gabala, 176–8
Simeon, 37, 60, 67
Six Books Dormition Apocryphon, 25–6, 130–65, 179–81, 202–3, 232–3, 240; date, 133–4; Epiphanius's knowledge of, 151–2; liturgical use, 130–1, 134, 143; Roman governor in, 136–7, 139, 158; Syriac manuscripts, 133; veneration of Mary in, 136–7. See also Bread

offerings; Kollyridians; *Ps.-John Dormition of Mary*
Smith, Jonathan Z., 13
Smith Lewis, Agnes, 132–3, 144, 157–8
Socrates Scholasticus, 67–8
Sodom, 117
Sophia of Jesus Christ, 88
Sozomen, 175–6, 219
Spain, 170–1, 173–4, 184
Stegmüller, Otto, 72–3
Stephen, 220
Sub tuum praesidium, 23, 68–73, 96, 99, 127, 199, 201, 231
Syria, 61, 85–6, 176, 208

Tatian, 85–6
Temple (in Jerusalem), 37, 49, 51, 53, 59–60, 123, 197, 225
Tertullian, 65–7, 96–7, 119, 157
Testament of Solomon, 123
Thecla, 12, 16–21, 146, 150, 165, 173, 194–5, 200–4, 235–6
Theodosius (Palestinian monk), 183
Theodosius II, Emperor, 205, 211–12, 216–17, 226

Theotokos, 3–4, 16, 27, 67–72, 141, 166–7, 177, 180–2, 189–90, 192–3, 199–200, 203, 206–10, 212, 214, 222–8, 235, 238
Thrace, 152
Tomb of the Virgin, 20, 122–3, 140, 185–6
True Cross, discovery of, 134
Tyre, King of, 120

Veneration, 9–10. See also, *Six Books Dormition Apocryphon*, veneration of Mary in
Verina, Empress, 221
Vespers, 161, 188
Virginal Conception/Birth, 4, 32–3, 35, 43–5, 53–5, 61–2, 65–6, 169, 229
Virginity, 14, 67, 124–5, 169–73, 203, 219; *in partu*, 53, 62, 66–7, 169. See also Perpetual Virginity
Vopel, Hermann, 197

Wellen, Gerard, 198
Women's ecclesiastical leadership, 75, 78, 134, 145, 150, 157–63, 232–3.
Wright, William, 132

Zacharias, 53